National Image & Competitive Advantage

Eugene D. Jaffe & Israel D. Nebenzahl

National Image & Competitive Advantage

The Theory and Practice of Place Branding

Copenhagen Business School Press

National Image & Competitive Advantage
The Theory and Practice of Place Branding

© Copenhagen Business School Press
Printed in Denmark by Narayana Press, Gylling
Cover design by Morten Højmark
1. edition 2006

ISBN 87-630-0172-1

Distribution:

Scandinavia
DJØF/DBK, Mimersvej 4
DK-4600 Køge, Denmark
Phone: +45 3269 7788, fax: +45 3269 7789

North America
Copenhagen Business School Press
Books International Inc.
P.O. Box 605
Herndon, VA 20172-0605, USA
Phone: +1 703 661 1500, fax: +1 703 661 1501

Rest of the World
Marston Book Services, P.O. Box 269
Abingdon, Oxfordshire, OX14 4YN, UK
Phone: +44 (0) 1235 465500, fax: +44 (0) 1235 465555
E-mail Direct Customers: direct.order@marston.co.uk
E-mail Booksellers: trade.order@marston.co.uk

Table of Contents

Preface to the Second Edition

In today's globalized world, both a powerful global company and a powerful country need to have "strong" brands that can attract and hold consumers and investors... As we move into a world where everyone has the same hardware and everyone is being forced to get the same software to go with it, a country's brand, and the unique bond it can build with its foreign investors, becomes even more important.

Thomas Friedman, author of *The Lexus and the Olive Tree*

The idea that countries have a "brand" or "image" is not new. Corporations have images (or identities), stores have images and so do individuals (especially actors and politicians). All of these entities are concerned about their identity and try to shape and improve it, if need be. A positive brand image is a valuable asset when interfacing with one's audience or stakeholders. What is true for corporations, stores and individuals, is also true for nations regions and even cities. Every location has an image, favorable or unfavorable, positive or negative. Some nations are viewed as benevolent and progressive, others as contemptible and repressive. Some are noted for engineering prowess, others for design skills. International as well as local regions have unique images and so do major cities. Whatever these views are, they color both investors' and consumers' perceptions of a locality's "brand". And, these perceptions partly determine the "brand's" marketability, whether in the form of exports or as a place to establish a subsidiary. While a locality's "brand" or image is certainly of concern to its leaders, it is equally important to private and public organizations that are trying to stimulate both incoming investment and tourism and encourage cooperative alliances between business firms.

A locality's "brand", or image, as viewed by outsiders, is an outgrowth of its economic, political and educational systems, in short its culture. Therefore, how this image is formed, and what form it takes, should be of concern to government, industry and individual firms. Managing this image correctly may well determine a locality's success in selling its goods in other markets. In spite of the convincing evidence that a country's image affects consumer perception of its products, decision makers from government to firms have rarely taken these effects into consideration (Papadopoulos et al, 1987, 5).

National Image and Competitive Advantage: The Theory and Practice of Place Branding culminates the authors' research and writing on country of origin effects during the past twenty five years. Many others have extensively investigated the subject over a period of forty years, resulting in several hundred academic journal and proceedings articles. In addition, a book of original papers, edited by Nicolas Papadopoulos and Leslie Heslop was published in 1993. In writing the first edition of *National Image and Competitive Advantage*, the present authors believed that the time had come to integrate the vast literature relating to country image in order to place more emphasis on strategy. In other words, we believed and still believe that proper management of a nation's image can give its business institutions a competitive advantage in world markets. Still needed are the tools that decision-makers can use to manage it. In the second edition we broaden the scope of the book from *country branding* to *place branding.* We start out in this endeavor by reviewing the theoretical basis for country image: What it is and how it can be measured. Then we turn to the subject of how it can be managed by countries, localities, industry organizations and firms. In doing so, we have collected much material never before published and material that has seen print, but largely ignored by theoreticians. For example, a good deal of quality research has been conducted by consulting firms on behalf of industry groups, government and business firms. The results of this research have been used to design national image campaigns for a number of countries. However, most academic writers have largely ignored it.

We are grateful to the Copenhagen Business School Press for encouraging a second edition of this book. As the book's title suggests, the second edition has been extensively expanded to include a section on the subject of branding nations, regions and cities. How this task can be successfully done is accompanied by case examples.

It is one thing to determine whether a country's image is positive or negative, and we have expanded the discussion in this regard, but it is equally important to determine what the monetary value of the image is. We have added a chapter on monetizing country image, based on the concept of brand equity.

This book has been written with several audiences in mind. It can be used in International Marketing and Business courses as a supplement to global product and advertising strategy. Most textbooks devote very little space to country of origin effects on planning and decision making. The present book fills this gap. A second audience consists of international marketing managers. Sections of the book that deal with country image implications for the firm will be of interest for them. Finally, those industry and government officials who must deal with the problems of creating and maintaining a country's national image will find this book useful.

Acknowledgments

The authors wish to thank a number of individuals and organizations who have encouraged the undertaking of this book. Professor Lauge Stetting, Publisher of the Copenhagen Business School Press took an early interest and guided the book to fruition. Two subsequent publishers, Axel Shultz-Nielsen and Ole Wiberg guided the second edition. We are also indebted to Hanne Thorninger Ipsen, Project Manager at CBS Press, who worked long hours to get the manuscript into a publishable product. The first author wrote a good deal of his contribution while on sabbatical as a Visiting Professor in the Department of International Economics at the Copenhagen Business School during 1999-2000. The revised edition was written while serving in a similar capacity at the Department of Marketing during 2004-2006, also at CBS. He is indebted to Professors Poul Shultz and Ricky Wilke and colleagues for creating a stimulating atmosphere conducive to research and writing. The second author worked on his contribution to the second edition while on sabbatical as an Arlene and Robert Kogod Outstanding Visiting Professor of Undergraduate Programs and as a Scholar-in-Residence at the Kogod School of Business, American University, Washington, DC, during 2003-2005. He is indebted to Professor Tomasz Mroczkowski and other colleagues for their support.

The authors are indebted to the Research Authority of Bar-Ilan University for covering some of the secretarial expenses in putting the manuscript together.

Some of the ideas presented in this book are the result of collaboration and/or discussions over the years with a number of colleagues, especially Shlomo Lampert at Bar-Ilan University and

Nicolas Papadopoulos at Carleton University. We are also indebted to a number of practitioners, especially Jack Yan who have shared their experience with us to enrich the examples in this book. Last, but certainly not least, we would like to thank our wives, Liora and Ora, as well as our children, for putting up with our long hours of collaborative research over the past twenty five years.

Copenhagen and Ramat-Gan, March 2006.

CHAPTER 1

Introduction:
Image, Images and Imagination

The way we imagine ourselves to appear to another person is an essential element in our conception of ourselves. In other words, I am not what I think I am and I am not what you think I am. I am what I think you think I am.

Robert Bierstedt

Introduction

Please complete the following sentence:

A luxury car made in Switzerland is…

Think for a moment about this question and try to answer it before proceeding with this book. If you are not familiar with such a product, use your imagination. Think about what a luxury car would be like if it were made in Switzerland.

Now think for a moment about a person buying such a car and complete the following sentence:

A person who buys a luxury car made in Switzerland…

Can you answer these questions? If you are a typical consumer, you can.

These are questions asked by the authors of this book and other researchers in numerous studies conducted during the past two decades. Like others reading this book, there is a certain image in your mind of the hypothesized car and its buyer. Now, you can rest assured that no luxury cars are made or have ever been made in Switzerland. Yet, you, like all typical consumers, have an image of the product that does not exist and its buyer whom you have never met. If that is so, you have images of *real* products made in various countries and these images influence your decision to purchase or not.

In this chapter we clarify what is meant by *image* in general and by *country image* or more general, *the image of a place*, in particular. Where do brand and country images come from and how do they enter the mind of consumers? How uniform or varied are these images? Can we influence the formation of images and their perception and if so, how? Can existing images be changed, and if so, what does it take to bring about such changes and in what time frame? What are the implications of brand and country images to consumers, companies and governments? These are some of the questions we try to answer in the remaining chapters of this book.

What Do We Mean by Product, Brand and Country *Image*?

"Image is the set of beliefs, ideas, and impressions that a person holds regarding an object" (Kotler, 1997, 607). It should be noted that the true attributes of the object are not included in the definition of *image*. Thus, an image is comprised of the subjective perceptions of the person about the object. These beliefs, ideas and impressions are mental images that may or may not be congruent with objectively defined attributes of the object. It is interesting to note that the object does not have to exist in order for a person to have a mental image of it. More than 750 years ago, the Jewish philosopher Maimonides, in discussing the superiority of the human mind, asks his readers to imagine a metal ship that can fly in the air (Gorfinkle, 1966, 41), an object that was out of the realm of reality at his time. While today we can actually fly in such a ship, for hundreds of years it existed only in the minds of scholars who read the writing of Maimonides or were otherwise exposed to the idea of such an object. In a similar manner, marketing researchers who engage in concept testing attempt to describe consumers' images of products yet to be designed. What is important for our discussion is the understanding that for the individual, the image *represents* the object, or even *is* the object.

"A *Product image* is the particular picture that consumers acquire of an actual or potential product" (Kotler, 1997, 317). The inclusion of "potential" in this definition leaves some room for the imagination.

"*Imagination* is defined as a "conscious mental process of evoking ideas or images of objects, events, relations, attributes, or processes never before experienced or perceived" (Microsoft Encarta, 2000). Thus, Kotler's definition of product image accepts the possibility noted in the previous paragraph of having an image even of non-existing products.

Brand, country and other place images are similarly defined as the mental pictures of brands, countries and localities, respectively. Like product image, these images exist in the consumer's mind. We are concerned about these images because "People's attitudes and actions toward an object are highly conditioned by that object's image" (Kotler, 1997, 607). Thus, what motivates consumer behavior is not the "true" attributes of products but rather mental images in the minds of consumers. Accordingly, "while *identity* comprises the way that a company aims to position itself and it's products, *image* is the way the public perceives the company or it's products. A company designs an identity or positioning to shape the public's image, but other factors may intervene to determine each person's resulting image" (Kotler, 1997, 292). Two of the key intervening factors are *brand* and *country images* of the company and its products.

Whatever is stated below about country image can be generalized to the image of other localities. For example, Berne, while being a part of Switzerland, has its own image as a capital city rich with history. At the same time, Switzerland itself is a European country. Thus, unless otherwise stated, our discussion below of "country image" can be extended to include smaller or larger localities, such as cities, states, or regions.

We now turn to the mental processes involved in forming perceptual images.

Learning Processes

A complete review of learning processes is beyond the scope of this book. The following is an abridged description of categorization theory that describes the most relevant learning processes involved in the perception of objects such as products and services. The roots of this theory can be found in Bruner, Goodnow and Austin's seminal work, *A Study of Thinking* (1956). Reviews of its application in consumer behavior can be found in an issue of the Journal of Consumer Research (1987) devoted to the subject.

Categorization, Abstraction and Generalization

The individual is constantly bombarded by numerous signals from the environment. To attend to all details received is beyond human capacity. To handle this situation, by means of selective attention, perception and retention, the individual attends and responds to only a small fraction of the information received. Learning controls the perception of information and reaction to it. It involves two parallel mental processes, abstraction and generalization.

Abstraction involves the formation of categories and the placement of objects in categories. In the words of Bruner, Goodnow and Austin (1956, 1), "To categorize is to render discriminately different things equivalent, to group the objects and events and people around us into classes and to respond to them in terms of their class membership rather than in terms of their uniqueness." When information about an object is received and there is an appropriate category for it in the person's mind, it is classified as being a member of that category. Indeed, the same object may be classified as belonging to more than one category. If no relevant categories are available, new categories will be formed or the object and all information about it will be ignored. By classifying an object within a category, some of its properties are learned to belong to that category while some properties are ignored. This loss of details is what is meant by *abstraction*.

Generalization is the opposite process. Once an object has been placed in a category, the person ascribes to it all the properties of the category, even when no relevant information about the object confirms the validity of these properties with regard to the particular object. This projection of attributes from a category to objects is *generalization*. Learning also involves reclassification of objects based on experience. To summarize, perceptual learning involves the creation of categories, the placement of objects within categories, the ascribing of common features to all members of categories and the revision of categories and/or classification of objects within categories based on experience.

Categorization, the joint process of abstraction and generalization, is primarily functional. By grouping objects that are alike in important respects together, we enhance information processing. Such organized knowledge structures allow us to identify novel items, respond to them in terms of their class membership and make evaluative judgments (Cohen and Basu, 1987). Brand name and country-of-origin may be considered such categories that impart properties to novel products and elicit consumers' evaluative judgments.

Bruner, Goodnow and Austin (1965, 2) delineate two ways of categorizing, namely, identity and equivalence. In identity categorizing, we identify things that seem to be different in their details as belonging to the same entity. For example, we view pictures of a person during different stages of his/her life and identify all pictures as belonging to the same person. In equivalence categorizing, things that are in reality different are conceived as being similar by their nature, by their belonging to the same class. In this book we are concerned with equivalence categorizing only.

For a simple example of equivalence categorizing, consider a person who learned to classify certain four-legged animals in the category of "dogs". Some of these animals may also be classified in the "friendly pets" category, or alternatively, in the "dangerous animals" category. A person may classify a new animal he sees as a dog and as a friendly pet. From now on all attributes of dogs and of friendly pets are ascribed to that animal. Friendly pets may be played with and patted. Being bitten by the animal may cause its reclassification as being a dangerous animal rather than a friendly pet. Wrongly classifying a wolf in the forest as being a friendly dog may lead to results that do not leave enough time for its reclassification as a wild beast.

Of key interest to us are Bruner, Goodnow and Austin's (1956, 11) clues to the formation of categories and their social use. In their opinion, the law of parsimony is a determining factor. The cues of classes are selected so that the signs defining a category are those that provide identification as early as possible. Categories are formed so as to minimize surprise of the environment. Since the individual views the world around him in terms of categories, and since individuals can communicate with each other only in terms of concepts they share (Schramm 1955), communication with others is conducted by the same category terms. Category learning is therefore, one of the principle means by which an individual is socialized (Bruner, Goodnow and Austin, 1956, 231). In this way, categories that one comes to use habitually are part of culture.

Two alternative theories of the categorization process, holistic and analytic, were suggested in the literature (Alba and Hutchinson, 1987). Holistic processing refers to classifications that are based on overall similarity, disregarding its relevance to the task at hand. In analytic classification, particular attributes specify class membership while others are ignored. To illustrate the distinction between these alternative processes, Alba and Hutchinson (1987, 419-420) cite a Ford advertisement that compared the quietness of the LTD with that of the Mercedes-Benz. Analytic processing of the ad might increase the perceived importance of quietness as an attribute of luxury cars and establish the fact that the LTD is a quiet, and therefore, a luxury car. Holistic processing of the ad might increase the perceived similarity of the LTD with the Mercedes and, in addition to quietness, be influenced by other settings in the ad, including the implied social class of the driver. We may add that holistic processing may also associate the LTD with consumers' perceptions of German made cars.

It is of great significance to the study of country image effect that empirical evidence shows that holistic processing is facilitated by stimulus complexity, time pressure, lack of motivation and incidental learning conditions (Alba and Hutchinson, 1987, 421). These are the typical situations in the evaluation of multinational brands of consumer products. Indeed, in a recent empirical study, Lee and Ganesh (1999) applied categorization theory to the study of country image and concluded that both low and high familiarity consumers rely on overall country image in their product evaluation. They also found that, as predicted by the holistic processing theory, overall country image affects the image of a country as a producer of a particular product class.

We can now apply the theory of categorization to the concepts of image defined earlier. In general, an image of an object is comprised of the attributes ascribed to it via the categories in which it is classified. Examples of classes that relate to the image of a product are its functional use, size, packaging, price range, brand name, related country images, etc. A strong brand, such as Sony, may be a category by itself, attributing to products sold under its name certain physical, economic and social qualities. Less known brands may be classified into groups of brands, such as specialists in style, those providing good value for the money or made-in a certain country. Unknown brands may just be ignored in the market place because their perception requires more effort on the part of consumers than brands with which the consumer is familiar.

The image of a country is influenced by the perception of its people, level of economic development, quality of its products, products in which it has comparative advantage, etc. The image of a less known country may be highly influenced by the country category in which it is classified. For example, a developing African country will yield a different image from that of a developing Asian country, and both countries will have a totally different image when compared with an industrialized and highly developed Scandinavian country. When a salesperson emphasizes that a certain product, unlike competing ones, is made in Japan, he parsimoniously conveys a lot of information about the quality of the product. Indeed, the salesperson uses the country cue to influence the image of the product to be formed in the mind of the customer.

At long last, you, our reader can now understand the basis for your own image of a luxury car made in Switzerland. While such a car has not been produced yet, you used your imagination to assign attributes to the imaginary car that stem from its classification in your mind as "luxury cars" and "made-in Switzerland" categories. In thinking about its buyer, you might have added your assessment of the psychological, wealth, attitude to spending, propensity to take risk, social status or similar attributes that a made-in Switzerland luxury car might possess. Since no additional information was given about the buyer, the image of the buyer serves as a mirror of the social value of the imaginary car.

Symbols

The theory of categorization emphasizes the need for parsimony. Symbols, in conjunction with categories, further increase the parsimony of communication. Symbols are arbitrary names assigned to things and qualities. Common examples of symbols are names for objects, letters, and numbers. Whereas a schema or image represents a specific experience, such as sight or sound, a symbol is an arbitrary representation of an event. The letter *A* is a symbol, and children use schemata, images, and symbols in their mastery of the alphabet. By using symbols, such as brand and country names to represent categories, the category and its attributes are quickly recalled and impact perceptions. The relationship between symbols and categories is further accentuated by the definition of symbols in Britannica (1999-2000): "Symbols are used in the development of higher cognitive units called concepts. A concept, or category, may be thought of as a special kind of symbol that represents a set of attributes common to a group of symbols or images. Concepts are used to sort specific experiences into general rules or classes, and conceptual thinking refers to a person's subjective manipulations of those abstract classes." This definition of symbols helps us to understand the importance of assigning brand names to products. Brand names serve as abstract symbols for attributes of products. The fact that a brand name may be the only common element linking otherwise unrelated products together does not diminish from its ability to make them share common perceptions and images. In a similar manner, a country or region name is a symbol that joins together a broader range of products and services, which, despite their diversity, have some common desirable or undesirable attributes.

Generalization versus Discrimination

"Generalization is the process inferred when a response elicited by a stimulus is also elicited by a different but similar stimulus" (Engel, Kollat and Blackwell, 1973, 233). In previous paragraphs we detailed the mental processes involved in generalization. It is time to draw attention to *discrimination*, the opposite process. Engel, et al (235) define *discrimination* as a process whereby an organism learns to emit a response to a stimulus but avoids making the same response to a similar but somewhat different stimulus. Discrimination occurs when an individual realizes that an object does not fully fit categories it shares with similar objects. When alternative classifications are utilized, different images result. The more we know about an object, the more detailed is its classification and less is left to the imagination. Thus, even if a number of diverse products made in the same country initially have a similar image, usage and other experiences with them over time may lead to discrimination and to the perception of a more distinct image for each.

Brand and Country Image Compositioning

The concept of compositioning in a business context was introduced by Ruttenberg, Kavisky and Oren (1995). It was further elaborated in Ruttenberg, Oren, and Honen (1998, 330) where it is described as "a new marketing-advertising concept…whereby a composition is formed between brands from existing product categories and each brand brings its own relative advantage to the Compositioning… Compositioning is developed with the purpose of carving out a unique positioning in the target audience's perceptual map or creating a new map all together". The most famous example of compositioning is the "Smart Car" introduced by Mercedes and Swatch. The Mercedes brought to the marriage the image of an established respectable producer of high quality and reliable automobiles while Swatch brought the image of excellence in design. Mercedes is associated with Germany while Swatch with Switzerland. Thus, it was intended that the Smart car would be perceived by consumers as being a high quality stylish car with German quality and Swiss precision. A simple form of compositioning is co-branding, where two or more brands are assigned to a single product or service. For example, American Airlines made an agreement with Citibank to issue Visa and MasterCard credit cards that carry both names. Global co-branding (each brand from a different country) situations may occur because of acquisitions or joint ventures (e.g., Fuji-Xerox), strategic alliances (e.g., British Air-USAir), the formation of composite products (e.g., the Dutch brand Friesche Flag yogurt with the Israeli Jaffa citrus brand) and joint promotions (e.g., Goodyear and Audi). Consumer attitudes toward a co-brand comprised of brands from two different countries may be formed not unlike that of domestic co-brands. However, in the case of global co-branding, there may be a joint effect (Nebenzahl and Jaffe, 1996; Jo et al, 2003) of brand and country images on consumers' evaluation of the brand alliance. We also expect that subsequent judgments of both individual brands and country images will be influenced by such a brand alliance.

The theory of categorization described above can serve as a theoretical basis for explaining how compositioning works. Each of the joined brands is a symbol associated with a category or categories. The presence of each symbol triggers an association in the mind of consumers with the respective images of the related categories. By joining more than one brand, an image that is a composite of all categories emerges. It should be stressed, however, that both desirable and undesirable properties interact in forming the new image. The resulted image is not necessarily positive. There is a story about a conversation between Marilyn Monroe and Bernard Shaw in which Monroe told Shaw "imagine that we will have a child that will be as smart as you and as good looking as I." To which Shaw responded "but what if the child will be as smart as you and as good looking as I?"

We can extend the concept of brand compositioning to brand and country compositioning. One of the authors of this book in his early work on country image was presented with the challenge of positioning a joint venture between an American and a Japanese car manufacturer to assemble passenger cars in Mexico from Japanese and American made components (Johansson and Nebenzahl, 1986). The new car could have been given a brand name of the American partner or of the Japanese partner. The car could have been positioned as an American car, concealing the Japanese partner and minimizing exposure to its Mexican assembly. Similarly, it could have been positioned as a Japanese car. Alternatively, the car could have been positioned as Mexican. One could also conceive of a composite image, presenting the car as having a Japanese power plant and transmission, American body and Mexican assembly. The composite image would have had American, Japanese and Mexican attributes. In addition, the chosen brand name would add its contribution to the image of the product. Consider the case of emerging country manufacturers attempting to achieve market entry in developed countries. A good strategy would be to find a well-known brand ally in the target country. Of course, a potential brand ally would have to carefully determine if brand erosion would occur as a consequence of co-branding.

Another example of brand and country compositioning is a series of studies conducted by the authors on production sourcing of leading brands. We studied the effects of producing American brands in Japan and Japanese brands in the USA (Nebenzahl and Jaffe, 1996). We also studied what would be the effect on both American and Japanese brands of East European made-in labels (Nebenzahl and Jaffe, 1991). We found that the result is a composition of the respective brands and countries. We also found that, in addition, the resulted images were functions of the relative strength of the brand and country images and that a country with a better image than the brand will slightly improve the image of the end product. On the other hand, the effect of a low-image country could be disastrous even to a very strong brand. It can be concluded that country image and its effect should not be taken lightly.[1]

Extending the scope of country image to other localities the role of compositioning is further demonstrated. Consider, for example, the image of Tel-Aviv and Jerusalem as tourist attractions. Both cities share the image elements of being Israeli and parts of the Jewish State. Yet, Tel-Aviv has the image of a modern Western-culture Mediterranean city with a gorgeous beach and vibrant night life. Jerusalem has the image of *The Holy City* that is sanctified by the three monotheistic religions. Thus, while Jerusalem is the main attraction for pilgrimage tourists, Tel-Aviv attracts those who seek a more glamorous environment, replete with a vibrant nightlife.

Misconceptions of Country Image
The discussion up to this point should have convinced the reader that the concept of country image is not a simple unidimensional one and

---

[1] A more detailed discussion of this subject is given in Chapter 5.

that its interaction with brand image further complicates matters. In the past, the subject was sometimes treated in an overly simplistic manner, leading to some serious misconceptions.

Companies often ignore the country image effect altogether, treating the world as a single market and source of products. There is a tendency to make sourcing decisions based on comparative advantage and cost differentials only, to the exclusion of image considerations. As will be shown in this book, such exclusion may cause serious damage to the image of the sourced products, a damage that may far exceed the economic benefits of low costs.

Some researchers have treated country image as a single variable measured on a semantic differential scale. However, no country excels in all attributes, or vice versa. Countries do have an image of excelling in some aspects, such as design, quality control, value for the price, etc., but not in others. Furthermore, simply labeling countries as being underdeveloped, developing and developed also leads to misconceptions. Until recently, Israel had been classified as a developing country. Yet, in contrast with most other countries so classified, it is a world hi-tech leader. Similarly, Denmark is considered by many as an agricultural exporter, while for many years its industrial exports far exceeded its export of processed food and produce.

Another misconception is the assumption that country image is completely independent of products. Afghanistan is considered as a third world underdeveloped country. Asked about its products, most would rate them at the bottom of the scale. Yet, Afghan rugs are highly valued in world markets.

The most serious misconception is probably the consideration of country image as a static phenomenon. To the contrary, the image of countries changes over time. While the image of a country affects the image of its products, experience with these products causes revisions in the country image. A related misconception is that country image is not subject to intentional managerial influence. In most studies it is taken as given. To the contrary, governments, industry, trade and professional organizations can and do formulate communication strategies aimed at improving the image of their respective country. Along the same lines, country image effect was considered as either a halo effect—a stereotyped country image that colors brand image, or a summary effect—the average image of the country's products which, in turn, affects the image of new brands or products coming from the country. Our contention is that both summary and halo effects exist.

These supposedly inconsistent effects are compatible, once it is accepted that the country image effect is a complex rather than simple phenomenon.

To date, legal aspects were generally considered out of the realm of the country image literature. With the advent of the European Union with it's legitimacy of the EU label on the one hand and of individual countries on the other, and with local and international rulings, it is important to include legal aspects while considering the management of country image.

What Lies Ahead

In this introductory chapter we clarified what is meant by image in general and by country and brand images in particular and outlined how such images are learned. We showed that that the combined affect of different images may be considered as a form of compositioning. Finally, we listed common misconceptions whose clarification is one of the motives for writing this book. The remaining chapters are devoted to an in-depth discussion of the subject, putting structure in the analysis and discussion and providing guidelines for managerial action. A unique feature of this book is the depth of discussion on one hand and the numerous real-life examples on the other. It provides theoretical models that facilitate future research in the field. It also presents detailed descriptions of country image campaigns never before published in one compendium.

Chapter 2 outlines a taxonomy that defines the boundaries and elements of country image. This taxonomy is used throughout the book. The chapter also addresses the issue of how country image can be measured and suggests a universal scale that may be used for this purpose. This is followed by a discussion of theory. Based on theoretical elements found in the literature, it provides a theoretical model that utilizes the taxonomy defined above to structure the dynamic relationships and interactions between brand, country and product images. It suggests circular dynamic influences where country image affects brand image that in turn affects product image. We noted that image is a perceptual concept. The perceived image in the mind of a consumer is a result of elaborate information processing. Chapter 3 shows how country image can be valued in monetary terms. Suggestions are given as to how country image equity can be measured. Chapter 4 focuses on consumers and their perceptions of brands and countries. It further extends and elaborates concepts touched upon earlier. Moving from the consumer to the organizational level, Chapter 5 deals with the management of CI by the firm. Here one will find evidence for the two-way interaction between brand and country images with suggestions for potential future strategies. Utilizing conceptual elements of the theoretical model and considering consumer and legal environments, Chapter 6 deals with past experience in the management of CI by industry organizations, national and municipal governments and provides suggested guidelines for the future. Here the reader will find material on past and present industry and government promotional campaigns. Chapter 7 discusses the legal aspects of country-of-origin. It surveys labeling requirements, statutory ordinances in leading countries, and rulings of world trade organizations and documents the use of the made-in label as a trade barrier.

The last chapter is the only one that is not grounded on past research and theory. Here the authors contemplate about the role of brand and country images in the age of electronic commerce highlighted by the World Wide Web (www) and suggest some areas for future research.

CHAPTER 2

The Theory of Country Brand and Product Images

He who loves practice without theory is like a sailor who boards a ship without a rudder and compass and never knows where he may cast.

Leonardo De Vinci (1452-1519)

Introduction

In chapter 1 we clarified what is meant by *image*. We now consider the meaning of *country image* and *country image effect*. A review of the literature shows that these terms mean different concepts to different people. While there is a common understanding of what is meant by the word *image*, *country image* is ill defined. Since error free communication can take place only when all communicators have common understanding of terms and symbols (Schramm, 1955, p. 6), we devote the following section to a clarification of the taxonomy of country image to be used in this book. Once the definition of *country image* is clarified, the second section deals with issues of its measurement. The remaining sections of this chapter provide a model that will give structure to the ensuing discussion. We do it by introducing a theoretical framework that clarifies the main concepts and suggests cause and effect relationships. For the sake of brevity and clarity, we refer in this chapter exclusively to *country*, and as noted earlier, this term can be replaced by places of different dimensions, such as *city* and *region*.

Country Image Taxonomy

Two efforts (Samiee 1994; Jaffe, et al. 1994) to provide a common conceptual framework of the country image effect distinguished between consumer perception of the country with which a product/brand is identified (e.g., Honda identified as a Japanese product) and the country of manufacture (e.g., Honda assembled in the United States). Most country image studies to date failed to make this distinction. Distinguishing between the two concepts is important because of the increased sourcing of production by multinational firms and their use of global, standardized advertising for their products (Han and Terpstra 1988; Nebenzahl and Jaffe 1991). Following this approach, we suggest that in addition to the country of manufacture (made-in cue), one should add the country of design, the associated country, the country where main parts are made and the country of assembly. In addition to these countries that are linked to the image of products, the home country of the consumer should also be considered a part of the country image domain. Such an inherent consumer nationality bias has been identified by Cattin, et al. (1982); Morello (1984); Lumpkin and Crawford (1985) and more recently by Ettenson (1993) and Amine (1994). Accordingly, we would like to suggest the following taxonomy:

HC Home Country. The country in which the consumer permanently resides. HC has cultural and social impact on the consumer, both in reference to consumption patterns and in shaping his attitudes towards products made in different countries.

DC Designed-in Country. The country in which either a part of or the entire finished product is designed. Italy is famed for its talented design and "Italian design" of products is promoted even when production takes place elsewhere. The emphasis of the country of design, DC, in overall marketing strategy has been rarely used and then mainly in the automobile and fashion industries. When used, it may influence consumer evaluation of product attributes.

MC   Made-in Country. The country whose name appears on the "made-in" label. It is usually the country where final production takes place. A certain minimum local added-value is usually required for the display of the made-in label. Domestic legislation will determine the extent to which country of manufacture must be labeled.

The traditional "made-in" label implies that production takes place in one country. It ignores sourcing of parts. Taking into consideration such sourcing, we add two additional definitions:

PC   The country that is the source of identified key parts or components. For example, when these authors ordered new computers for their office, it was recommended by the university's purchasing department that they should select personal computers of any make "as long as the hard disc drive is made in Japan."

AC   The country where final assembly took place. It is identified by the "assembled-in" label.

In all definitions above, each country actually contributes something to the product. Due to historical reasons, sometimes a country may be associated with a product via a brand name, even when it has no real contribution to it. This will often be the case of strong brands of companies that become multinational. This observation leads to the following:

OC   Country of origin. The country which a consumer associates with a certain product or brand as being its source, regardless of where the product is actually produced. For example, many consumers consider GE to be an American brand even though some GE products are produced outside of the USA.

HC, DC, MC, PC, AC and OC may represent up to five different countries when international sourcing takes place.[2] For example, a General Motors branded car may be designed in Italy (DC), have the engine and transmission components produced in Japan (PC), be assembled in Mexico (AC) and may be associated with the USA (OC)

---

[2] Five instead of six because either AC or MC are identified, but not both.

by a consumer residing in France (HC). It should be noted that when DC, PC and AC are the same country, it is identified as MC. When PC and AC are both specified, they replace the more general MC. This is an example of increase discrimination by providing more detailed categories. Of course, OC=MC when global brands are manufactured in the origin country, e.g. Sony made in Japan or Black & Decker made in the United States.

The distinction between DC, PC, AC, MC and OC is important since we assume that either or all may impact consumers' perceptions of products or brands. We need HC to note that consumers may be affected not only by the countries associated with the product, but also by their own nationality and culture (Chasin, Holzmueller and Jaffe 1989; Amine, 1994). Amine and Shin (2002) found that students' HC affected their evaluation of foreign products.

Now, that we defined the different classes of countries that may be involved in shaping the image of brands and products, we turn to the image of the countries themselves. Based on all we know about a country, an image is formed in our mind about its attributes, strengths and weaknesses. Exactly how these images are formed is the subject of later sections of this chapter. For the present, it suffices to realize that images are formed. Accordingly, and based upon our nomenclature of different country situations, we define corresponding country images:

DCI   The image of a country as a source for designs of products.

PCI   The image of a country as a production location of the relevant product components incorporated in products.

ACI   The image of a country as an assembly location of products.

MCI   The image of a country as a production and assembly location of products.

OCI   Origin-Country-Image. The overall image of a country that is considered to be associated with brands or products.

The main reason for our concern with the different types of country images is their *effect* on the image of brands or products. This leads to the definition of CIE:

CIE   The effect an image of a country has on brands or products related with the country. Any of the country images defined above may have its particular effect.

It seems that CIE remains an abstract concept that describes the effects of either OCI, or MCI. A survey of the literature shows that what has been purported to be CIE has been either the effect of OCI (Nes 1981; Han and Terpstra 1988; Nebenzahl and Jaffe 1991) or of MCI (Schooler 1971; Nagashima 1970; Chasin and Jaffe 1979; Johansson, Douglas and Nonaka 1985; Johansson and Nebenzahl 1986; Darling and Arnold 1988; Ettenson, Wagner and Gaeth 1988; Chasin, Holzmueller and Jaffe 1988; Papadopoulos, Heslop and Beracs 1990a). Due to this inconsistency, comparison of research results of different studies may be invalid. In the discussion below, whenever there is a need to make a distinction among different country image effects, we will use one of the detailed definitions listed above. Otherwise, we will use CIE as a reference to the overall country image phenomenon.

There is some evidence that CIE is more meaningful in reference to a specific product line (Gaedeke 1973; Wang 1978; Cattin, Jolibert and Lohnes 1982; Heslop, Liefeld and Wall 1987; Han and Terpstra 1988; Eroglu and Machleit 1989) or that there is linkage between product categories and country image perceptions (Roth and Romeo 1992). Accordingly, the taxonomy is expanded to include reference to specific product lines. We suggest the following:

DCIP   The image of a country as the design location of a given product line, P.

PCIP   ACIP, MCIP and OCIP are similarly defined for the parts, assembly, made-in and associated countries.

In correspondence with the above, we suggest the following symbols for brand images:

BI   Brand Image. The overall brand image.

BIP   The image of a product line, P, when sold under the corresponding brand name.

For the sake of brevity we do not distinguish at present among the detailed particular images of brands as associated with design, manufacturer or assembly and suggest broader categories. Yet, it should be kept in mind that just as countries, brands may be perceived as having particular strengths and weaknesses in the different aspects of products and business.

Finally, marketers are interested in the image of a particular product, given all its attributes, its brand and its related countries. Accordingly we define:

PI   The relative image of a specific product offered in the market.

PI results from the different image effects that impact the product. These include the product physical attributes, price, service, etc., as well brand and country images.

Now that the variables representing country image and its effect have been clarified, we turn to their measurement.

Measuring Country Image Dimensions

Multiple Independent Image Items and Dimensions
In one of the first studies on country image, Nagashima (1970) compared Japanese and American attitudes toward foreign products. Country image was assessed in this study by twenty semantic differential questions relating to five dimensions: Price and value (e.g. reliable-unreliable); service and engineering (e.g. technically advanced-technically backward); advertising and reputation (e.g. recognizable brand names-unrecognizable brand names); design and style (e.g. large choice of size and model-limited choice of size and model); and consumers' profile (e.g. more for men-more for women). The mean of each question was computed and the means of items classified in each of the above dimensions were presented together. Even within dimensions, different questions were not averaged together into a summary scale. From the type of analyses performed, it is clear that Nagashima considered country image to consist of a series of related but independent image items rather than an overall image. Nagashima's research was replicated by other researchers who adapted some or all his scale items without questioning their validity and reliability. Other researchers used the same methodology but designed their own dimensions of what they considered to constitute country image (e.g., Laroche, et al, 2005; Ashill and Sinha, 2004; Nebenzahl, Jaffe and Usunier, 2000).

Multi-Item Image Scale

The next step in the development of measurements was to consider the independent image dimensions as belonging to a multivariate scale. This method is exemplified by the authors of this book who selected 13 of Nagashima's original semantic differential items that could be taken as having negative-positive direction and computed their grand mean (Jaffe and Nebenzahl, 1984). The resulted mean was taken to represent the overall country image.

Statistically Derived Multi-Item Image Dimensions

While Nagashima (1970) intuitively grouped his twenty image dimensions into five broad classes prior to collecting the data, other researchers used statistical techniques for that purpose. For example, Nebenzahl and Jaffe (1984) used factor analysis to group thirteen of Nagashima's items into broad classes. They found that two dimensions, product-technology and price-value, summarized the information contained in the thirteen questions. This result implies that CIE is comprised of at least two distinct perceptual dimensions that should be measured separately. This method has two advantages over previous methods. First, the identified image dimensions relate to consumers' response rather than to what the researcher believes these dimensions should be. Second, instead of considering country image to consist of many perceptual dimensions as in Nagashima's method, fewer and more meaningful perceptual dimensions are derived. In contrast with the method that artificially averages unrelated image concepts into a single averaged score, this Jaffe-Nebenzahl method provides clues to the dimensions actually perceived by consumers.

Consumer-Sourced and Statistically Derived Multi-Item Image Dimensions

All the above methods have one major flaw, they are based on rating questions that stem from what the researchers consider to relate to country image. However, consumers' perceptions do not have to follow the logic of researchers. There is a need, therefore, for country image scales that are based on consumers' rather than researchers' frame of reference. For international marketing research, it would be advantageous if such scales could be applied in different countries and yield comparable results.

In the past few years, the authors of this book developed a consumer-oriented scale that was proven to be valid and reliable for the measurement of country image across countries. In the first development stage of the new scale, consumers were asked to describe home electronic products and the type of a person who might buy them when made-in different countries.[3] This study, conducted in the United States, France and Israel resulted in 64 perceptual scale items. It should be stressed that most of these consumer-sourced items were never included in studies designed by researchers. In the second stage, these 64 rating scale items were included in questionnaires administered in France, Mexico and Israel. Using factor analysis and other statistical techniques, the list of items was reduced to thirty. To assure reliability and validity, the reduced set of questions was included in questionnaires administered in Canada, France and Israel.

In both the second and the third stages, the selected questions were grouped into five meaningful perceptual dimensions. It was found that consumers perceive the image of countries along these distinct dimensions. Furthermore, in developing the scale we were careful to assure that the grand mean of all thirty questions is a valid measure of the overall country image. Thus, using this measuring instrument, we can now describe and compare the image of different countries in the eyes of the consumers. We can also assess differences in these images by consumers who reside in different countries. The resultant scale items and questionnaire format are shown in Appendix 1.

Having defined the key variables and their measurement, we next outline a theoretical framework that clarifies the main concepts, suggests cause and effect relationships and leads to the development of a comprehensive dynamic model of the formation of country image and its effects.

The Need for a Theory of Country, Brand and Product Images

Albaum and Peterson (1984: 162-3), commenting on the findings of several authors' evaluation of the state of international marketing research, concluded that "with few exceptions, existing research on international marketing issues is fragmentary, generally atheoretic, and not sufficiently programmatic to offer anything other than simplistic and incomplete insights into the underlying phenomena of interest." Moreover, some scholars express disappointment that international marketing lacks a central research paradigm (Soldner 1984). What is true for international marketing in general is also true for country image, the subject of this book.

---

[3] See questions at the beginning of Chapter 1.

As the globalization of marketing efforts continues, the relationships between country, brand and product images on purchasing behavior become more important. To understand these relationships we need a theory. A theory serves two functions. First, assuming that a theory is valid, it provides a basis for managerial decisions. Second, it provides hypotheses that can be empirically tested. When these hypotheses are tested and accepted, the theory is validated and its application by managers is further justified. If the hypotheses are rejected, the theory has to be revised or replaced by an alternative theory, a process that increases our understanding of the phenomena considered. Thus, by providing a comprehensive theory, we increase our understanding of country image and strengthen our ability to provide guidelines for managerial action.

A Framework for Theory Development

The term *theory* has many meanings. For the purpose of our discussion we define theory as *the analysis of a set of facts in their relation to one another* (Merriam-Webster Collegiate Dictionary, 2000). In the behavior science, we have a valid theory within a desired context when we can meaningfully replace each of the words in the following sentence as a factual statement:

> *Who [verb] what, when, where, how and why.*

The *[verb]* in the above sentence should be replaced by a relevant word that relates to the topic in question. In marketing it typically relates to exposure, perceptions, retention, knowledge, attitudes, and behavior. For example, who *knows* where a product is made? Do consumers *look* for the "made-in" label? Do consumers *prefer* products made in one country over those made in another? Are they willing to *pay more* for products made in this country?

The *who, when* and *where* in the above sentence show what constraints are placed on theory (Dubin 1978). For example, *who* are the consumers that are influenced by the country image (CIE) of products they evaluate? Are there differences among consumer segments? Are managers influenced more (or less) by the country image of products they purchase for their respective organizations than are consumers? Does gender modify the country image effect (CIE) assumptions? The *when* adds the dimension of time to theory, recognizing that the same phenomenon may have a different effect over different time periods. For example, we may theorize that the effect of country image changes as international trade increases. Country image may also dynamically change as consumers gain experience with products made in certain countries. The *where,* adds the dimension of location. For example, is the *country image effect (CIE)* concept universal, i.e.; does it operate in the same way in all countries? Does it have the same effect in buying over the Internet as when buying in a retail store? Does the made-in country have the same effect on consumers in self-service as in other types of stores?

According to Dubin (1978) the *what* of theory asks which constructs logically should be considered within the boundaries of the country image effect (CIE) concept and which variables define its constructs. For example, does the effect relate only to the made-in country or also to the country of design? Which scale constitutes a valid measure of "country image"? Is it a single variable or multi-item scale? The *[verb]* as described above, may be considered a part of the *what* dimension of the theory statement. For example, is product selection a valid measure of what constitutes a country image effect? Once the *what* has been identified, the *how* specifies the interactions between the constructs or variables. For example, how will a shift of production location impact product image? Together the *what* and *how* elements constitute the domain or subject of the theory (Whetten 1989). While the *whats* and *hows* describe relationships, a further step is needed to explain *why* the proposed relationships occur.

Up to this point we treated each element in the theory statement as a source for questions to be clarified. This does not constitute a theory but rather curiosity. To be a valid theory, the sentence should make a factual statement that may be true or false. A few examples of appropriate theoretical statements should help clarify this point:

> *Israeli consumers look for products made in Japan by reading the "made-in" label when shopping for home electronic products in department stores because they believe such products are of superior quality in comparison with products made in other countries.*

This is a complete statement with all the elements of theory defined.

> *American consumers prefer to purchase American-made products in order to support the local economy.*

Even though this statement does not include all elements specified above, it is still a valid theoretical statement. Here the missing *when, where and how* imply that under all conditions American consumers prefer American made products, irrespective of *when, where* and *how* the purchase is made. Similarly, the missing elements in the following statements imply that some elements may be generalized and thereby ignored.

When shopping for fashion shoes, European women look for those made in Italy because they believe these products excel in design.

Some Australian consumers consider Sony VCRs to be better than those sold under the GE brand name because they consider Sony to be a superior brand and because they believe these VCRs are made in Japan.

All examples above provide theory statements because they define at least *what, how* and *why*. However, the following is not a proper theory statement because the missing *why* cannot be ignored:

French consumers prefer British to German made cars.

In summary, a theory should at least specify *what, how* and *why*. It may also have constraints that are placed on the theory and limit its application.

Theory-Based Approaches to CIE

Now that we understand the requirements of theory, we can proceed in the development of the theory of country, brand and product images. While there is no consensus definition of the country image effect (Sauer, et al 1991), it is generally understood to stand for the impact that generalizations and perceptions about a country have on a person's evaluations of the country's products and/or brands. Until recently, all the generalizations deduced from the combined literature on country image had no integrating theory (Liefeld 1993). Most past studies are descriptive and some are limited by methodological flaws (cf. Bilkey and Nes 1982; Jaffe and Nebenzahl 1984; Johansson 1989; Martin and Eroglu 1993; Obermiller and Spangenberg 1989). Two major flaws are the fact that many studies are overly limited by being univariate or by being static.

To overcome the univariate objection, some multi-attribute relationships were empirically tested in recent studies. Variables tested include product variability (Eroglu and Machleit 1989; Hooley, et al 1988; Howard 1989; Obermiller and Spangenberg 1989; Roth and Romeo 1992); familiarity with the product (Erickson, et al 1984; Heimbach, Johansson and MacLachlan 1989; Han 1989; Hong and Toner 1989); the use of product information (Han and Terpstra 1988; Heimbach, Johansson and MacLachlan 1989; Hong and Toner 1989; Hong and Wyer 1989; Obermiller and Spangenberg 1989; Kiecker and Duhan 1992); brand (Han and Terpstra 1988; Seaton and Vogel 1985; Tse and Gorn 1992; Witt and Rao 1992); price (Jaffe and Nebenzahl 1988; Johansson and Nebenzahl 1986; Seaton and Vogel 1985; Wall, Liefeld and Heslop 1991); warranty (Thorelli, Lim and Ye 1989); store image (Lin and Sternquist 1992, Morgansky, and Lazarde 1987); promotion (Chao 1989; Ettenson, Wagner and Gaeth 1988; Head 1988; Nebenzahl and Jaffe 1991a.); attitude toward political systems (Chasin, et al 1989; Han 1988; Wall and Heslop 1986); gender (Johansson, Douglas and Nonaka 1985; Seaton and Vogel 1985); and age and income (Johansson, Douglas and Nonaka 1985).

While these studies shed some light on the variables involved in forming consumers' attitudes towards brands and countries, they are still limited by being static. It should be obvious that relationships dynamically change over time. Thus, what is needed is a multidimensional comprehensive and dynamic model that integrates what can be summarized from the past univariate or static studies. It should be extended to include theorized relations that can be tested later. Such a model was recently suggested by Nebenzahl, Jaffe and Lampert (1997) and is the basis for the following discussion.

Country Image Effect:
A Combined Halo and Summary Construct

A number of researchers have posited that the country image effect may be explained as either a halo or a summary construct (Erickson, Johansson and Chao 1984; Johansson 1989; Johansson, Douglas and Nonaka 1985; Shimp, Samiee and Madden 1993). These constructs are explained below.

The halo construct assumes that even when a person has neither prior knowledge of, nor experience with products made in a certain country, s/he will still have a certain image of the country as a source of products. This image is based on whatever knowledge that person has about the country, including its people, and its level of economic, political and social development. In this case, a consumer's perceptions about the Made-in Country (MCI) directly impact attitudes towards products in situations where the consumer knows little about a country's products. Han (1989) proposes that the halo construct implies that (MCI) affects beliefs about product attributes that in turn affect brand attitude (product evaluation). In Han's formulation of the halo construct, this relationship is hypothesized as:

(MCI) => beliefs about attributes => brand attitude

We can formulate it as a theory statement:

Due to the need to evaluate products while having limited information (why), consumers utilize their perceived country images (how) to formulate brand attitudes (what).

The summary construct assumes that country images are based on experience with a country's products and the resulted perceived attributes of products made in it. Experience is not necessarily that of the individual, but individuals are influenced by the experience of others through information flows such as word-of-mouth and mass media. By generalizing these perceptions to attributes of unfamiliar products made in this country, country image, in turn, affects consumers' attitudes toward the brand (Crawford and Garland 1988; Hong and Wyer 1989; Howard 1989) or the specific product. Han (1989) presents this proposition as:

Experience => beliefs => (MCI) => brand attitude

This can be formulated into a theory statement:

Due to the need to evaluate unfamiliar products while having limited information (why), consumers utilize information about other products made in a certain country (how) to form their perceived country images and, in turn, brand attitudes (what).

Are the summary and halo constructs good theoretical models for explaining the country image effect? In a study of Israeli consumers, Jaffe and Nebenzahl (1988) found some evidence for the presence of halo effect only as a surrogate variable when the consumer has no familiarity with products made in the rated country. In a study conducted in the USA, Han (1989) found that the summary construct showed good fit for USA-made TV sets and automobiles, while the halo construct showed good fit for Korean-made TV sets and Korean and USA-made automobiles. Neither model showed a good fit for Japanese-made TV sets or automobiles. Why did country image operate as a halo for Korea and as a summary model for the United States? Why was neither construct relevant in the case of Japan? Han's explanation was that when consumers are unfamiliar with a country's products (the assumption in the case of American consumers vis-à-vis Korean-made goods), country image operates as a halo from which product attributes are inferred. Based on both the Jaffe and Nebenzahl (1988) and Han (1989) studies it can be concluded that lacking familiarity of a country's products, country image acts as a halo effect.

Does it follows that as consumers' experience with products or brands coming from a certain country increases, a summary construct becomes more apparent? Han (1990) suggested this possibility in an empirical study that only partially confirmed the halo effect. Another intriguing question is how could both models operate in the case of American-made automobiles in Han's (1989) study? Could it be that in evaluating complex products consumers are influenced by a halo effect even when there is product familiarity? If so, familiarity should interact with the country image effect.

The Effect of Familiarity on the Salience of the Country Image Cue

Johansson (1989) developed a model in which CIE serves as a summary of known product attributes, indicating that the higher familiarity, the stronger the influence of CIE. A more complex approach is presented in a dynamic model suggested by Lampert and Jaffe (1998). According to this model, a dynamic process begins with country image acting as a halo effect when there is no familiarity with a country's products. As consumers gain experience with products of the country they gain familiarity with the true attributes of these products. If only a few brands from the country are available, or when attributes of different brands stemming from the country are relatively uniform in certain key attributes, this information will revise the country image with respect to these attributes. From there on, country image will act as a summary effect for these and other brands. On the other hand, if products originating from the country are perceived as having wide variance with regard to most attributes, there will be no summary effect. When this occurs, CIE will be a less influencing factor in forming consumer perceptions.

This model implies that over time a country's image changes owing to consumers' exposure to and experience with products made in the country, or by changes in the quality of such products. Take, for example, the image of Japan. In early studies (Lillis and Naranya 1974; Nagashima 1970) Japan's image as a manufacturer of consumer goods was found to be lagging behind the USA and other Western countries. In later studies (Nagashima 1977; Johansson and Nebenzahl 1986; Han and Terpstra 1988), it was found to be ahead.

What additional empirical evidence regarding familiarity is available? A number of studies have found a positive correlation between product familiarity and use of the made-in cue (Johansson, Douglas and Nonaka 1985; Johansson and Nebenzahl 1986; Johansson, 1989). Other researchers tried to show that use of the made-in cue is a function of the interaction between familiarity and the confidence and predictive value of this cue (Heimbach, Johansson and MachLachlan 1989; Eroglu and Machleit 1989). While a positive association was found between product familiarity and the made-in cue (Heimbach, et al p. 465), the correlation coefficients were low. Knight and Calantone (2000) suggested a flexible model that includes both halo and summary components. In a static comparative empirical experiment, the flexible model was found to be superior to the halo and summary models when tested alone. When consumers have low familiarity with a given country's products, product beliefs were assumed to affect attitudes more than country image. On the other hand, when familiarity is high, country image was assumed to have a greater effect on attitudes than product beliefs. Although these assumptions are interesting, the results of the experiment were inconclusive. In a recent study, Laroche, et al (2005), found that both country image and product beliefs affected product evaluations regardless of consumers' level of familiarity with foreign products.

Noting that in all these studies only static cross sectional data were used, it can be concluded that there is some evidence that country image may act as a summary as well as a halo effect and that both effects may operate simultaneously. Accordingly, we would like to suggest here a revision of the halo and summary models by merging the two independent and supposedly alternative models into a single unified multi-stage dynamic rather than static model. This model is presented in Figure 2.1.

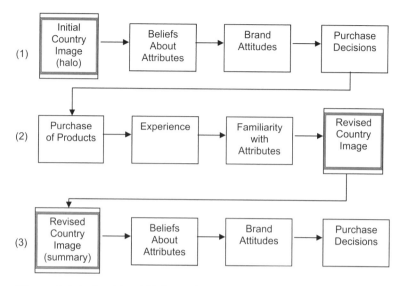

Figure 2.1 A Combined Halo and Summary Model of Country Image

In the first stage, prior to having meaningful experience, the image of a country acts as a halo in impacting beliefs about the expected attributes of products, which result in attitudes toward the brand or product. In the second stage, following purchase, experience serves to revise the knowledge about attributes of products that is followed by a revision of the country image. The more the country image is based on actual experience, the more it becomes a summary as distinct from the halo effect. In the third stage, the revised country image serves to form expectations (beliefs) about products attributes.

We can formulate the above as theory statements:

Due to the need to evaluate products while having limited information (why), consumers utilize their perceived country images (how) to formulate brand attitudes (what). Having experience with products made in a country (how) leads to a revision of that country image as a producer (what). For the sake of efficiency or need to evaluate new products (why), the revised country image is utilized by consumers (how) to formulate attitudes toward these and other products or brands made in the country (what).

To summarize, the dynamic model presented above implies that over time the role of country image may shift from a halo effect when no information is available about a country's products to a summary effect as familiarity from product experience becomes more salient. This model is based on the assumption that if consumers perceive different brands originating from a given country as having the same attributes, e.g. quality (little variance between similar attributes of more than one brand), country image becomes a summary concept. In these cases it increases in importance because it is a more efficient way for consumers to process information. If consumers perceive a number of Japanese brands to have the same level of attributes - new, unfamiliar Japanese brands entering the market will be evaluated by a more salient country image cue than by brand name. However, if consumers' experience results in the perception of high variability among attributes of different brands of a given country, country image becomes less salient in effecting perceptions.

This dynamic model may provide, at long last, a solution to the conflicting empirical evidence dilemma presented above. Studies conducted on products imported from newly exporting countries, such as Korea in Han's (1989) study, provide evidence for the initial halo effect. Studies conducted on products made in countries with whose products consumers have extensive experience over time, such as TV sets made in the USA in Han's (1989) study, document the resultant summary effect. Studies that found neither halo nor summary effect, as in the case of Japan in Han's study, show evidence for the transition stage. Finally, studies that support simultaneously both halo and summary effects, as is the case of USA-made automobiles in Han's study, show that for high familiarity countries and complex products, experience does not erase the overall country image halo effect. In conclusion, the empirical studies found in the literature that reported conflicting evidence simply measured different phenomena.

Even the dynamic model presented in Figure 2.1 is incomplete, since it does not fully detail the relationships between brand and country images. It also ignores the possibility that the images of more than one country are involved. A more complete model that attempts to cover the gamut of possibilities is presented in the next section.

An Integrative Dynamic Model of Country, Brand and Product Images

Nebenzahl, Jaffe and Lampert (1997) integrated the dynamic model of Lampert and Jaffe (1998)[4] with the dynamic halo-summary model presented above and extended it into a more general model. This model attempts to present a more complete theory of country image by showing the elements and their interactions involved in forming consumers' attitudes toward products made in certain countries. It also shows how these images are revised over time with added experience and other marketing information. The country image phenomenon is viewed as a dynamic process in which country and brand images interact to eventually impact product choice. All these attitudinal images, in turn, are revised by consumers' experience with the alternative product choices that were previously made.

The suggested model is based on an assumption that there are overall brand and country images, as well as specific product line images that affect the perception of attributes of products associated with the country or being sold under the brand name. A key concept of this integrative model is the relativism of perceived images. All product, brand and country images are considered to have meaning only in relation to other products, brands and countries, respectively. Thus, when we say, for example, that Japan is perceived as a relatively high quality source for home electronic products, we mean that such products are perceived to be of higher quality than those made in other, lower quality-image countries. Similarly, when Italy is perceived to excel in shoe design, it is in relation with other countries that are viewed as less capable in this regard. The same holds true for brands and particular branded product lines. The implication of this premise is that perceived improvement in the image of any one product, brand, or country leads to perceived relative deterioration of the competing products, brands or countries, respectively, even when the latter have not changed. In competitive markets this model makes a lot of sense, since purchase decisions are based on relative rather than absolute levels of attributes of competitive products.

Figure 2.2 presents an overall summary of our model. For all products available in the market (PIj), consumers receive information about the made-in country (MC), country of design (DC), country of association (OC) and brand. Based on the information and relative image of each cue and the perceived attributes of the competing

---

[4] The authors of the 1997 article had prior exposure to the 1998 publication.

products purchase, decisions are made. Purchases lead to new experience with different products, experience that leads to a revision of all images by means of feedback. In this manner, all country, brand and product images are revised, thus affecting future purchase decisions.

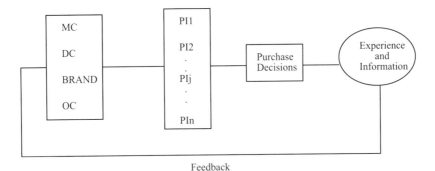

Feedback

Source: Nebenzahl, Jaffe and Lampert (1997)
Figure 2.2 An Information Processing Model of Relative Product Image

We now turn to a detailed description of the model. In this model we further propose that there are two-way interactions among all image components. To demonstrate these propositions, our exposition begins at the relative brand and country image level and works its way to relative product image and product choice, as presented in Figure 2.3. It proceeds from product experience back to brand and country images, as presented in Figures 2.4 and 2.5. We consider the first section, shown in Figure 2.3 to be a static part of the model, as has been done in most country image studies. The remaining parts of the model add the dynamic nature of the process.

Figure 2.3 shows the hypothesized causal paths leading to relative product image (PI) and eventual product choice for a consumer residing in a given country (HC) during time period t.

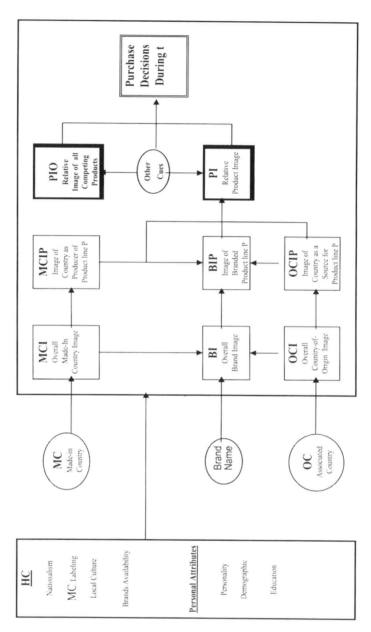

Source: Nebenzahl, Jaffe and Lampert (1997)

Figure 2.3 The Formation of Relative Product Image, Given the Consumer's HC

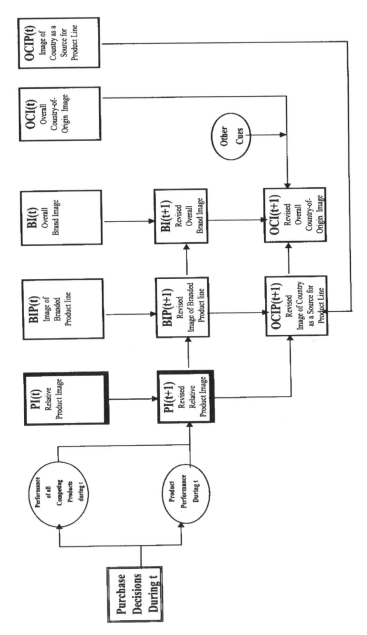

Source: Nebenzahl, Jaffe and Lampert (1997)

Figure 2.4 The Formation of Revised Origin Country Image, OCI, Given the Consumer's HC

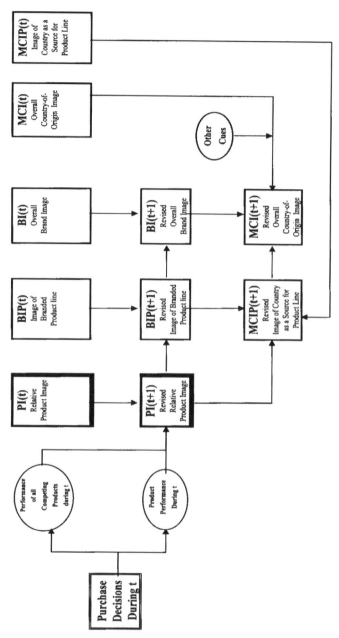

Source: Nebenzahl, Jaffe and Lampert (1997)

*Figure 2.5 The Formation of Revised Made-in Country Image, MCI,
Given the Consumer's HC*

The model begins with individuals that reside in a given country, noted as HC. It is assumed that due to cultural and environmental differences, residents of different countries may have different perceptions of a given country's products and services (Amine 1994). That is why it is important to first note the country of residence of the consumers whose behavior is to be studied. Examples of domestic variables that affect the process are degree of nationalism and ethnocentrism in the country, made-in labeling requirements, and availability of brands in the local market. Personal attributes, such as age, gender and education are also considered as impacting the process. HC variables that have been investigated include attitudes toward political systems (Han, 1988; Wall and Heslop, 1986; Chasin, et al, 1989); gender (Johansson, Douglas and Nonaka, 1985; Seaton and Vogel, 1985); age and income (Johansson, Douglas and Nonaka, 1985). Accordingly, HC is shown to impact all stages of the information processing in the formation of relative product image. It can be concluded that one should take extreme caution in generalizing results found in a given country to other countries.

We now explain the details of the interrelations of the static part of the model presented in Figure 2.3. The process begins with consumer exposure to a branded product in the market. Perceived information cues are assumed to include the brand name and the made-in country name (MC). The information transmitted by these cues may trigger recall of one or more overall relative images associated with the product that may affect its evaluation. These include the relative images of the respective brand (BI), the made-in country image (MCI), the image of the country where the product was designed (DCI) (not shown in the figure), the image of the country of assembly (ACI) (not shown in the figure) and the image of the country where the consumer believes the brand originated (OCI) (not shown). All recalled images are mentally processed and integrated to eventually form an image of the exposed product (PI).

The Effects of the Made-In Country (MC)

Let us begin with the made-in country cue (MC). It triggers recall of MCI, the individual's overall perception of the country's ability as a manufacturer. This overall image (halo for unfamiliar countries or summary for familiar countries with consistent qualities) will influence perception of the country as a manufacturer of the given product line (MCIP), say VCRs. While the overall country image (MCI) impacts the image of the specific product line (MCIP), the perceived images

49

are not necessarily the same. For example, a highly favorable country image (MCI) does not guarantee a highly favorable country image as a source for a certain product line (MCIP). This may be illustrated by the fact that the image for Russian-made automobiles may be significantly lower than the overall image of Russia. Conversely, the image of Russian-made vodka may be significantly higher than the corresponding overall image of Russia.

It is generally accepted that the country image effect (CIE) is product category specific (Etzel and Walker 1974; Halfhill 1980). The question is, what is the span of influence that country image carries? In some cases, country image is confined to a type of product within a product category (Gaedeke, 1973; Heslop, Liefeld and Wall 1987), at times it relates to a whole product category (Nagashima 1970; Wang 1978). Thus, England has a positive country image in the United States for luxury cars, due to Rolls Royce and Jaguar. Yet, its image for other types of cars is weak. In contrast, Japan has a strong image for medium-priced cars, but not for the high end. Yet, Japan has a strong image for cameras over the whole range of camera types. Germany, Japan, France and Italy have strong images in several product categories: Japan in cars, cameras and consumer electronics; France in wines, perfume and clothing; Italy in furniture, shoes and sports cars. Looking at these realities, it appears that country image can spillover from one product class to another. For this reason, our model shows a causal relationship from overall country image (MCI) to the image of a specific product line (MCIP). However, such spillovers are more likely to occur among product categories sharing common characteristics. Japan and Germany have established their image in products having a high level of technology; France is associated with fashion, while Italy in product categories involving attractive design. Thus, the boundaries for establishing country image are not confined to specific product categories.

While the made-in label triggers beliefs about the made-in country (MCI), a similar perceptual process is invoked by the country of design (DC) when it is specified on the product label or via other marketing communications. The country of design (DC) acts much the same as the made-in country (MC) in invoking its image of the country as a source of design (DCI) and triggering and impacting the image of that country as a design location of the specific product line DCIP. Similar comments can be made about AC, the country of assembly. Since the flows of relationships stemming from knowledge of the country of design (DC) or country of assembly (AC) are parallel with the made-in country (MC) throughout the model, for the sake of brevity and clarity they are omitted from the presentation. As a note of caution, it should be stressed that this convenient omission should not reflect on the importance of the countries of design or assembly and their potential utilization in marketing tactics.

The Effect of Brand Name

Next, we turn to the brand name (BI). Past studies have linked brand image to consumer perception of product quality (Jacoby, Olson and Haddock 1971). As is the case with country cues, consumers' overall beliefs about a given brand (BI) may vary by specific product lines produced under the brand name. For example, consumers perceive Pierre Cardin to be a fashionable brand (BI). The image of a specific branded product line or product item (BIP) may vary from the overall brand image (BI), even though it impacts all specific product lines sold under the brand name. For example, if camping equipment were to be sold under the Pierre Cardin label, the resulting product line image (BIP) would most likely be lower than its overall brand image (BI). The product line brand image (BIP) is also impacted by the relative image of the country as a source for the respective product line (MCIP).

Nebenzahl and Jaffe (1991b) confirmed these relationships in their study of the perceived brand image of Sony and GE (BIP) home electronic products as production is sourced from Western to Eastern European countries (MC). In their study, they measured the image of each brand without reference to a country, the image of Eastern European countries as producers of home electronic products and the image of the brands when sourced from the studied countries. All measurements were done using the same multi-item scale. It was found that the image of each brand when sourced from an Eastern European country was between the original image of respective brand and country images.

The Effect of the Perceived Country of Origin (OC)

The brand name cue evokes not only beliefs about the brand itself (BI), but also triggers recall of the country associated with it as its country of origin (OC). For example, regardless of where Philips products are produced (MC), consumers may also associate them with the Netherlands (OC), thus triggering the relative overall image of this country (OCI) and its image as a source for the specified product line (OCIP). As is the case for the made-in country, the associated country affects the brand image of the product line (BIP) and moderates the effect of the brand image alone.

The determination of the image of a particular make and model (PI) completes the brand and country information processing. When a product's made-in country (MC) is known to consumers prior to exposure to the product's attributes, the image of the country as a producer of the product line (MCIP) affects product image (PI) through the image of the branded product line (BIP). If a product's made-in country (MC) is made known when the product's attributes are evaluated, the image of the country as a producer of the product line (MCIP) directly affects the product image (PI). In this case, the made-in country (MC) functions as an attribute of the product (Hong and Wyer, 1990). In addition, product image (PI) is influenced by other exogenous cues such as price, store image and product warranty. This possibility, presented by a circle in the model, is discussed below.

The Effect of Extrinsic Cues on Product Evaluations
In addition to the salient brand and country effects, the integrative paradigm also includes other predictor and/or moderating extrinsic cues such as price, promotion and store image (Dodds, Monroe and Grewal 1991; Rao and Monroe 1989; Zeithaml 1988). The effect of price on perceived product quality and buying intentions has been well documented in the marketing literature (cf. Monroe 1979; Monroe and Krishnan 1985).

Comparative Evaluation and Purchase Decisions
As noted earlier, product image is meaningful only in relative terms, that is, in comparison with alternatives. This is represented in the model by the presence of PIOs, the relative image of all competing products. According to this model, consumer choice and purchase decisions are based on the relative image of each alternative product that is considered in comparison with those of all other alternatives. In addition, decisions are also influenced by the additional extrinsic cues.

The Interaction among Determinants of Product Image
Up to this point we have described information cues that affect the image of each alternative product and product choices. But are there interactions among these cues? In the presence of competing cues, does each still exert its effect? Does the interaction lead to stronger or weaker effects? Studies of the interaction effects of multiple cues show mixed results. Andrews and Valenzi (1971) and Render and O'Connor

(1976) found that price produced a stronger effect on quality perception than brand or store image, while Gardner (1974) found a moderate effect for price and brand name. Dodds, Monroe and Grewal (1991) studied the effect of price, brand and store information on buyers' perceptions of product quality and value, as well as their willingness to buy. They found that price had a positive effect on perceived quality, but a negative effect on perceived value and willingness to buy. Favorable brand and store information positively influenced perceptions of quality, value, and willingness to buy.

In one of the few multiple-cue studies incorporating country-of-origin (Seaton and Vogel 1985), it was found that the made-in country had the most effect on consumer evaluation of product quality, while brand name had a moderate effect and price an insignificant effect. Wall et al (1991) found that country-of-origin information was more important in affecting product quality assessments than price and brand information. Thorelli, Lim and Ye (1988) studied the effects of country of origin, product warranty and store image on perceived quality, overall attitude and purchase intention. They found that all three independent variables affected product quality and overall attitude, but not purchase intention. However, they also found that country of origin had the least effect when it interacted with the other two cues. In a related, multi-cue study of store image and made-in country effect on consumer perceptions, Lin and Sternquist (1992) found that the made-in country was the only cue that influenced consumers' product perception, while store prestige did not. Morgansky and Lazarde (1987) studied the effect that store type, brand type and import status had on apparel quality. Although they found that a store's association with imported merchandise can lower the quality perception for that store, their experiment was limited because no brand names were used (only type of product) and no specific countries were named (only imported versus domestic product). In the Thorelli et al (1988) study, brand was not included. As a result, in both studies the influence of brand name was not measured and in the last named, country of origin was not included. Therefore, future studies should examine the interaction of country-of-origin and other extrinsic cues.

Dynamic Aspects of the CIE

As noted above, a country's image changes over time. Moreover, there may be a two-way influence between a product's brand image (BI), made-in country image (MCI) and the perceived origin country of the brand (OCI). For example, a well known global branded product such as a Sony VCR when sourced in a weak-image country such as Russia may improve the country image of Russia (MCI) while eroding the brand image of Sony (Nebenzahl and Jaffe, 1991b). When production takes place in Russia, the erosion of Sony's image may subsequently erode the image of Japan (OCI) due to their association (OC), even though the product was not produced there. The same holds true for the countries of design (DC) and assembly (AC). Thus, the image of a number of countries may be affected by experience with a single branded product. These dynamic perceptual image revision processes are (with the exclusion of DC and AC) modeled in Figures 2.4 and 2.5.

The link between the static part of the detailed country image model presented in Figure 2.3 and dynamic parts presented in Figures 2.4 and 2.5 are the purchase decisions made during period t. Thus, the ending node of Figure 2.3 is the beginning node of Figures 2.4 and 2.5. When we overlap these nodes, we integrate the figures into a single unified dynamic model.

Given the experience with products purchased during period t, consumers evaluate the relative satisfaction from these and other purchases. The evaluation made by an individual customer is not limited to his or her own purchases. By way of word-of-mouth and mass media communications the individual is exposed to the experience of others as well. Thus, the evaluation is a learning process that integrates experience information from varied sources. This evaluation leads to a revised relative product image in the following period PI(t+1) as shown in Figures 2.4 and 2.5. As illustrations, we show the effect of experience on the image of the country of association (OCI) and the made-in country image (MCI) in Figure 2.4 and Figure 2.5. Revisions of the images of the countries of design (DCI) and assembly (ACI) operate in the same way as the made-in country (MCI).

As shown in Figures 2.4 and 2.5, experience with products purchased during period t and earlier causes a functional chain of reactions that result in a revision of all brand and country images in later periods. By linking each revised image at t+1 with the corresponding image during t, the dynamic model stresses that the revision of images is a long run updating process in which experience leads to some revision in prior perceptions rather than their immediate total replacement. This is consistent with the combined halo and summary model developed above. As shown in Figures 2.4 and 2.5, experience initially operates at the brand level, where the revised product image PI (t+1) leads to corresponding revisions in the image of the brand as a producer of the product line BIP (t+1) and the overall brand image BI (t+1). While the model does not show it graphically, it should be understood that the image of the brand as a source of the product line (BIP (t+1)) is impacted by all products of the branded product line and that the revised overall brand image (BI (t+1)) is impacted by all product lines sold under the same brand name. Following and in parallel with the revision of brand images, country images are also updated. Figure 2.4 shows that the image of the country associated with the brand as a source for the particular product line (OCIP (t+1)) is impacted by the revised brand images of the respective product lines (BIP (t+1)) of all branded products associated with the country. In addition to the above, the overall country image (OCI (t+1)) is also impacted by the revised overall brand images (BI (t+1)) of all brands associated with the country. As shown in Figure 2.5, a similar parallel process leads to updating the image of the made-in country as a source of the product line (MCIP (t+1)) and the overall made-in country image (MCI (t+1)).

To follow the logic of the model consider, for example, what would happen if consumers were to be highly dissatisfied with, say, Sony VCRs made in Malaysia. This experience will result in the erosion of Sony's image as a producer of VCRs (BIP (t+1)), in the overall image of Sony (BI (t+1)), in the image of Malaysia as a producer of VCRs (MCIP (t+1)), in the overall image of Malaysia, (MCI (t+1)), in the image of Japan as a source of VCRs (OCIP (t+1)) and in the overall image of Japan (OCI (t+1)). Consider next that consumers are relatively satisfied with such products, but consider them of lower value than Japanese-made Sony VCRs. In this case, one can expect erosion in the images of Sony and Japan while those of Malaysia will improve.

Even though there are a modest number of longitudinal studies describing the direction and duration of changes in country image (Dornoff, Tankersley and White 1974; Jaffe and Nebenzahl 1989; Nagashima 1970, 1977; Schieb 1977; Wood and Darling 1992), they do not adequately explain why observed changes have occurred and therefore do not meet the requirements of theory. The duration of each time period, t, in the model, during which all relative images are revised, has not been empirically studied. Future empirical studies should address this issue. It should be short enough to allow for capturing short-term changes. On the other hand, it should be long enough to allow experience with new products to yield valid assessment of changes in product attributes rather than just random fluctuations in measurements. Given the length of time it took to observe changes in the image of brands and countries, (Nebenzahl and Jaffe 1991a), we believe that the time duration of t should be measured in years for country image and in months for brand image when the brand is extensively promoted. With this frame in mind, it is likely that brand images can be intentionally revised within a year or two. The length of time required to *intentionally* change the image of a country will depend on the marketing efforts exerted by government of the country and by companies associated with it. Given the paucity of data on the time required to bring about significant image changes, future studies should be devoted to the dynamics of image revision processes.

Conclusion

Following the logic of the dynamic model of this chapter, we posit that the role country image plays in product evaluation changes in a predictable way. Initially, when there is no consumer experience with products in a given product line, relative country images play a decisive role in determining brand and product perceptions. This is the situation that Nagashima (1970) found in 1967 when American (and Japanese) respondents believed that "made-in Japan" was synonymous with cheap, mass-produced goods. When a country's brands are introduced in a foreign market, if there is low variability in their attributes, the initial halo role of country image will gradually be replaced by a summary role, which is a function of the true attributes of the country's products. This is what Nagashima (1977) observed in his 1975 study that showed the image of Japanese products had improved. If, on the other hand, there is a high variability in the attributes of brands associated with a country, country image will have a minor influence, which only colors, rather than strongly impacts the perception of products. These observations imply that for country image to change, a consistent and sustained long-term experience is required. Indeed, the notable, post-war changes in the images of Japan and other East Asian countries took decades, rather than years to occur.

In this chapter we presented a conceptual theoretical model for the explanation of brand and country-of-origin effects. The graphic presentation of the model facilitates the formulation of numerous theory statements. In Figures 2.3, 2.4 and 2.5, each arrow can be translated to a theory statement or proposition. For example, the arrow linking *brand name* with the country-of-origin associated with the brand (OC) in Figure 2.3 can be formulated into the following:

Due to prior knowledge that a given country is associated with a certain brand in the mind of consumers (why), exposure to the brand name (how) triggers recall of that country and its attributes.

Each of these theory statements or propositions may be further translated into a hypothesis for empirical testing by providing operational measures for the included variables and their interactions. The structure of the model also suggests which variables are exogenous, which are intervening and which are functions of other variables. As noted throughout this chapter while discussing the model, some of the theory statements included in the model have been previously tested empirically. Others call for future research. There also remains much work to be done in order to test the interrelationships between made-in country image, origin country image and brand image.

The two-way interaction between brand and country images has interesting strategic implications for both government and multinational companies. What strategies can be employed by a firm, industry and government to improve country image in each stage of the product life cycle? What elements of the marketing-mix should be used to change country image over the long run as opposed to those that may compensate for a negative image in the short run? What are the ramifications of the international legal environment? These are some of the topics to be covered in the remaining chapters of this book. Before getting into these details there is a need to find ways for the assessment of the monetary implications of country image. This is done in the next chapter.

CHAPTER 3

Monetizing Brand and Country Images

Measure what is measurable, and make measurable what is not so
Galileo Galilei (1564-1642)

Introduction

It should be noted that practically all measures of country image discussed in the previous chapter are based on rating scales that elicit consumers' attitudes toward countries. Such scales are deficient in that they do not provide a measure of the economic consequences of these attitudes. Intuitively, it should be self evident that, *ceteris paribus*, a country having a better image than others, especially as a source for a product, has a comparative advantage that should translate to economic value, and vice versa.

The need to estimate the economic value, or to *monetize* country image, is of utmost importance for managerial sourcing decisions as well as national image policies. Presently, in sourcing decisions, cost-benefit analyses of production and shipping costs are considered while consumers' perceptions are ignored. Given that low production costs are usually associated with low country image; will the benefits of cost savings be higher than the loss in revenues resulting from the low image? Similarly, knowing that a certain country has a highly positive image is valuable information in itself. But should that country invest in maintaining its image? And if yes, how much is it reasonable to invest? And conversely, should a low image country engage in an image promoting campaign? To answer such questions there is a need to link images with their corresponding values. Accordingly, in this chapter we review recent developments in the assessment of brand equity, show the relationship between brand image and brand value as well as between country image and its value, and discuss how these concepts and procedures can be applied to the assessment of country image value.

Brand Image, Brand Equity and Brand Value
- From Consumer Perceptions to Measurable Values

In the past two decades, brand equity and its assessment were key topics in the marketing literature. Aaker (1991) and Keller (1993) provided the conceptual basis for most research that followed. According to Aaker (1991, p. 15), brand equity is "a set of assets and liabilities linked to a brand, its name, and symbol, that add to or subtract from the value provided by a product or service to a firm and/or to that firm's customers." Given its impact on subsequent research, let us highlight the concepts encompassed in this definition. First, we note that Aaker considers both assets and liabilities, that is, both positive and negative elements and their impact. This is in line with our understanding of brand or country image and their effect. However, the word *equity*, due to its use in finance as the value of owners, is positively biased. As a result, in the bulk of the literature equity is taken to represent only the positive contribution of the brand, neglecting the other possibility. Second, in this conceptualization, brand equity is an antecedent to value. As we will see shortly, this relationship is often lost and equity and value are used as synonyms, or value is considered a subset of equity. We contend that the original conceptualization of Aaker should be kept. Third, equity affects the value to the firm or its customers. This led to the study of brand equity from two different perspectives, a *firm-based brand equity* and *customer-based brand equity* (Capon et al, 2001). The first is based on the finances of the firm while the second considers consumer perception and behavior as equity. Only recently Gupta and Lehmann (2003) merged the two approaches in a model described below.

Keller (1993) conceptualizes brand equity from the perspective of the individual consumer, his knowledge, and the implications of this knowledge for marketing strategies. Keller defines consumer knowledge in terms of brand awareness and brand image. He defines customer-based brand equity as the differential effect of brand knowledge on consumer response to the marketing of the brand, namely, "a brand is said to have positive (negative) customer-based brand equity if consumers react more (less) favorably to the product, price, promotion, or distribution of the brand than they do to the same marketing mix element when it is attributed to a fictitiously named or unnamed version of the product or service" (Keller, 1993, p. 8). With the exception of the customer-based focus, this definition of equity is similar to that of Aaker. Thus, while there are some differences in terminology and focus, both the Aaker and Keller conceptualizations of brand equity are rather similar.

Operationalization of the brand equity concept has proved to be a far greater challenge (for a comprehensive review of the literature see Hoeffler and Keller, 2003). We identify two operationalization stages in the literature; the first entails specifying the dimensions of brand equity and the second the development of scales for the measurement of these dimensions. The dimensions identified by Aaker (1991) are *brand awareness*—the ability of a potential buyer to recognize or recall that a brand is a member of a certain product category; *brand association*—anything linked in memory to a brand; *perceived quality*—the consumer's judgment about a product's overall excellence; and *brand loyalty*—"a deeply held commitment to rebuy or repatronize a preferred product or service consistently in the future, despite situational influences and marketing efforts having the potential to cause switching behavior" (Oliver, 1997, p. 392). With the exception of brand awareness, all these dimensions can be identified as elements of brand image, indicating how close the two concepts are.

Keller (1993), as noted earlier, conceptualized brand equity as consisting of brand awareness and brand image. The dimensions of brand image are consumer perceptions about the product attributes, perceived benefits and attitudes toward the brand. These, in turn, affect consumer behavior, or reactions to marketing stimuli, such as price.

With regard to measurement of the conceptualized dimensions, Keller (1993) makes detailed suggestions for indirect and direct measures. Indirect measures assess consumer perceptions, that is, elements of brand image. Direct measure estimate the results, such as the premium or discount consumers are willing to pay in comparison with unbranded similar offers. Aaker (1996) suggested a ten-item scale for the measurement of these dimensions and of market behavior—the brand's market share and its relative price and distribution system. While the original dimensions are all consumer related, the added "market behavior" dimension reflects company policies rather than consumer perceptions, digressing from the original conceptualization. Of particular interest to us is a concept called *price premium,* the first scale item suggested by Aaker for the measurement of loyalty, which is the amount a customer will pay for the brand in comparison with other brands that offer similar benefits. Aaker (1996, p. 107) states that this measure "may be the best single measure of brand equity available because, in most contexts, any driver of brand equity should affect the price premium. The price premium thus becomes a reasonable summary of the strength of the brand." We fully agree with this observation and consider price premium not a part of brand equity, but its consequence, namely, the consumer-based relative brand value, to be discussed shortly.

We can now summarize the above discussion by modeling the relationship between brand awareness, brand image, brand equity and brand value. As Figure 3.1 shows, brand awareness and brand image are antecedents to brand equity. What this relation states is that, in addition to positive brand image associations, a brand has to be first identified by the consumer in the market. Brand equity, in turn, leads to behavior which results in brand value. This model was recently tested in a number of empirical studies. In their development of a brand equity scale based on Aaker (1991) and Keller's (1993) conceptualization of brand equity, Yoo and Danthu (2001) assumed that brand equity is composed of four dimensions. However, their results confirmed only three factors, brand loyalty, perceived quality, and brand awareness/associations. Thus, they could not distinguish between brand awareness and brand associations. This result with regard to awareness/associations could stem from the limited number of scale items (10) included in their measurement. Their analysis did confirm the relation between brand equity and consumer-based brand value. Baldauf et al (2003) tested the same Aaker (1991) and Keller (1993) conceptual model and confirmed it empirically. They found that brand equity, measured by awareness, perceived quality and loyalty, significantly affects brand value, measured by sales, brand profit-ability, and customer perceived value. Hsieh (2003) tested and confirmed a mathematical version of this model at the consumers' country of residence level (HC). They derived separate parameters of the model for consumers residing in a number of different countries and show how results by country can be aggregated to a global brand value. De Mortanges and van Riel (2003) used Young and Rubicam's BrandAsset Valuator (BAV) (Young & Rubicam Group, 2005) as a measure of brand equity and found that it is positively related to brand value as measured by shareholder value. It can be concluded therefore, that recent academic studies have verified the validity of this model.

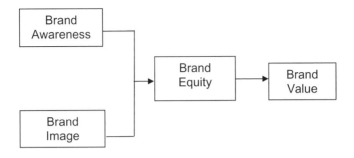

Figure 3.1 Brand Equity Model

Country Image, Country Equity and Country Value

We can now extend the image, equity and value concepts from the product-brand to the country-brand level. Let's consider first the impact of country image at the product or service level. In Chapter 2 we presented the relationships between country image and brand image. To recall, the country of origin and the made-in country images are impacting brand image. A highly positive country image as a source of the product will, therefore, add to the positive image of the brand and as a result to its equity and value.

Second, considering the recent trend towards place branding, we can view a country name just as a 'brand name' associated with products. In a seminal paper on the subject, Papadopoulos and Heslop (2002) contend that countries are not unlike large corporations. They state (p. 308) that "a country is a 'corporation' that produces many products, not a unitary 'product'. As such, it needs a *corporate* positioning strategy based on its core competencies, which today arise not from raw materials or low business costs *per se,* but largely from people, ideas, approach, and styles of doing business. The competencies of Switzerland, for example, (accuracy, trustworthiness, etc.) are transferable and actionable in unique ways to the different 'product lines' of the country, such as tourism, banking or the exporting of watches and premium dairy products." Accordingly, just as GM, a corporation producing diverse products is a corporate brand having equity and value, so is Switzerland. Thus, country image leads directly to country equity. But, just as is the case with company brands, country image will lead to country equity only if there is also consumer awareness of the country either by the made-in label or by perceived associations. Country equity leads to consumer-based country value, where country value is the differential value to the consumers when the country is associated with products. That is why products coming from developed countries can be priced higher than products sourced in less developed countries. It also leads to nation-based country value, namely, the difference in the overall value of all products produced in a country in comparison with the corresponding value had they been produced in other countries.

Estimating Relative Customer-Based Brand Value

Methods for estimating relative brand value follow the definition of customer-based brand value, namely, the added value contributed by the brand name to a product. As a result of this added value, consumers are willing to pay more than for other products. Some researchers define "other products" as unbranded products (Keller, 1993; Yoo and Donthu, 2001). Accordingly, their estimation methods pit the branded product against a similar but unbranded one (Simon and Sullivan, 1993). Others define "other products" as "competitive brands" (Winter, 1991; Aaker, 1996; Usunier, 1996; Crimmins, 2000). According to this definition, relative brand value is the premium (discount) that consumers are willing to pay in order to get the branded product in comparison with that of a competing brand (Crimmins, 2000). Given that by and large, unbranded products are not available in modern markets, this becomes a theoretical concept unfamiliar to consumers. For this reason, we prefer the second definition and suggest that brands should be pitted against each other, for example, the valued brand in comparison with its strongest competitor, in determining relative value.

It should be noted that all the definitions above focus on the consumer. It is, therefore, expected that measures proposed for the assessment of brand value will be operationalized at the individual consumer level. In one such method utilized in a number of past studies (Aaker, 1996; Crimmins, 2000; Boosi, 2003), consumers were presented with a branded product having a certain price tag. They were then asked how much more or less they were willing to pay for a similar product but bearing an alternative brand name. The required premium or discount, measured in monetary terms is the relative brand value. For example, in Boosi's (2003) study, Israeli respondents were asked to rate the image of Honda and Subaru passenger cars. Their average ratings on the brand image scale were 4.97 and 3.39, indicating that Honda was considered as having a relatively higher brand image and equity. Respondents were also given a base price for Subaru of NIS 100,000 and were asked how much more or less they were willing to pay for a similar car but bearing the Honda brand. The average price was NIS 113,144, yielding a premium of NIS 13,144. It can be concluded that the value of Honda in comparison with Subaru is this premium sum. In order to facilitate comparison among brand values of products having divergent price ranges, the monetary premium or discount can be converted to a percentage. In our example, respondents were willing to pay a premium of 13 percent for the Honda brand.

Brand Image and Brand Value

What is the relationship between brand image and brand value? In order to answer this question, Boosi (2003) measured two competing brand images on a multi-item scale and relative brand value. She then regressed the relative brand value as a function of image. In an initial survey employing self administered written questionnaires; respondents rated pairs of brands and assessed their relative value. By subtracting the image score of one brand from the other, this method facilitated computing not only the relative brand values but also their relative brand image differences. Table 3.1 presents the results of regression analyses of the two image measures.

Product Line	N	Constant	B	F	Adjusted R^2
First Study					
Passenger cars					
Relative image	130	-0.04	0.08	143	0.523
Brand image	130	-0.63	0.13	119	0.477
Soft Drinks					
Relative image	126	-0.08	0.15	201	0.614
Brand image	126	-0.97	0.23	143	0.529
Airlines					
Relative image	124	-0.05	0.14	130	0.509
Brand image	124	-0.78	0.18	71	0.359

Using F test, all equations are significant at $\alpha < 0.000$

Source: Adopted from Boosi, (2003) Table 6, p. 68.

Table 3.1 Regressions of Relative Brand Value as a function of Relative Brand Image and of a single Brand Image (Self-Administered Questionnaire)

It should be noted that the first regression for each product line, which takes into account the image of both brands, has consistently higher R^2 values than the second, which utilizes the image of only one of the brands.

In a follow up telephone survey, respondents rated only one of the brands. Table 3.2 presents the results of this survey.

Product Line	N	Constant	B	F	Adjusted R²
Passenger cars	151	-0.04	0.14	77	0.335
Soft Drinks	150	-0.03	0.13	59	0.280
Airlines	145	-0.09	0.16	42	0.221

Using F tests, all equations are significant at $\alpha < 0.000$

Source: Adopted from Boosi, (2003) p. 88.
Table 3.2 Regressions of Relative Brand Value as a function of a single Brand Image (Telephone Survey)

Here the image variable power in explaining the relative brand value is somewhat lower, as is evident from the corresponding F and R^2 values. This difference is caused by the mind-set respondents had due to the research instrument. In the first survey, by rating both brands before giving their relative values, the pros and cons of each brand were considered in estimating their relative value. In the second survey, the pros and cons of only one brand were considered prior to estimating the relative value of the brands. In this case, less information was utilized by respondents, resulting in less accurate results.

As noted earlier, the method described above is operationalized at the consumer level. Individual consumer data can later be aggregated to the corporate level for brand related decisions. Such data are highly useful in making brand promotions and other branding decisions.

Estimating Relative Country Image Value

Johansson and Nebenzahl (1986) made the first attempt to "monetize" the country image effect by measuring the relative consumer-based value of the images of different countries. The methodology they employed is similar to that of relative brand image. It shows consumers an anchor price for a product when made in its country of association, OCI. Respondents are then asked how much more or less than the anchor price they are willing to pay for the same branded product when made in another country. Using this method they determined that manufacturing a Buick or a Chevy car in Mexico, in place of the United States, reduced the value of the cars by approximately $1,500, from $9,000 to $7,500. The same methodology was utilized recently by Seaton and Laskey (1999) who found that a change in the assembly location of a $17,000 automobile from the

USA to Mexico would result in a reduction in perceived value of $1,952.

Nebenzahl and Jaffe (1993) realized that the raw data derived by this method of questioning facilitates more detailed analysis than just computing the average price change. Using the cumulative frequency distribution of the prices cited by respondents, they extended this methodology by estimating quasi-demand preference curves. In these preference curves, the "price" is defined as the percent discount or premium from the anchor base price. "Quantity" is the proportion of consumers that would purchase the sourced product at the given price or higher, assuming that those willing to purchase at higher prices will also purchase at the considered price. Table 3.3 presents such data for shifting production of a Sanyo microwave oven from Japan to West Germany and South Korea. Figure 3.2 presents these data as preference curves.

As can be observed in Table 3.3 and Figure 3.2, the preference curves show the relationship between a price discount or premium and expected change in sales. We first note that the German curve is consistently above the Korean one, indicating that when Sanyo microwave ovens are produced in Germany they can be sold for higher prices than if produced in Korea. At a discount of sixty percent, no sales would have been lost due to a shift in production location. Only eight percent of the respondents were willing to purchase a Korean-made Sanyo microwave oven at the same or at a higher price as one made in Japan. Less than one percent were willing to pay any premium for it, while most required a substantial discount. In contrast, very few respondents expected a discount in order to purchase the same microwave oven when made in Germany. Seventy eight percent would have purchased the German-made product at the anchor price or higher while 22 percent were willing to pay a significant premium.

Percent Price Change	Percent willing to Buy at Price Change or Higher When made-in:	
	S. Korea	W. Germany
-60	99.7	100.0
-50	97.7	100.0
-40	76.6	98.8
-30	65.8	98.0
-20	44.0	95.8
-10	18.3	86.8
0	**8.2**	**77.9**
10	0.8	22.1
20	0.8	10.4
30	0.3	3.2
40	0.3	2.2
50	0.3	2.0
60	0.0	0.2

Source: From Tables 4 and 6 in Nebenzahl and Jaffe (1993), pp. 168, 170.

Table 3.3 Percent of Israeli Consumers willing to Purchase Sanyo Microwave oven when made in S. Korea and W. Germany instead of Japan

In addition to the above analysis, Nebenzahl and Jaffe (1993) show that elasticities based on these preference curves can also be computed. These elasticities can help in setting up prices for sourced products. Finally, as was already done for brand image and brand value (Boosi, 2003), when both a multi-item image scale and a monetized assessment are included in the same questionnaire, one can regress the expected price change with the image score and assign economic value to perceived country image. This regression shows the expected premium (discount) that will result for each unit improvement (deterioration) in the relative image of the country.

While the applicability of relative value of brand and country images for managerial decisions in the areas of sourcing, pricing and promotion are self evident, their applicability for national policy making requires some elaboration. In deciding about overall image promotion policies, policy makers can start by selecting their country's key industries and major brands within each industry. For each industry/brand combination, they should then collect image and relative value data in comparison with their strongest world competitors. Combining the resulted value functions with the concurrent total sales of the related industries can yield the gross monetary value of changes in country image by industry. These data can support decisions concerning country image promotions by industry and overall. A similar analyses but for contending brands can yield the data needed for decisions concerning assistance for companies interested in making FDI in the country. In this case, the impact of improvements in country image resulting from the entry of strong multinational brands can be taken into account.

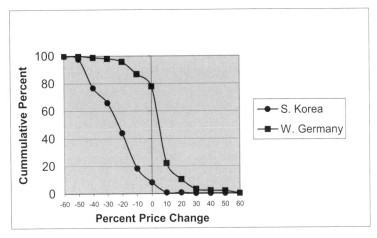

Source: Based on Figure 2-2 in Nebenzahl and Jaffe (1993), p. 173.

Figure 3.2 Preference Curves for Sourcing Sanyo Microwave oven in S. Korea and W. Germany instead of Japan

Long-Term Valuation of Customers

The advantage of the relative brand and country image value methods is their focus on competitive forces in the marketplace. They view brand image as contributing to added value, or the premium that products bearing the brand name can charge over competition. This is a micro approach. Corporations, let alone countries, also have interest in more macro approaches, those that focus on the overall value of a brand. In this section we review a valuation method that while being customer-based, provides the means for estimating the overall value of a brand. Thus, this method bridges between customer-based and firm-based conceptualization of brand value.

In a series of articles and a book, Gupta and Lehmann (2003; 2004; 2005) propose a model and method for valuing customers as assets of the firm and show that the result is a valid method for estimating the value of the firm even when standard accounting methods fail. Our interest in this model stems from two of its key parameters, customer margin and retention, which are highly impacted by brand image. The following exposition is based on Gupta and Lehmann (2003) "Customers as Assets" article.

The modeling begins by considering an individual customer of the company. Over the long run, the consumer is expected to remain a customer for a certain number of years, n, and in each year, t, his marginal contribution to profits, namely, the revenues he generates minus the costs of serving him, is expected to be m_t. Using traditional discounting formula, equation (1) below provides the present value of the discounted cash flow generated during the lifetime of the consumer as a customer,

$$(1) \quad CLV = \sum_{t=1}^{n} \frac{m_t}{(1+i)^t}$$

where CLV is the customer lifetime value and i the discount rate.

This formula requires considerable amount of data and sales projections per customer but it can be greatly simplified by making a number of reasonable assumptions. First, rather than considering each individual, let the model represent the average customer. Second, assume that the average margin is constant over time, thus $m_t = m$. Third, rather than specifying the length of time the average consumer will remain a customer, for which data is not readily available, consider the company's overall retention rate of customers per year, r, as the probability that a customer stays with the company in any one year. Fourth, assume that this retention rate is constant over time. Under these assumptions, and considering the length of the planning horizon to be infinite, equation (1) can be simplified to:

$$(2) \quad CLV = m\left(\frac{r}{1+i-r}\right)$$

where CLV is the customer lifetime value, m the expected margin by customer, r the retention rate of customers and i the discount rate.

The right hand side of (2) includes two parts, the margin, m and r/(1+i-r), which the authors term *margin multiple*. While the margin can vary widely among companies, from less than a Dollar to thousands of Dollars, the margin multiple, being a function of just the discount and retention rates, has a rather limited practical range. The following table provides the computed margin multiple for a selected range of discount and retention rates.

	Discount Rate				
Retention Rate	0.08	0.10	0.12	0.14	0.16
0.50	0.86	0.83	0.81	0.78	0.76
0.60	1.25	1.20	1.15	1.11	1.07
0.70	1.84	1.75	1.67	1.59	1.52
0.80	2.86	2.67	2.50	2.35	2.22
0.90	5.00	4.50	4.09	3.75	3.46
0.95	7.31	6.33	5.59	5.00	4.52

Margin multiple = $r/(1+i-r)$

Table 3.4 Margin multiple for Selected Discount and Retention Rates

Let us consider the implications of this model to the estimation of brand and country image values.

The Value of a Brand's Customer Base and Brand Value

Once the customer lifetime value is estimated, the brand value can be estimated by simply multiplying CLV by the brand's total number of customers, or its customer base. Since the value of the customer base reflects the discounted value of all future net earnings of the brand, it provides a measure of the value of the brand or the company just as well. By comparing such estimates with stock market valuation of selected firms, the authors show that indeed it is a relatively good proxy for the value of the firm. Furthermore, this model can serve for the valuation of companies for which standard accounting measures such as P/E ratio cannot be computed. Consider, for example, the valuation of young Hi-Tech or Internet companies. These companies experience losses for a number of years as they expand their customer base. Computing conventional profitability ratios for these firms is meaningless. By taking into account the discounted earning from current and yet to be acquired customers, this model provides a reasonable estimate of their true market value.

Acquisition of New Customers

As noted in the previous paragraph, there are companies that spend significant amounts for the acquisition of new customers. Considering these customers as assets of the firm, the customer acquisition costs should be considered investment rather than expense. How much is it logical to invest in customer acquisition? The customer lifetime value, representing net earnings, provides an upper limit for such investments, per customer, as any higher spending will result in a present-value loss.

Implications for Brand Image and Brand Value

Let us consider brand image and brand value in light of equation 2. For ease of exposition, we will consider the Honda-Subaru example cited earlier. Recalling the definition of brand value as the added value which consumers are willing to pay, one immediate implication is that the company of the stronger brand can charge more for its products than the other company. Being players in the same market, both companies are likely to employ similar technologies and should have, therefore, similar cost structures. Thus, the added premium due to brand name translates, therefore, to higher expected net income. This is represented by a higher margin, m, in equation 2. Being interested in the contribution of the brand name to CLV, let us consider just the differences between the brands. As noted above in our example, respondents were willing to pay a premium of NIS 13,144 for a Honda branded car. Assuming that, on the average, new car buyers purchase a new car once every three years, we divide the above price premium by three to derive the share in Honda's annual margin attributed to its brand name, namely, NIS 4,381. Assuming a discount rate of 12 percent and retention rate of 80 percent, the margin multiple, as seen in Table 3.4, is 2.50. Computing CLV, we conclude that the brand name of Honda should be valued at 4,381 times 2.50, or NIS 10,953 per Israeli customer.

Of even greater significance is a consideration of the other two parameters of equation 2 which compose the margin multiple, namely, the discount and retention rates. Being in the same market, the two firms should have approximately the same discount rate. Honda, the stronger brand, probably represents lower risk, may master somewhat better discount rates, but, as is obvious from reading across rows of Table 3.4, the impact of small differences in the discount rate are relatively minor and can be ignored. This is not the case for r, the customer retention rate. In practice, wide variations in retention rates can be observed for different companies serving the same market. As can be seen by reading across columns of Table 3.4, changes in the retention rate greatly impact the margin multiple and with it the customer lifetime value. To demonstrate this point, Gupta and

Lehmann (2003) estimated that a five percent increase in the retention rates of Capital One and E*Trade, shows an increase of 22 percent and 37 percent, respectively, in their customer lifetime value.

As noted earlier in discussing the conceptualization of brand equity, one of its dimensions is consumer loyalty (Aaker, 1991, Keller, 1993). By definition, higher levels of loyalty translate to higher retention rates in equation 2, and as a result, also much higher customer lifetime value. Let's assume that the average retention rate in the passenger car industry is 80 percent, as in the example above. Let's also assume that due its strong brand loyalty, this rate is 90 percent for Honda. What difference will this higher rate make to the brand value of Honda? Checking again Table 3.4, the margin multiple is 4.09. Applying this value to m=4,381 estimated above, we get a brand value of NIS 17,920 as compared with brand value of NIS 10,953 derived when the retention effect of loyalty was ignored.

Implications of the Contribution of Country Image to Brand Value

Earlier in this chapter, we discussed the relative value of country image and its estimation. We cited studies that documented the decline in the value of American brands of passenger cars if production is shifted from the USA to Mexico (Johansson and Nebenzahl, 1986; Seaton and Laskey, 1999). Let's consider the more recent study and compute the long term impact of sourcing in Mexico. Seaton and Laskey (1999) found that a change in the assembly location of a $17,000 automobile from the USA to Mexico would result in a reduction of perceived value of $1,952. In the same year, the pre-tax net earning of the automotive division of GM in North America was 6.25 percent (General Motors Corporation, 1999, p. 39). Applying this rate to $17,000 yields a pre tax income of $1,062. Shifting assembly to Mexico, before accounting for cost differentials, results in a loss of $890. Since we are dealing with a loss, we cannot compute CLV on the basis of margin. To overcome this hurdle we compute CLV for gross income per average customer for cars assembled in the USA and in Mexico and then derive the net difference.

Assuming, as we did in the case of Honda, that the average new car buyer makes a purchase once every three years, the base price of $17,000 translates to $4,250 per year. Assuming again, a discount rate of 12 percent and retention rate of 80 percent, the CLV of the gross income from a customer who purchases an American assembled car is:

Gross American assembled car CLV = $4,250 * 2.50 = $10,625

By shifting assembly to Mexico, the expected price per car declines to 15,048, or $3,762 per customer per year. In addition to the immediate loss in revenues, brand loyalty of the Mexican assembled cars is expected to decline as well. Assuming a decline in the retention rate of 10 percent, we find in Table 3.4 that the multiplier for a 12 percent discount rate and a 70 percent retention rate is 1.67. Applying this value, we can now compute the gross CLV for the Mexican assembled cars.

Gross Mexican assembled car CLV = $3,762 * 1.67 = $6,283

The difference between the two customer lifetime values is $4,343.

We can now understand the contribution of the long term consideration. If we were to consider the short term only, we would reach the conclusion that if the difference in assembly costs between the two countries is more than $1,952, it pays to source assembly in Mexico. By taking into account the long term effects of customer loyalty, the breakeven point is more than twice that amount.

Estimating Brand Value by Means of Firm-Based Financial Data

Taking a macro rather than micro approach, a number of research organizations have estimated brand value by analyzing publicly available and/or proprietary financial data. The advantage of this approach is in its estimation of overall brand value that stems from all products sold under the company's brand name rather than making detailed analyses by product. The disadvantage is the requirement that the company has a single brand for all its products.

Interbrand, a London based company, was the first to put a value on a brand name (Interbrand, 2004). In recent years, the company has published the ranking and values of the best global brands. To be considered a global brand, a firm has to have at least a third of its business outside its home country. Interbrand's methodology was adopted by others, such as the Financial World (Meschi, 1995) that publishes its own valuation and ranking of brands. The basic concept behind this methodology is that the unaccounted intangible income of the brand represents the core of the brand value. Using Kellogg's brand as an example, the following is an adaptation of how Financial World computes brand values (Meschi, 1995).

In 1994, worldwide sales of all the products bearing the Kellogg's name reached $5.5 billion with operating income of $1 billion. This operating income is reduced to account for all known other sources for intangible income. First, the median capital-employed-to-sales ratio is computed for the related industry, 32 percent in the case of the prepared food industry. Using the industry's median and the sales of Kellogg's, the amount of capital employed by the company is estimated to be $1.76 billion. Assuming that a private label in the food industry would earn a 5 percent return on capital, $88 million (5 percent of $1.76 billion) of intangible income can be attributed to return on capital and is subtracted from operating income. The resulting $912 million figure is considered as brand-related pretax profit. Second, the brand's net income is computed by subtracting the applicable tax rate. In the case of Kellogg's, the USA tax rate of 34 percent is applied to the pretax profit, resulting in the brand's net income of $602 million. In order to smooth short term random fluctuations, Financial World uses a two-year weighted average of the brand-related pretax profit. Interbrand, on the other hand, makes a discounted five-year forecast of the same, varying the discount rate according to it's estimate of the level of risk of each assessed brand.

Finally, brand value is derived from the brand's net income by multiplying it by *Interbrand Strength Multiple*. This multiple is determined by the brand's leadership, stability, market strength, internationality, trend, communication support and legal protection. In 1994, Kellogg's Interbrand Strength Multiple was 18.76, resulting in a brand value of $11.3 billion.

While this method provides a good ballpark estimate of brand value, its accuracy is questionable. First, the method is limited to single brand corporations or those that provide financial data by brand. Second, even after accounting for the value of capital and the effect of taxes, the brand's net income includes other intangibles, such as monopolistic conditions, control of resources, and the like. Third, Interbrand's five-year forecast further reduces the objectivity of the data. Fourth, Interbrand's strength multiple is an adjustment whose validity, accuracy and reliability was not reported in the academic literature. It is very likely that both the five-year forecast and the multiplier are affected by the same factors, exaggerating differences among companies. Even with these limitations, the conceptual basis behind the method is sound, and the brand's income before it is multiplied by the adjustment factor is a relatively good estimate of the current margin due to brand name. This margin that can be computed on the basis of publicly available data for publicly owned companies can be entered as m in Gupta's CLV for the estimation of long-term value.

Using published financial data of more than 400 companies in conjunction with its own proprietary measurements, Corporate Branding, LLC showed that there is a significant association between brand image on the one hand and market share, cash flow multiples and stock market valuation, on the other (Gregory, 2001, pp 49-66). Its measure of brand image, *CoreBrand Power*, is a proprietary 100-point scale based on the brand's familiarity and favorability. It should be noted that *CoreBrand Power* is a measure of brand equity while market share, cash flow multiples and stock market valuation are all measures of brand value. To conclude, this methodology can be utilized to assess the overall impact of brand image on brand value at the corporate level.

Extracting Brand Value from Share Prices and the Firm's Financial Data

A number of researchers developed models for estimating brand value by extracting it from stock market valuation in conjunction with the firm's financial data. Simon and Sullivan (1993) review these models and suggest their own. The basis for all these models is the economic theory assumption that the stock-market is efficient. In an efficient stock-market, a large number of independent investors weigh all information about all traded companies and estimate their future prospective. Thus, the current market value of any firm (share price times number of issued shares) represents an unbiased estimate of the present value of all its future net cash flows. This value of total equity is composed of the firm's tangible assets, a value available in the company's financial data, and the unknown intangible assets. Thus, subtracting the tangible assets from the market value provides an unbiased estimate of the unknown intangible assets.

Tobin (1969), one of the first to take this approach, defines an index, Q, computed by taking the ratio of the market value of the firm by the replacement cost of its tangible assets. A value of Q greater than 1 indicates the presence of intangible assets and their magnitude.

It should be noted that brand equity is just a part of intangible assets of the firm. Other intangibles include profits arising from monopolistic conditions, firm-specific assets, control over raw material resources, R&D investments, and the like. Accordingly, the value of intangibles has to be further adjusted in order to derive brand value. As a case in point, Simon and Sullivan (1993) developed a model that is based on

Tobin's Q but accounts for the effect of firm specific factors not related to brand equity and market specific factors that lead to imperfect competition. It further directly accounts for determinants of brand value, namely, past and current advertising expenditures, advertising share, age of the brand, and order of entry to the market.

In considering this strand of models it should be noted that while the estimates of intangible assets are sound and simple, estimating the brand equity component requires elaborate adjustment and the results are less reliable. Furthermore, for companies having more than one brand, unless data are available for each brand as a profit center, the result is a joint effect of all brands.

Implications to the Measurement of Country Value

Can such methodologies as described in the last two sections be adopted for the measurement of country value? While we are not aware of any attempt to do so, it is an interesting challenge to develop corresponding methodologies that will be based on national accounting data relating to international trade and/or input-output matrixes.

Conclusion

To summarize, in this chapter we suggested a taxonomy that can help in assuring that researchers have the same meaning for different country-image concepts. We reviewed the development of measuring instruments for the assessment of the perceived country image and its economic value. It can be concluded that recent developments facilitate the inclusion of country image effects in cost-benefit analyses that will consider not only cost accounting estimates but also the expected impact of country image on product acceptance. Tools are available today to aid in a decision where production should take place and what changes in prices have to be made, given the selected product location.

In addition, we completed the description of measurement issues by showing how brand or country equity and value can be assessed. We presented a model that shows the relationship between image, equity and value, where image is antecedent to equity and value is the consequence of equity. We described in detail a number of methods for the assessment of country or brand value. By presenting them alongside each other, it becomes apparent that some of the models can be utilized for the estimation of parameters required by others. Specifically, the long-term model of Gupta and Lehmann, which is solidly based on economic theory and financial reasoning, requires the input of three parameters, profit margin, retention rate and discount rate. The discount rate is of limited range and can be easily determined. The profit margin can be estimated by means of the relative customer-based brand (country) model. It can also be estimated by means of financial models that extract current brand value from stock market and published financial data of companies. The retention rate, being a direct function of loyalty can be estimated from measures of image or equity. Some companies even provide the retention rate in their annual reports (Gupta and Lehmann, 2003). The resulted synergy greatly enhances our ability to estimate the long-term value of brands and of countries as brands.

CHAPTER 4

It's All in the Eyes of the Consumer

"What is it you are researching?"
"Denmark's image in Britain"
"Oh! How interesting"
..."What is it you are researching?"
"Denmark's image in the U.K."
"What makes you think Denmark has an image?"

Malene Djursaa, 1989

Introduction

In the preceding chapters, we discussed the theoretical aspects of the made-in country as an evaluative cue in consumer decision making. French perfumes, German cars, Japanese television sets, Danish and Swiss dairy products are just some of the examples where national image is synonymous with quality, workmanship, durability, style or taste. When national image produces a favorable consumer response, manufacturers and indeed, country administrations are keen to promote them. In this chapter, we look at the empirical evidence of the made-in cue.

To what extent do consumers look for the made-in label in search for information provided by this cue? Is it of real concern to the consumer whether a product is domestic or imported? Does this concern differ by product category? That is, is labeling more important for cars and other durable products than for food and clothing? Nearly every country of origin study has assumed that consumers look for the made-in label when judging the characteristics of a product. Surprisingly, little empirical evidence has been forthcoming in academic research as to whether consumers ask about the origin of a product when making a purchase decision. These issues are examined in this chapter.

What Do We Know About National Images in the Eyes of Consumers?

National images are not static, but change over time. These changes are an outgrowth of many factors as explained in Chapter 2. The purpose of this section is to review what we know about images of countries and to show, where possible, how they have changed over time.

Consumers' Place of Residence (HC) Effect on Perceived National Images

In order to determine the country image of UK products, the consulting firm Wolff Olins (1995) undertook a study among a sample of 200 marketing and communications directors of Fortune 500 companies. The findings showed that 57 percent of the European, USA and Canadian respondents believed that the image of UK industry has improved "over recent years", compared to 35 percent who believed that it remained the same and 10 percent who believed that it has deteriorated. Fifty three percent of UK respondents believed that the UK country image had improved, while about half of Far Eastern respondents believed that the image had improved. Of individual country managers, the Germans held the most favorable opinion about the UK's country image; 80 percent believed that it had improved, while only about 40 percent of the Italian respondents held the same beliefs. These findings not only show opinions about changes in a country's image, but also demonstrate that it is very home country (HC) specific as specified in our general theoretic model. Moreover, the perception of country image also differs by industry type. Breaking down the same respondents by industry showed that those from transport and communications tended to believe that the UK's image had favorably changed, while significantly fewer in the utilities and financial services held the same belief.

Looking at components of country image, e.g., design, shows perceptual differences by respondent country. Only 26 percent of UK respondents perceived UK-made products to be well designed compared to 39 percent of the French respondents and 74 percent of the US respondents.

A survey was carried out in 1999 for the British Council in thirteen "key countries" by the consulting firm Market & Opinion Research International (MORI) to determine what the respondents think about British society and culture. Two hundred respondents aged 24-35, defined as well-educated, either studying for a post-graduate qualification or employed in a key position in government or industry were interviewed. The findings show that the UK's image is less positive than the USA and Japan. For example, while 62 percent of the respondents agree that Britain has a good reputation for scientific and technological innovation, the UK was ranked well behind the United States, Japan and Germany (Ratcliffe and Griffin, 1999). A similar finding emanated from a study carried out among its European subscribers by Time magazine (*Country Images II*, 1997), in which the UK was ranked seventh as a technologically advanced country. In addition, UK products were ranked in eighth place for attractive design, well behind Italy and France. However, 25 percent of the respondents agreed that the UK's image was improving, while only Spain, Portugal, Poland and Ireland's images were believed to have improved more. Finally, UK consumers have a relatively low regard for their country's image. Only 27 percent perceive British products as excellent or good – even the Japanese (32 percent) have a higher regard for British products (Leonard, 1997).

A number of research studies have tried to gauge either an overall image of a country or an image based on a specific attribute, such as quality, workmanship or luxury. An example of a study that focused on overall quality is a survey (JMA Research Institute, Gallup Organization, 1993) undertaken among 20,000 consumers in 20 European, Asian, Central, South and North American countries[5] that asked: "In general, how would you rate the overall quality of goods produced in [country[6]]: excellent, very good, good, only fair, or poor?" The overall quality leaders were Japan (38.5 percent of respondents), Germany (36.0 percent), and the USA (34.3 percent). Mexico and Russia were at the bottom of the list with 6.2 percent and 5.8 percent,

---

[5] The countries surveyed were Canada, Chile, Columbia, Costa Rica, Dominican Republic, France, Germany, Guatemala, Hungary, Iceland, India, Italy, Japan, Mexico, Nicaragua, Spain, Taiwan, Thailand, United Kingdom and the United States.

[6] The rated countries included Canada, China, France, Germany, Italy, Japan, Mexico, Russia, Spain, Taiwan, United Kingdom and the United States.

respectively. However, an ethnocentric bias was apparent when the results were broken down by location of the respondents. Table 4.1 shows that more European respondents selected Germany as the quality leader than Japan or the United States; American respondents chose the USA as the quality leader ahead of Japan and Germany and Asian respondents chose Japan as the quality leader ahead of Germany and the USA. Canada entered the list of the top five quality leaders only when rated by American respondents. Again, this shows that an ethnocentric bias exists both on a country and regional basis.

European Respondents	Percent of Respondents
Germany	44.3
Japan	35.0
USA	26.9
Britain	21.9
France	20.6
USA Respondents	
USA	40.8
Japan	36.0
Germany	30.1
Canada	21.3
Britain	19.8
Asian Respondents	
Japan	50.3
Germany	34.5
USA	32.8
Britain	26.8
France	23.3

Source: "The Importance of National Image in the Global Marketplace", JMA Research Institute, Inc. and the Gallup Organization, 1993.
Table 4.1 Overall Quality Image – by Residence Area

Even geographic location and size may affect how people view a country's industrial ability. In a survey of British managers (Djursaa, 1988), about 75 percent believed that Denmark was mainly an agricultural country, while "distant and ice-bound" was a frequent response regarding its geographic location.[7] In reality, manufactured (non-food) goods account for 72 percent of Denmark's exports. About one-third of her exports are technology intensive.

Constructs of Country Image

One of the most comprehensive studies was undertaken in France, Germany and Italy during 1992 by RISC, an international consulting company. The study looked at associations between seven countries and ten product attributes. Approximately 2,500 respondents in each of three countries, France, Germany and Italy, were asked to select from a list of seven countries that country or countries that they associated with the ten attributes listed in Table 4.2. The results show that France and Italy are associated with "style", "design" and "refinement", Germany with "reliability", "after sales service", "solidity" and "quality" and Japan with "attractive prices", "value for money" and "technology." Among the other countries other than the respondents' own country, the United States was not outstanding on any attribute, with the exception of "technology", (23.4%) but still lower than Germany (29.8%) on that attribute. Great Britain and Spain showed the lowest overall associations.

Country	France	UK	Germany	Italy	Japan	Spain	USA
Reliability	19.6*	6.8	65.3	13.3	22.4	1.5	11.4
Style	38.8	16.4	18.0	42.9	7.4	4.4	8.6
Design	32.4	7.0	17.0	47.6	14.9	3.9	12.7
Attractive prices	11.1	2.5	10.5	21.6	43.1	25.3	6.2
After sale service	22.5	4.3	50.5	19.2	13.8	1.4	6.8
Solidity	13.0	6.7	70.4	10.0	16.8	1.1	9.1
Quality	22.6	7.8	59.2	17.6	21.2	2.0	10.6
Value for money	19.9	3.3	32.8	19.8	35.0	5.6	7.9
Technology	11.2	1.9	29.8	7.0	61.9	0.8	23.4
Refinement	48.5	11.3	19.6	33.5	10.0	2.5	15.3

N = 7582.
*Read: 19.6% of respondents selected France as the best country for reliability. Rows add up to more than 100 since multiple answers were possible.

Source: Dubois and Paternault, (1997), p. 82.
Table 4.2 Associations Between Countries and Attributes

---

[7] Even nationals of a country have interesting perceptions about their country's size:
"Denmark seen from foreign land looks like a grain of sand – Denmark as we Danes conceive it is so big you won't believe it" (Piet Hein, first stanza of a Grook).

These country images seem to form two constructs: (1) design, and (2) reliability and value for money. This two-construct solution was confirmed by a principal components factor analysis (Dubois and Paternault, 1997).

Country Image Varies by Product line

An earlier study (Djursaa, 1988) undertaken among a convenience sample of respondents in the UK looked at overall and specific product images of the UK, the then West Germany, Denmark and Sweden:

UK Respondent Perception of Products Made in:

	UK	West Germany	Sweden	Denmark
High Quality	46%	87%	64%	51%
Value for money	35%	43%	19%	15%
Attractive styling/design	38%	58%	52%	56%
Modern	54%	88%	60%	67%
Easy to maintain/service	45%	60%	35%	20%

Source: Djursaa (1990), p. 31. Reproduced by permission of MCB University Press.
Table 4.3 UK Respondent Perception of Products

When rating an overall image, UK respondents scored West Germany the highest on all five attributes and their own country second best on only two, "value for money" and "easy to maintain/ service." Both Scandinavian countries were rated relatively high on "attractive styling/design" and "modern", while Sweden was also rated high on "quality." However, when asked to rate the same countries by product line, the image perceptions changed. When asked to rate three food products, five products where design is an important component, and six industrial products by country of origin, it was found that Britain and Denmark ranked in first place for food products, Britain ranked first in fashion, home textiles, glass/china and pottery, and second in furniture, and West Germany ranked first in four out of six industrial products. Conversely, Denmark ranked last in all categories of Indus-trial products, with the exception of agricultural machinery, which is consonant with its image in the UK of being mainly a food producing country. Sweden ranked second in furniture products and cars (tied with the UK). The ratings of the four countries on "quality" of industrial products are shown in Figure 4.1. In the overall ratings, Britain ranked lowest on the "quality" attribute. However, when product types are considered, Britain tied for first on agricultural machinery, second on machine tools, electronics, cars and steel. It was rated highest among the four countries on medicines.

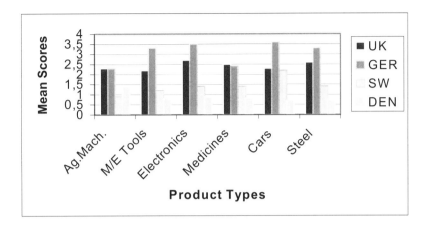

Source: Djursaa (1990), 31. What Consumers Say About the Effect of Country Image. Reproduced by Permission of MCB University Press.
Figure 4.1 Product-Quality Ratings

Both Denmark and Sweden seem to have a stereotyped image among UK consumers, probably representing a "Scandinavian" profile, rather than distinct country images. Denmark stands out for agricultural machinery, while Sweden for cars. Mostly, their ratings are relatively low, regardless of the fact that Sweden has a well-developed electronics industry and Denmark exports a significant amount of pharmaceuticals. However, national images are a given fact and it is up to government, industry and individual firms to deal with them. The extent to which affinity to a country's culture affects its image is an important concern for policy makers, industrial groups and individual firms. The chairperson of a joint Canadian Commons-Senate Committee argued that his country's positive cultural image could help sell Canadian products. The committee even went so far as to propose that artistic groups should accompany ministers on trade missions (The Economist, 1994). For individual firms, a positive country image may help promote a global brand. British Airways, for example, studied how UK culture was seen around the world (Curtis, 1997). Depending upon the results, the company decided to position itself as a British brand rather than adopt a more global image. For example, the national colors of England were displayed on BA aircraft. This subject is discussed in detail in Chapters 5 and 6.

Country Image and Purchase Intentions

To this point we reviewed research on country image that focused on image per se. But does image affect intentions and behavior? In this section we survey what consumers say about nations and how these thoughts color their opinion about the goods and services offered for sale.

A nation's image has many facets. It is a product of its culture, which includes economic, political, and education systems, religion and social structure. There is also a tentative finding of an association between a company's environmental friendliness and country image (Manrai, et al, 1997). While this list is not exhaustive, it does cover a lot of ground. Several studies, for example, have shown a relationship between stage of economic development and country-of-origin effects (Schooler, 1971; Wang and Lamb, 1983; Verlegh and Steenkamp, 1999; Chinen, et al, 2000). That is to say, there may be an inherent perceptual bias against developing countries' products, serving as an entry barrier to industrialized markets. In a survey of American consumers (Chinen, et al, 2000), willingness to buy a country's products was found to be related to its economic development. In general, American consumers are more receptive to products from developed countries and less so from developing countries. The results of this survey are shown in Table 4.4

COUNTRY	WILLINGNESS TO BUY
India	4.04
Indonesia	4.10
Israel	4.30
Greece	4.33
Spain	4.77
Norway	4.78
UK	4.83
Canada	4.85
Sweden	4.87
Germany	5.42
Japan	5.53
United States	5.87

Source: Adapted from Chinen et al, (2000). Scale values ran from 1 to 7, with 7 being the most favorable.

Table 4.4 Willingness to Buy and Economic Development

Can Consumers be Segmented by their Attitudes?

Given the evidence presented thus far, it is clear that consumers and industrial buyers perceive countries as differing in their images. The question remains as to how uniform are these images; that is, can consumers be segmented by their attitudes? We have identified four consumer segments, three of which relate to emotions towards one's own country in contrast with other countries, (1) *Patriots*, (2) *Cosmopolitans and*, (3) *Traitors* and one relating to emotions toward a particular foreign country: (4) *Hostiles*. *Patriots* are consumers who prefer to buy domestically made goods even though their image may not be as good as that of imported goods. *Hostiles* will not buy imported goods from certain countries they consider to behave badly in the international arena, e.g., by contributing to environmental spoilage, and violating human rights. However, unlike *patriots*, they do not have an inherent bias in favor of locally made goods. In contrast with *patriots*, *traitors* have a clear preference for imported, rather than domestic goods. Typically, residents of less developed countries believe that locally made goods are inferior. Furthermore, in some countries the ownership of foreign products serves as a social status symbol. Finally, *cosmopolitans* are consumers who do not have a bias against either imported or domestic goods and judge all products on an equal basis. Cosmopolitans do not ignore the country of origin. They consider it an attribute of products and brands. A discussion of these consumer segments follows below.

Consumer Ethnocentrism and Patriotism

Most country image studies have been made in developed countries. Not surprisingly, these studies show that consumers in those countries prefer products made-in either their own country or in other developed countries to those from emerging, developing or Eastern European countries. Surveys have shown that Americans prefer American-made products (Bruskin Report, 1985; Gallup, 1985). However, actual sales figures show that in many categories, imported products command significant market shares. For example, in 1995, imported footwear in the United States had a 73 percent market share; luggage made from leather, 71 percent; household audio and video equipment, 61 percent; motor vehicles and bodies, 42 percent; and household consumer durables, 29 percent. So, many American consumers do not purchase domestically made products if given a better alternative from imports. These consumers are *cosmopolitan* and judge a product not so much by its origin, but rather for its attributes such as price, quality, and workmanship in comparison with alternative products.

Patriots

Patriots, or ethnocentric consumers are found in many countries. There may be segments of American and other nationalities of consumers that do prefer to buy locally made products, regardless of product attributes. Stephen Lande (1995) claims that some American consumers believe that by purchasing domestic products, they are contributing to the economy and see this as a patriotic duty. Olsen et al (1993) have likened American consumers that purchase domestic products as a form of assistance to employment of workers whose jobs may be threatened by competing imports. They found that the willingness to help by consuming domestic products was dependent upon the salience of the problem (looming unemployment), inequity of the situation and identification with the workers. Many consumers care more about the country of origin of products when competition from imports in a particular industry and the subsequent loss of jobs has been widely publicized. Just over half the number of respondents in a Gallup survey in 1994 (FTC, 1995), said they pay more attention to the country of origin for cars and clothing, than for other product categories. At the time, foreign competition of these product categories was publicized by labor unions and manufacturers organizations. As a result, patriotic consumers tend to rate domestic-made products more favorably than imported products and are more likely to buy the former.

Kaynak and Dalgic (1988) observed that some Irish consumers would buy domestic-made products in order to help the unemployed. Okechuku (1994) found that American, Canadian, German and Dutch respondents to a survey preferred TV sets or car radios made in their country, followed by brands made in other developed countries.

Wall and Heslop (1986) found that approximately one half of Canadian respondents surveyed claimed that they would not only prefer Canadian-made products, but would be willing to pay higher prices for them if they were of equal quality to imports. Other studies have revealed segments of patriotic consumers. Surveys of Finnish (Darling and Kraft, 1977) and French (Baumgartner and Jolibert, 1977) consumers have shown that both groups rated domestic-made goods over foreign ones.

In the 1992 RISC study cited earlier in this chapter, respondents were asked the question: "In your opinion which country best understands the idea of luxury and reflects it through its products and brands?" Indications of the extent of patriotism are shown in Table 4.5.

	Surveys in:		
	France	Germany	Italy
France	62.7%	39.1%	35.0%
Britain	7.3	3.8	3.5
Germany	6.7	23.6	4.2
Italy	4.8	11.1	43.2
Spain	0.1	0.9	0.3
Japan	4.6	5.7	2.6
USA	8.5	14.4	10.9
Other	5.3	1.3	0.2
	N = 2569	N = 2522	N = 2491

Source: Dubois and Paternault (1997).
Table 4.5 Best Country for Luxury

From the above results it is clear that patriotism affects perceptions. In each country, the "national" score is much larger than that of the other two countries. French respondents gave their own country a 62.7 percent rating, compared to the ratings of the Germans (39.1 percent) and the Italians (35.0 percent). The Germans rated their own country 23.6 percent compared to the French rating of only 6.7 percent and the Italian rating of 4.2 percent. The Italian respondents rated their own country 43.2 percent, compared to the French rating of 4.8 percent and the German rating of 11.1 percent. Moreover, both the French and Italians rated their own country first in Luxury, compared to all other countries. Only the Germans rated France first and their own country second. Looking at all the ratings, it would seem that the French respondents are the most chauvinistic among those surveyed in the three countries. Less than ten percent of French respondents identified any other country as being first in luxury. In contrast, both German and Italian respondents identified France and the USA as excelling in this respect.

In a study of Polish consumers, Supphellen and Rittenburg (2001) found that when foreign brands are clearly better than domestic alternatives, ethnocentric consumers seem to conform to the consensus belief that foreign brands are indeed superior, but express their ethnocentric feelings by rationalizing their preferences for domestic brands ("they have good qualities as well"). Acceptance of the consensus that foreign brands are superior is a form of social desirability, even though ethnocentric consumers believe that domestic brands are just as good and will act accordingly. Supphellen and Rittenburg (2001) suggest that brand managers of superior products sold in Eastern Europe should appeal to the social desirability of purchasing them. On the other hand, the objective of managers of relatively inferior domestic products should be to change the general opinion that foreign is better, a task that the authors admit is difficult to achieve. Therefore, they suggest forming strategic alliances with Western companies in an attempt to improve brand image.

According to Annholt (Nations Brands Index – Q3 Report, 2005), a nation's brand is a sum of people's perceptions of a country across six areas of national competence: Tourism, exports, people, governance, culture and heritage, and investment and immigration. Using these parameters Annholt (2005) conducts a panel survey in ten countries to determine how each population rates their country and others as well. Americans tend to place their own country first in every category. This self-rating is in contrast with the perceptions of other people who rate the United States much lower, with the exception of export brands and investment potential. Canadians also are *patriots*, ranking their country first in all categories, except culture. At the other end of the continuum are the Poles and Russians, who tend to rate themselves relatively low on most of the above parameters.

Klein et al (2000) found that Chinese and Russians generally perceived domestic products inferior to imported ones. However, unlike the Russians, the Chinese believe that it is inappropriate or immoral to purchase imported products. While this finding contradicts the conventional wisdom, its efficacy is dependent upon the extent to which the small samples used in their study can be generalized to the Chinese population at large. For example, some manufacturers try to give their products a Western image. Gilley (1996) reports that Chinese manufacturers pass off local products as Western. This apparently became so extensive that the government in the city of Guangzhou banned the use of foreign names on locally made products. However, this action was not followed by similar, central government regulations. Another question is to what extent the patriotism of the Chinese reported by Klein et al (2000) will be translated into actual purchase behavior. The same question can be asked about another study (Ziamou, et al, 2000) from a former Socialist country, Bulgaria, which found that Bulgarians preferred domestic brands of cosmetics to Western-made products, even though consumers believed that the imported products had a better image and superior packaging.

Traitors

Not all consumers believe that they have a patriotic duty to purchase domestic products. As pointed out by Klein et al (2000), most studies of ethnocentrism among consumers were carried out in Western or developed Asian countries like Japan, where it is plausible that consumers judge domestic-made products favorably. The same authors ask whether the construct of consumer ethnocentrism extends to countries where domestic goods are viewed less favorably than imports. For example, Jaffe and Martinez (1995) found that Mexicans value locally made household electronic products much lower than those made in the United States and Japan. Consumers in former Socialist countries prefer imported products because they have been conditioned over the years to consume inferior goods made in state-owned factories that were protected against foreign competition (Ettenson, 1993). Batra, et al (2000) also found that consumers in developing countries prefer foreign "non-local" goods because they believe it is more prestigious to own them. The preference for foreign-made goods was stronger among consumers who were influenced by normative pressures and for product categories that had high social value.

Identifying Patriots, Cosmopolitans and Traitors

Who are these so-called "patriotic" or "ethnocentric" consumers? How are they differentiated from non-ethnocentric or non-patriotic consumers? The first researchers to identify ethnocentric consumers were Shimp and Sharma (1987) who defined them as those who believe that buying domestically-made products is morally justified and patriotic because by doing so the home economy is supported. They found that consumers who had higher levels of ethnocentrism held more favorable attitudes towards domestic-made products and negative, stereotyped attitudes towards imports. They developed a seventeen-item scale, presented in the Appendix, to measure consumer ethnocentrism, known as the CETSCALE (consumer ethnocentric tendency scale), which has been validated in a four-country study by Netemeyer et al (1991) and has been since widely used by researchers around the world.

An individual's ethnocentrism is measured as the summed scores of the seventeen items of the CETSCALE. Based on a 7-point scale, a person's score may range from a low of 17 to a high of 119. Those scoring high on the scale are considered to be ethnocentric consumers.

In studies conducted by Shimp and Sharma (1987), in four United States cities, the mean scores were 68.58, 61.28, 57.84 and 56.62.

Ethnocentrism is believed to be influenced by consumer demographics, such as education, income and social class. Generally, it is believed that older consumers and those having relatively lower education and income are more prone to ethnocentric consumption. These and other factors that influence consumer ethnocentrism are shown in Figure 4.2.

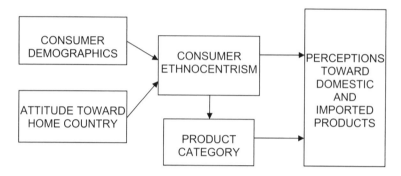

Adapted from Durvasula et al (1997), p. 77.
Figure 4.2 A Framework of Consumer Ethnocentrism

Brodowsky (1998) studied the effect of ethnocentrism on the evaluation of domestic and imported products. He found that among low ethnocentric consumers, country of origin explained more variation in product evaluation than attitude. Low ethnocentric consumers are more likely to use country of origin cues as objective information about product quality. In contrast, high ethnocentric consumers use country of origin cues to express patriotic sentiment and are influenced by this in their purchase decisions. Moreover, high ethnocentric consumers tended to believe that domestic products were of higher quality than comparable imported ones. In a later study (Borodowsky, et al 2004), the authors found that highly ethnocentric American consumers have more positive beliefs about American-designed-and-manufactured automobiles than purely Japanese ones. However, these consumers would be more likely to purchase Japanese-brands of automobiles that are manufactured in the United States. One of their conclusions is that these sorts of consumers consider the "morality" of purchasing foreign made products as more important than the quality of the products themselves.

In addition to consumer demographics, it has been found that the extent to which consumers have a positive or negative attitude toward their home country affects their evaluation of domestic versus imported products. Thus, it is believed that those having a high regard or concern for their country ("patriots") will have higher levels of ethnocentrism (Netemeyer, et al, 1991). We have emphasized that consumer evaluations of country of origin are product specific. That is, a country's image may vary by product category. Therefore, it is likely that the degree of consumer ethnocentrism will also vary by product category. Products that are thought to be more essential to the economy (and provide more employment) may generate more ethnocentric behavior than those that are not. Product type also directly moderates beliefs about the attributes of domestic and imported products.

Mexican Patriots versus Malinchismas (Traitors)

The concept of *malinchismo* in Mexico is ingrained in local culture. The term – synonymous with "traitor" – is believed to originate after the Spanish conquest of Mexico. When the Spanish army arrived in Mexico commanded by General Cortez, it communicated with the Aztec King Montezuma II through a female translator known as La Malinche. It was claimed that her translations on behalf of Cortez were misleading and contributed to the destruction of the Aztec Empire. Since then, traitors have been euphemistically termed *malinchismas*. So, a Mexican consumer who purchases imported goods and thereby harms the local economy is a *malinchista*. Who are the so-called Mexican *malinchismas*?

Some information about the socio-demographic characteristics of *malinchismas* in Mexico were identified by Baily and Gutierrez de Pineres, (1997) in an application of the CETSCALE among a sample of middle and upper-class Mexicans regarding their preferences for imported, American food products. The results of the study are shown in Table 4.6.

Survey Question	Low (1-2)	Medium (3-5)	High (6-7)
Only those products that are unavailable in our country should be imported.	193 (48.6%)	105 (26.5%)	99 (24.9%)
Mexican products, first and foremost.	216 (54.3%)	128 (32.1%)	54 (13.5%)
Purchasing foreign goods is un-Mexican.	102 (26.0%)	156 (39.7%)	135 (34.3%)
It is not right to purchase foreign products because it puts Mexicans out of job.	164 (47.6%)	156 (39.6%)	74 (11.9%)
A Mexican should always buy Mexican-made products.	125 (31.4%)	171 (42.9%)	102 (25.6%)
We should purchase products made in Mexico instead of letting other countries get rich off us.	197 (49.4%)	139 (34.8%)	63 (15.8%)
Mexicans should not buy foreign products because this hurts Mexican business and causes unemployment.	178 (44.6%)	155 (38.8%)	66 (16.5%)
It may cost me in the long run, but I prefer to support Mexican products.	197 (49.4%)	152 (38.0%)	29 (12.6%)
I buy imports only if local not available.	78 (19.6%)	61 (15.3%)	259 (65.1%)
Import buyers are costing Mexican jobs.	156 (39.3%)	97 (24.4%)	144 (36.3%)

Responses range from 1 = Strongly Disagree to 7 = Strongly Agree.

Source: Baily and Gutierrez de Pineres, (1997)

Table 4.6 Mexican Responses to the Cetscale

The first column of Table 4.6 shows the proportion of non-ethnocentric consumers. For example, 54 percent of the respondents do not believe that Mexican products are "first and foremost", only 26 percent believe that "purchasing foreign goods is un-Mexican", while 49 percent do not agree with the statement that "it may cost me in the long run, but I prefer to support Mexican products." In short, all the results in column one of the table lead to the conclusion that most respondents in the Mexican study are not ethnocentric consumers.

A regression analysis between those who are more prone to purchase imported products and socio-demographic characteristics shows that there is a strong relationship with high income and education, larger households and the age group 31-35. These findings correspond with those of Mascarenhas and Kujawa (1998) who found that non-ethnocentric consumers tend to be young, well educated and have higher occupational status. The fact that "patriotic" Mexicans are older and less educated agrees with similar findings based on American samples (Schooler, 1971; Han, 1988; Howard, 1989).

Hostiles and Friends: The Animosity-Affinity Model of the Purchase of Products from Certain Countries

In some situations, a made-in or associated country label may trigger an affective, rather than a cognitive response. That is, a person's feelings and emotions about the made-in country may directly influence a willingness to buy its products, without regard to what that person actually thinks about them. A consumer who has strong positive feelings toward a country may purchase its products even when s/he realizes that these products are not superior to other offerings. For example, Jews residing in Western countries purchase Israeli government bonds, even when alternative bonds have a higher yield, as a token of support of the country. The same appeal is utilized in the Israel Direct in its Internet e-marketing cite, whose web page appears in Figure 4.3, which offers Israeli products in special gift packages. The purchase of ethnic products by emigrants is often motivated by feelings of affinity with the country from which they have emigrated. In contrast, the consumer may have a high regard for the country's products, but will not buy them because of animosity toward that country. This is not necessarily the patriotic consumer who prefers domestic products for the reasons stated above. For example, while some positive attitudes were held about industrial products made in several former communist countries, purchasing agents in the United States expressed an overall dislike for them (Chasin and Jaffe, 1979, 1987). This dislike for Eastern European-made products may have resulted from a negative view, or disdain for their Communist regimes of that time. However, the authors did not examine if a relationship exists between animosity towards the country's political system and stereotyped images of its products.

Israel Direct
... your holyland source

Kosher Food and Wine

Instructions?

┌ **Honey & Olive Oil Gift Pack**

Decorative Reusable Box

Citrus blossom Honey
Cold Pressed Extra Virgin Olive Oil (250 ml)
Honeycomb Candles (3)
Mango Tea

$49.82 including air shipment

Land of Canaan Olive Oil
the finest Israel has to offer

Cold Pressed, Extra Virgin Olive Oil

┌ 250 ml of Cold Pressed, Extra Virgin
Olive Oil from the Galilee
$22.13 including air shipment

┌ 500 ml of Cold Pressed, Extra Virgin
Olive Oil from the Galilee
$26.00 including air shipment

Source: http://www.israeldirect.co.il/Food-wine.html
Figure 4.3 Utilizing Affinity: Ethnic Appeal in e-marketing

Klein et al (1998) developed a definitive test for consumer
animosity. The authors theorized that animosity toward another nation
can be an important predictor of foreign product purchase, even when
this enmity is unrelated to beliefs about the quality of products
produced in that country. This relationship is shown in Figure 4.4.

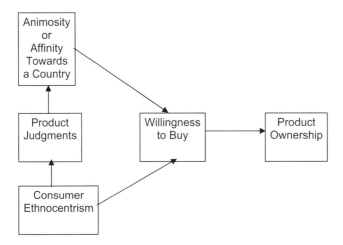

Source: Adapted from Klein et al, 1998. Reprinted with permission from the *Journal of Marketing*, published by the American Marketing Association, Klein, Jill Gabrielle, Richard Ettenson and Marlene Morris, 52 (January).

Figure 4.4 The Animosity-Affinity Model of Foreign Product Purchase

The model of Klein et al hypothesizes that animosity toward a country directly influences a person's willingness to buy products made by that country independently of product judgments. Moreover, it is hypothesized that animosity is a construct distinct from ethnocentrism. In this book we propose to replace *animosity* by an *animosity-affinity* construct. In our opinion, there is a continuum of attitudes towards an individual country that ranges from animosity through indifference to affinity. To reflect this approach, we added *affinity* to *animosity* in Figure 4.4

Klein et al (1998) tested the animosity model on a sample of adult consumers in the city of Nanjing, China's 11th largest city with a population of 2.5 million (1990). The results show that Chinese consumers' animosity toward Japan (apparently for World War II crimes against the local population) was related negatively to their willingness to purchase Japanese products, and more important, this effect was independent of what they thought about the quality of Japanese products. Moreover, the authors found a correlation between animosity toward Japan and ownership of Japanese products. The greater the animosity toward Japan, the lower the incidence of Japanese product ownership.

Can these findings be extrapolated to a wider Chinese population? Trade figures shows that China has the greatest volume of trade with

Japan. Japanese goods accounted for about 20 percent of China's total imports during 1999 (MOFTEC, 2000). This would seem to negate the assumption that Chinese animosity towards Japan minimizes the consumption of Japanese-made goods. However, approximately 80 percent of these imports consisted of capital and industrial goods, which may be less influenced by feelings of animosity. The remaining 20 percent of Japanese exports to China are concentrated in processed foods and textiles, products that hold small market shares in China. Imported textiles accounted for 8 percent of total consumption, processed foods, 3 percent and clothing only 1 percent (ITC, 2000).

It would seem that the Chinese animosity towards the Japanese is reciprocated. A random sample of approximately 2,000 Japanese over the age of 20 taken at the end of 1998 was asked: "Do you have positive feelings toward the United States, the People's Republic of China, the EU member countries and the ASEAN countries?" The results are shown in Table 4.7. Only about half of the Japanese respondents have some positive feelings about Mainland Chinese, but even less positive feelings about the ASEAN countries. Interestingly, the Japanese hold the most positive feelings about the United States (almost 80 percent of the respondents), in spite of the atomic bombing of Japanese cities during World War II and the ongoing trade friction between the governments of the two countries. Trade figures show that about 45 percent of Japan's imports originate from ASEAN (13 percent from China) countries and another 25 percent from the United States. Apparently, the volume of trade with ASEAN countries is not related to the relative lack of positive feelings toward them.

	USA	CHINA	EU	ASEAN
Have positive feelings	40.0%	12.0%	16.7%	6.3%
Have generally positive feelings	37.6	36.9	38.9	24.7
Don't really have positive feelings	12.2	29.9	21.4	32.4
Don't have positive feelings	7.9	17.6	15.3	24.3
Don't know	2.3	3.6	7.7	12.5

Source: Opinion Survey on Foreign Affairs, Prime Minister's Office, Tokyo, 1998.

Table 4.7 Japanese Feelings Towards Countries

A Two-Dimensional Consumer Segmentation Model

The past research reviewed above indicates that consumers may be segmented by two distinct constructs: their degree of ethnocentrism-othercentrism (patriots-inferiors) and their degree of animosity-affinity (hostiles-friends).[8] Each of these constructs may be considered as a continuous scale. The first ranging from high degree of ethnocentrism, through cosmopolitan approach, to high degree of othercentrism. The second, ranging from high degree of animosity, through indifference, to high degree of affinity. Since the first relates to overall attitudes toward purchasing imported as distinct from locally made goods while the second relates to attitudes toward a particular foreign country, both constructs may interact in affecting consumer behavior. For example, a consumer may prefer foreign-made goods, while at the same time have hostile feelings toward a specific foreign country. Figure 4.5 presents a two dimensional model of these two constructs. For convenience, we divide in Figure 4.5 each of the two continuous dimensions into three broad categories.

Attitude toward Imports	Attitude toward a country		
	Animosity	Indifferent	Affinity
Othercentricity	1 Conflict	2 Dominated by Othercentricity	3 Strong attraction to imports from the country
Cosmopolitan	4 Dominated by Animosity	5 No emotional preference	6 Dominated by Affinity
Ethnocentricity	7 Strong repulsion of imports from the country	8 Dominated by Ethnocentricity	9 Conflict

Figure 4.5 A Two Dimensional Consumer Segmentation Model

---

[8] We prefer to use objective terms that describe phenomena rather than loaded terms that disclose the writer's biases. Patriot is a positively loaded word while chauvinist is a negatively loaded one describing the same phenomenon. Ethnocentric is unbiased. Traitor is a loaded word. Since the antonym of ethnocentric has not been defined yet, we coin here the term othercentric to define a person who prefers foreign made products. For the same reasons we replace hostility and friendship with animosity and affinity.

Four groups of cells, distinguished by shading can be identified in Figure 4.5. The three dark gray cells on the diagonal, consisting of cells 3, 5, and 7 are those for which the effect of both dimensions are in the same direction and are compounded. Being othercentric, consumers in cell 3 prefer imported goods in general and, at the same time have positive feelings toward the foreign country in question. These consumers are most likely to purchase imported products from that source. At the other extreme, consumers in cell 7 prefer locally made products over imports in general and are hostile to the particular foreign country. They are least likely to purchase imports from this country. Those in cell 5 have neither positive nor negative feelings toward either imports or the country and are more likely to consider products on their merits.

Being cosmopolitan, consumers in the white cells 4 and 6 are influenced only by their emotions toward the foreign country. Those in cell 4 are dominated by their animosity to the country, while those in cell 6 by their affinity to it. Similarly, consumers in the white cells 2 and 8 have no particular emotions toward the foreign country and their attitude is dominated by their attitude to imports in general as compared with locally made (HC) products.

Finally, those in the light gray cells 1 and 9 have mixed emotions. Consumers in cell 1 prefer imported products, but feel animosity toward the particular country. Those in cell 9 generally prefer locally made products, but have affinity toward the foreign country. Given their conflicting emotions, the behavior of these consumers cannot be predicted. While we can utilize the above model to conjecture how consumers are expected to behave, there is a clear need for future research to investigate the simultaneous effects of both emotional constructs. In particular, future research should also address the question how consumers with conflicting emotions behave.

Travel and Country Image of Visited Countries

Another consumer segmentation approach is by the extent of their foreign travel experience. Does travel effect one's perception of a country's products? Do consumers who have traveled to a foreign country evaluate its products more favorably than non-visitors do? Very few studies have attempted to answer these questions. An early study of Canadian consumers (Papadopoulos and Heslop, 1986) found that those who had visited Sweden held generally less positive attitudes than non-visitors towards both the country and its products. However, views about Japan's degree of technological advancement and the industriousness of its people were stronger among visitors. Nevertheless, visitors to Japan indicated a markedly lower inclination to purchase some of Japan's mainstay products, such as cameras and automobiles, than non-visitors. On the other hand, it was found that consumers who had visited Great Britain indicated a strong preference for British goods. The finding by Papadopoulos and Heslop (1986) that visits to countries do not necessarily lead to favorable attitudes towards its people or products is buttressed by a more recent study (Ratcliffe and Griffin, 1999), which showed that familiarity (although not necessarily based on tourism) with a country, the UK in this case, is not strongly associated with positive perception of it. As shown in Figure 4.6, respondents from countries along the "best fit" line (that links the mid-point score in familiarity and favorability) do show an association between the two variables. Respondents from Poland, Malaysia, South Africa, India and Saudi Arabia fit this cluster. Those from Mexico and Russia form another cluster of respondents whose favorability is relatively higher than their familiarity. Germans and French have a lower opinion of the UK, given their familiarity with it.

What is the reason for the less favorable images of Sweden's and Japanese goods among visitors to their countries? The authors of the research posit that Sweden and Japan already enjoy generally, favorable images for their products, so that non-visitors also rate them highly. However, visitors become "exposed to daily life occurrences, and, in step with the adage that 'familiarity breeds contempt', think less positively...." about both the countries and their products (Papadopoulos, et al, 1997, 36). The opposite was believed to be the case with Britain, whose country image was not as positive as that of Sweden and Japan. So, visitors coming in contact with the UK environment, and supposedly having good experiences, rate British products more positively.

Studies by Hallberg (1996, 1999) of Dutch, British and German respondents who had visited Sweden found that tourism effects consumers' willingness to purchase products from visited countries. However, there were few significant differences (six out of 21 descriptors) between the visitors and non-visitors regarding attitudes toward Swedish products, although the visitors had more positive evaluations in all cases were differences were significant.

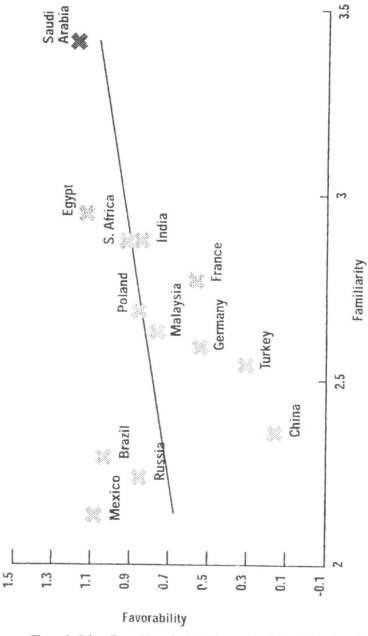

Source: *Through Other Eyes: How the World Sees the United Kingdom*, The British Council, October, 1999.

Figure 4.6 Favorability and Familiarity of Selected Countries

A Time, Inc. readership survey[9] showed that respondents who had visited Poland, the Czech Republic and Taiwan, had more favorable opinions about their products, trade relations and government than those that had never visited those countries and/or expressed no desire to visit them.

The few studies of country image and tourism leave many questions unanswered. Was the length of a visit or frequency of visits in a particular country associated with evaluation of the country and its products? Were measures taken of country and product evaluations before visiting so that before-after measures could be recorded? And, if so, how long a time interval after the visit were attitudes measured? Were there any differences in prior familiarity with a country's products between visitors and non-visitors? Are any travel effects moderated by demographics and/or ethnic affinity with the visited country? Countries that attract large numbers of foreign tourists have an excellent opportunity to promote their country image and goods and services. How this might best be accomplished will have to wait until more in-depth research is undertaken on this important issue.

From Attitudes to Behavior

Country of Origin Labeling – Do Consumers Care?

A number of surveys have been conducted in the United States by the Federal Trade Commission (FTC) and private organizations in order to measure consumer attitude about the importance of labeling imported products with the name of the origin country. If consumers do want to know the origin of a product, then it is incumbent upon governments to ensure that the proper labels will be prominent on the package or the product itself.

Some consumers prefer domestic made products in the belief that they have a duty to support the local economy. Just how widespread is this belief? A Gallup survey conducted in the United States during 1994 found that 84 percent of respondents prefer American-made products. More than half the respondents said that they either always or sometimes try to determine a product's origin before making a purchase decision. When asked their reasons for preferring American

---

[9] According to a survey undertaken by Time Inc. in 1997 among its Reader Panel consisting of Top Management (18%), Middle Management (14%), Professional (28%) and Government (6%) respondents residing in 11 European countries.

products, the response was that it helps the American economy and keeps workers employed (FTC, 1996).

However, these answers were not modified by product category. More consumers might be concerned about country of origin for durable goods purchases, than for clothing. For example, in another survey undertaken by Gallup (FTC, 1995) among American consumers in 1992, about half the respondents reported that the country in which a watch is manufactured is important when making a purchase decision. A total of 59 percent said they would prefer a watch made in Switzerland. Yet, in a research study submitted to the FTC by the New Balance Athletic Shoe Company, none of the respondents mentioned country of origin of a shoe's components when asked about factors considered in making shoe purchases. These findings show that the importance of a made-in label varies by product category.

A survey sponsored by the Australian government found that 88 percent of the respondents prefer to "buy Australian", while 77 percent said that they are willing to "pay a little extra" for Australian-made goods (Australian Federal Government, 1999). In another survey (Patterson and Tai, 1991) of Australian consumers, it was found that 20.4 percent of the respondents said that they "always" look for the made-in label when they purchase clothing, another 28.1 percent "often" and 39.5 percent "occasionally" look for the label. Only 12 percent said they "never" look for the made- in label.

Since 1983, The Packer, a leading American produce industry newspaper, has sponsored consumer studies to track trends in the purchase and consumption of fresh produce. When asked whether they agree with mandatory country of origin labeling on produce, 63 percent of the respondents strongly agreed, implying that they look for the made-in label (Spezzano, 1999). The American Alliance for Honest Labeling, a lobby group that supports mandatory country of origin labeling on frozen food packages, claims that in a four city poll, two-thirds of the respondents favor a mandatory country of origin designation on frozen food packages.

Likewise, in a national survey sponsored by the Federal Government of Australia, it was found that 70 percent of respondents claimed that they look for information about a product's country of origin. In a survey of business owners, 55 percent agreed that consumers look for country of origin information when shopping (Australian Federal Government, 1999). While lower than the consumer response rate (which might be inflated), more than half of consumers searching for origin information is a significant figure.

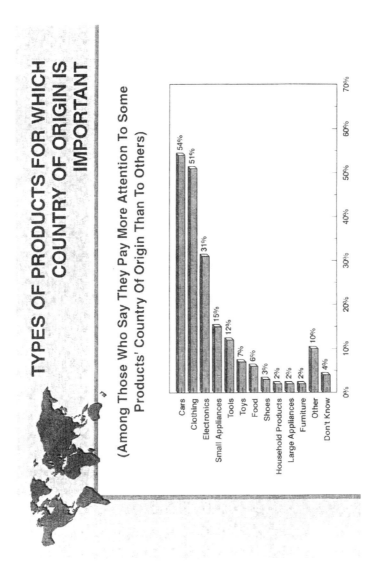

Source: Consumer Attitudes Toward Product Sourcing, IMRA, May, 1994

Figure 4.7 Importance of Country-of-Origin by product type

A Gallup survey sponsored by the International Mass Retail Association (IMRA, 1994) found that 34 percent of the respondents "always" try to determine the origin of a product when making a purchase decision. Another 44 percent said that they "sometimes" try to determine the origin, while 14 percent said "rarely" and only 8 percent, "never." For those who "always" try to determine the country of origin, 65 percent claimed that their purchase decision was based on country of origin. Next in importance was product features (38 percent), followed by warranty (36 percent), quality (35 percent) and price (32 percent). As pointed out in Chapter 1, country of origin effect is product specific. This is borne out by the Gallup study as shown in Figure 4.7. Here we see that the importance of country of origin is greatest in the purchase of cars, clothing and electronics. It is of little importance in the purchase household products, large appliances and furniture.

A survey undertaken among marketing and/or communications managers in a sample of 200 Fortune 500 companies found that 72 percent of the respondents replied that purchasing decisions for goods or services are affected by country of origin (Croft, 1995). The importance of origin in purchase decisions differed by product category. For example, 81 percent of respondents in financial service organizations replied that it was important, compared to 59 percent of the respondents from mining, quarrying and gas extraction.

Evidence for the Impact of Country Image on Purchase Behavior

Most studies cited above measured attitudes and opinions, but not actual behavior. Yet, we do have some evidence for behavior patterns motivated by country image. The effect of country image on consumer perception was demonstrated by research conducted by Publicis in the UK for the Renault Clio campaign. They found that the British perceived the French as having a more desirable way of life. This theme was integrated into the campaign, which ran from 1990 to 1998. As a result, Renault succeeded for the first time to enter the top 10 best selling cars in the UK (Cf. Yan, 1995).

Indian consumers were especially cognizant of the country of origin of TV sets when color TV transmission was introduced in 1982. Because domestic manufacturers did not have the resources necessary to produce color TV sets, the government allowed the importation of knocked down kits for local assembly. The kits were imported from South Korea, Japan and West Germany and assembled under Indian brand names. The Japanese and German assembled sets were in demand, but the South Korean ones were not. As "made in" country labels were not displayed for the kits' origin, consumers went to the trouble of opening the back of TV sets in order to ascertain from which country the components were imported (Khanna, 1986).

An extreme example of the effect of inferiority towards locally made products surfaced in the Nigerian automobile assembly industry. Nigerian consumers prefer foreign, high technology products. For example, Dutch, Japanese and South Korean-made TV sets are preferred for their perceived, technological advancement, reliability and workmanship over local, Nigerian brands. (Okechuku and Onyemah, 1999). The extent to which these attitudes affect on purchase behavior was documented in the case of Peugeot 504 assembly. The Nigerian preference for imported consumer products resulted in the reduction of the domestic assembly of the Peugeot 504-model car from 100,000 units in 1986 to about 4,500 in 1996, when import restrictions were eased.

Marcoux et al (1997) have found that the Poles are not patriotic consumers, especially in the consumption of status products such as clothing, cosmetics, and electronic products. Imported, Western products are preferred in order to enhance social relationships or to aspire to a higher social status. Anecdotal evidence was given by a manager of a company in Poland: "if you ask if it is important to buy Polish products, 90% say it is...but if you ask what shampoo they bought last week, 90% bought Western".

In an observational study of Israeli consumers' behavior in a department store, Nebenzahl (1998) found that in 34 percent of interactions concerning durable goods, the made-in country was mentioned by either the customer or the salesperson. The corresponding percentage in the sport shoes department was only 5 percent. These results clearly indicate that the importance of the country cue varies by product line. Given the importance of the country cue for durable goods, do consumers know where products are made? In a follow up survey of the consumers whose behavior was observed in Nebenzahl's study, it was found that when the made-in country (MC) was the same as the country of origin (OC), 64 percent of the customers could name that country. However, when production was sourced, 31 percent of the customers erroneously named the country associated with the brand (OC) as the country where the considered brands were made instead of the true made-in country (MC). Apparently, these consumers failed to perceive the made-in labels of the considered products.

In a comparable effort, Liefeld (2004) wanted to determine to what extent North American customers knew the country of origin of purchased products at the point of purchase. Consumers were interviewed as they left the cash registers at six different locations in

Pennsylvania, Missouri, California British Columbia Ontario and Nova Scotia, in shopping malls and general merchandise and hardware outlets. It was found that more than 93 percent of the purchasers did not know the country of origin of the product just purchased. Moreover, of the nearly seven percent who did know the country of origin, only 2.2 percent stated that knowledge of country origin might have influenced their product choice.

Contrary to survey results that exhibit consumers' lack of attention to the country-of-origin cue is the comment made by Heslop and Papadopoulos (1993) that there is a plethora of empirical evidence showing that country-of-origin influence does matter in consumers' evaluation of products, but that "for reasons we have yet to understand fully, people do not like to admit that it does." Building on this comment by Heslop and Papadopoulos, Liu and Johnson (2005) conducted an experiment to test the hypothesis that country stereotypes can be spontaneously activated by the mere presence of country-of-origin information in the environment, and they may influence product judgments even when consumers did not intend to base their judgments on country-of-origin. The results provided some support for the contention that country stereotypes can alter evaluation of brands.

Conclusion

Should Brands Fly the Flag? Should national images be used to promote domestic products? Can they be used to promote a global brand by literally waving the flag as Robert Morley did in an advertisement for British Airways?

We have tried to demonstrate in this chapter that consumer response to country-of-origin is not homogeneous. As national products may not have universal appeal because of the existence of consumer segments, the same is true for the effect of country branding. In the case of the overall country influence on brands or products (CIE), four consumer segments have been identified. Those responsible for national branding campaigns – whether on the firm or industry level – should bear them in mind when determining strategy.

We have also shown to what extent CIE impacts on consumer decision making. Two major conclusions have been found. First, consumers do form opinions about products made in different countries and these opinions influence their purchasing behavior. Second, the end result is that CIE is product specific. While consumers form overall images of a country's abilities to produce quality products, when it comes to making a purchase decision, this overall image perception is mitigated by a corresponding perception of the country as a source of the particular product line. A country may be perceived as a good producer of consumer products, but not necessarily of automobiles. These observations confirm the detailed theoretical model presented in Chapter 2 that includes overall image (MCI) and product specific (MCIP) components. Thus, it may be difficult to estimate the end result of all country image effects if there is a great deal of variability in the perceived quality of different product categories. These conclusions and others found in this chapter form the basis for strategy formulation at the firm, organizational and governmental levels, which is the subject of Chapters 5 and 6.

CHAPTER 5

Managing Country of Origin Effects by the Firm

"Made in Japan" used to be a sign of engineering excellence. At the moment, it reads more like a health warning.
A comment on the quality control problems of Mitsubishi Motors and Bridgestone tires in the *Economist*, September 18-22, 2000

Introduction

In previous chapters we have reviewed how country image affects consumers' perceptions of products and how these perceptions affect purchase behavior. In this and the next chapters, we discuss how country image may be managed on three levels: Firm, industry and government. An individual firm cannot control country image itself. Studies have shown that country image is influenced by exogenous factors such as a country's economic development, national identity, and its people, in short it's cultural environment. Therefore, firms, industry and government must work in concert if a national image is to be formed and successfully exploited.

Managing CI by the Firm

In an era of globalization, a firm's activities are integrated across multiple country markets. A major advantage of a global company is that it can configure parts of its value chain in different countries. An important criterion for this configuration is efficiency, performing activities where they can be the most productive. The ability to configure the value chain in this manner gives the multinational concern a competitive advantage over its domestic rivals that must perform most of these activities at home. An example of configuring a value chain is the placing of R & D centers at home and in a few select countries where native, high quality scientists can be readily found (e.g., India, Israel), perhaps at lower cost as well, without too much risk of dissipating whatever knowledge is created. Another example is the setting up of distribution centers at strategic crossroads (e.g., Holland, Singapore) and manufacturing facilities located in developing countries to take advantage of low-cost wages for labor intensive products. Not least this last consideration is of relevance to the subject of country image. Two facets of sourcing production in different countries have country image considerations. The first is that sourcing production in low wage countries that have unfavorable country images may save costs, but may also result in negative product evaluations by consumers. Second, and perhaps more complicated, is the fact that many consumer products have *multiple* country images. These are so-called *hybrid* products that contain components and parts that are sourced from more than one country. These products result from production sharing by manufacturers who design production lines across countries that have differential production costs. How do consumers evaluate a product that is assembled in one country, but contains components and parts made-in additional countries, and carries a brand name associated with yet another country? These are issues with which this chapter deals.

Production Sourcing

The trade off between lower costs and potential negative consumer demand must be determined before a sourcing decision is made.

The authors of this book carried out an experiment using a sample of students attending a large university in the New York Metropolitan area to determine what would happen to American consumers' perception of two well known brands if their production were sourced to Eastern European countries. The products were household electronics and the brands General Electric and Sony. The result of this experiment is shown in Figure 5.1 below. The figure has two axes, market presence (recognizable brand name, variety, easy to find) and product value (value for money, quality, and durability) and four quadrants.[10] The upper right-hand quadrant indicates a positive market presence and positive product value. The lower right-hand quadrant

---

[10] In an eight country study, Papadopoulos and Heslop (1990), found four dimensions: Product integrity, price-value, market presence and market response.

represents a positive product value, but a negative market presence. The upper left-hand quadrant indicates positive product value, but a negative market presence. The lower left-hand quadrant represents a negative product value and negative market presence.

The positions of the brands shown in Figure 5.1 predict a significant deterioration in brand value as both brands are shifted from their home countries to those of Eastern Europe. The deterioration is more serious for Sony than for General Electric, perhaps owing to the initial, much stronger product value enjoyed by the Japanese manufacturer. Sony made-in Japan (upper right-hand quadrant) was perceived as having a significantly higher product value than a similar product made by General Electric in the USA (upper left-hand quadrant). Both were perceived as having about the same market presence. If Sony sources its production to the USA (lower right-hand quadrant), its market presence declines somewhat, but its product value deteriorates even more, although it is still positive. The GE brand also loses market presence by shifting production to Japan, but gains slightly in product value. Apparently, either American consumers perceive Japanese made products to be superior in quality to American made ones (cf. Chinen, et al, 2000) and/or a made-in Japan label for electronic products has more value than a made-in USA label.

In any case, the experiment shows that both brands would lose significant equity if they carried a made-in label of any of the three Eastern European countries studied. While both brands lose in market presence, Sony loses more than GE in two countries, Poland and Hungary. It seems that it is easier for consumers to conceive of GE being made in East European countries. Even though the loss in product value of Sony is greater than the corresponding GE loss, its ending product value is still greater than that of GE for all shifts in production. This shows that the Sony brand name has more equity than GE and can withstand the negative made-in country images of the Eastern European countries. Firms that want to determine the effect on brand equity as manufacturing or assembly is sourced to countries that have negative country images must design similar, customized experiments.

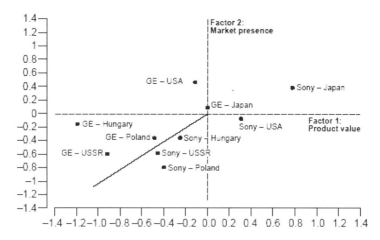

Source: Nebenzahl, I. D. and Jaffe, E. D. (1997) "Measuring the Joint Effect of Brand and Country Image in Consumer Evaluation of Global Products," Reprinted in: *Journal of Marketing Practice: Applied Marketing Science*, Vol. 3 No. 3, p. 200.

Figure 5.1 Market Sourcing and Perception

Additional evidence about the relative importance of brand and country of origin is found in a number of studies. d'Astous and Ahmed (1992) found that brand was more important than country of origin as an evaluative cue, although the results varied across product class. Tse and Lee (1992) found that a strong brand like Sony could compensate for a negative country image, buttressing the results of our experiment related above. Likewise, Hulland found that brands with positive equity, like Sony, tend to be considered more frequently for purchase than brands with negative equity (e.g. Citizen). Another study by Ulgado and Lee (1993) found that a known and favorable brand image could reduce the effect of a weak country image. Moreover, consumers tend to perceive the brand origin of a product to be associated with the country where the brand's corporate headquarters is located rather than the country where the product is manufactured (Thakor and Lavack, 2003). Consistent with the above findings, Ashill and Sinha (2004) found that for watches, brand rather than country of origin has a much stronger impact on purchase intention. Therefore, a strong brand equity could mitigate negative country of origin associations. Accordingly, a Sony product would benefit from its Japanese origin, no matter where it is produced. Nevertheless, Tse and Gorn (1993) found that the country cue was stronger than brand.

The above studies lead to the conclusion that while the image of a strong global brand is expected to erode when sourced in a weak image country, it can somewhat compensate for a negative country image. However, the pulling power of the brand is likely to be greater in the case of products whose qualities can be ascertained through experience. Consumers can evaluate the quality of global branded products that are manufactured or assembled in developing countries. However, the brands of many prestige and status products are strongly intertwined with country image. It is almost impossible to separate them. Rolls Royce and Land Rover *British* automobiles[11], Royal Copenhagen *Danish* china and Kosta Boda, *Swedish* crystal, owe their brand image to a strong country image for these product categories. The same is true of Swiss watches and perfumes made in France. For these products, offshore production or assembly is unthinkable. Even the purchase of Land Rover by the German BMW[12], while keeping production in England, may have had a negative effect on consumer perception of the brand.

Hybrid Products

Hybrid products are composed of components sourced in multiple countries. Examples of hybrid products are automobiles assembled in emerging or Eastern European countries like Mexico and Poland that contain components and parts made elsewhere. Witness the Pontiac Le Mans, assembled in South Korea but designed in Germany that contained parts from across the globe (see Table 5.1). Consider also the case of the 1989 Honda Civic that contained parts from at least three countries (See Figure 5.2). Honda management claimed that the car was 69 percent American made. The United States Customs asserted that it was only 45 percent American, while an audit by the University of Michigan determined that only 42 percent of its engine

---

[11] BMW, like Land Rover was planning to construct a factory for Rolls-Royce automobiles near Goodwood, UK when it planned to take over the brand in 2002. BMW's decision was partly due to the belief that Rolls-Royce cars should never be manufactured outside of England. Similarly, production of the 2001 model year Mini, a brand that BMW retained during the sale of the former Rover Group, have remained in England at BMW's Oxford facility. (The authors thank Jack Yan for calling this to their attention).

[12] On March 16, 2000, BMW announced the sale of its Rover cars division to Alchemy Partners, Ltd., a British venture capitalist firm. The new venture was to be called the MG Car Company. However, Land Rover was eventually sold to Ford Motor Company.

was made in the United States.[13] The question is of course, how do consumers evaluate such hybrid products? Are they aware of the complexity of manufacture, and if so, do they really care where the components originate from, or are they only concerned with the location of final assembly? Do consumers consider the Pontiac a South Korean or an American car? Is the Honda perceived as a Japanese or an American car? Are consumers aware of the Canadian parts incorporated in it?

Component or Part	Country
1.6 Liter Engine	South Korea
2.0 Liter Engine	Australia
Automatic Transmission and Transaxle	Canada and USA
Manual Transmission	South Korea
Brake Components	France, USA, South Korea
Tires	South Korea
Electrical Wiring Harness	South Korea
Sheet Metal	Japan
Fuel Injection	USA
Fuel Pump	USA
Radio	Singapore
Steering Components	USA
Windshield Glass	South Korea
Battery	South Korea
Rear Axle Components	USA and South Korea
Exterior Body Stamping	South Korea

Table 5.1 What's Inside The Pontiac Le Mans Assembled In South Korea, But Designed In Germany?

Decomposing Country of Origin

Given the above examples and questions, we can distinguish between four country-of-origin effects other than the country of manufacture whose name appears on the made-in label (see Figure 5.3). These are the country associated with the brand (OC), country of design or engineering (DC), country of components or parts (PC) and finally, country of assembly (AC). In the Pontiac example, the country of design (DC) is Germany; the country of assembly (AC) is South Korea. There are seven countries where components or parts originate (PCs). In addition, the brand name (Pontiac) brings out an association with the United States as its country-of-origin (OC). Each of these

---

[13] The final arbiter in such cases is the U.S. Customs.

individually or together is thought to affect the overall perceived attributes of the final product:

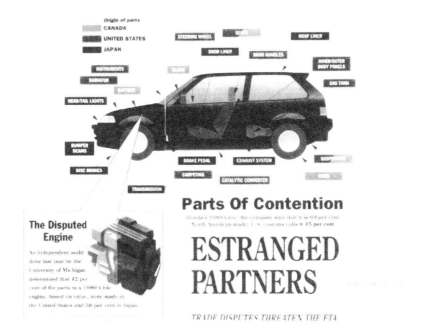

Source: Nancy Wood, "Estranged Partners", MacLean's, March 16, 1992.
Figure 5.2 Component Sourcing of a Honda Car

Consumers can be cued to the existence of a hybrid product only if the product contains a label to that effect. Some products carry an "assembled in" label either because the manufacturer believes that the country of assembly has a more favorable image than the countries where the parts are made, or when such a label is required by law (as in the case of cars sold in the United States). Of course, if manufacturers believe it is to their benefit they may emphasize the country of assembly, parts or design in advertising and sales promotion campaigns.

To what extent do the relationships depicted in the above figure operate in reality? A number of empirical studies have found mixed results depending upon the sort of product advertised or the country of assembly. For example, American university students were shown ads for Magnavox brand television sets described as either being assembled, designed or containing parts from the USA or Mexico

117

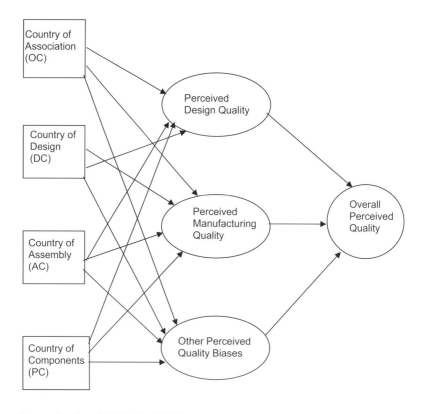

Source: Insch and McBride (1998).
Figure 5.3 Decomposed Countries of Origin Model

(Chao 1998). It was found that country of design only affects the perception of design quality, whereas country of assembly and country of parts affect the perception of product quality. However, Ahmed, et al (1994) sampled Canadian consumers and found that country of design significantly affected perceived product quality and value for a number of consumer products including cameras and VCRs. In a later study, Ahmed et al (1997) manipulated country of design and country of assembly between products originating in Canada, Japan, Mexico and the USA. They found that among American consumers, country of design influenced perceived product quality more than country of assembly for cars, VCRs and shoes. Among Canadian consumers, country of design was more important than country of assembly for VCRs, but for cars and shoes, country of assembly was more important.

Li, Murray and Scott (2000) also studied the effect of multiple country-of-origin effects. They surveyed students at an Australian university and concluded that DC was more influential in affecting evaluations of functional and symbolic product qualities than AC or OC. Their finding suggests that a strong DC may compensate for sourcing production in low cost assembly sites. Finally, in a study of New York State consumers, Brodowsky (1998) found that, as expected, those exhibiting high ethnocentric tendencies believed that cars designed and assembled in the United States were of higher quality than those designed and assembled in Japan.

Without exception, the above studies sampled diverse populations of students and household consumers. While the effects of consumers' product perceptions have also been examined among industrial buyers, research effort in this area remains relatively modest. The authors found only one published study (Dzever and Quester, 1999) of industrial buyers regarding the decomposition of country of origin. In this study, the quality perceptions of Australian purchasing agents for machine tools and component parts from seventeen countries were measured. Questions were asked in relation to either country of design or country of assembly. While this study also found that AC and DC affected perceptions of product quality, these perceptions differed by product attributes. For example, Japan was perceived as superior in terms of machine tool assembly technology, but not in design. Sweden was perceived as superior in terms of machine tool ease of operation assembly, but less in design. However, when it comes to component parts, Sweden was perceived superior in both AC and DC on the attributes of ease of operation and training. So, perception of AC and DC varies by product type and product attribute. Therefore, it would be misleading for a marketer having a good DC reputation to assume that this could be used to convince potential buyers that the quality of assembly would be equally good.

What do these studies have in common? They show that country image is decomposed in the case of hybrid products. In some cases, the country of assembly cue affects perception of product quality, in other cases it may be country of design. Granted that all of these may affect product evaluation; can a poorly perceived assembly location be compensated by a positive design location, or by a positive country of components? Can a weak AC, DC or PC be compensated by a strong brand name or by price?

In an experiment (Tse and Lee, 1993) using a home stereo system as the object, made-in country, country of assembly and country of design were manipulated among Japan and South Korea. It was found that a strong, global brand name (Sony versus Goldstar) could compensate for negative country of assembly and country of design stereotypes, although the brand name affect on AC was much stronger. Seaton and Laskey (1999) found that brand name was relatively more important that AC and PC, in that order, among American consumers. The ability of a strong brand to neutralize to some extent a negative AC or DC is much like the sourcing case of Sony and GE shown above. The stronger global brand (Sony) outperformed the weaker brand (GE) as production was shifted out of the home countries. This experiment took place in the United States. In another experiment using Canadian and People's Republic of China subjects, Ahmed and d'Astous (1999) manipulated AC, DC, brand, price and warranty for VCRs and shoes in Canada and refrigerators, cameras, and t-shirts in China. Contrary to Tse and Lee (1993), they found that brand name is a less important cue than DC and AC in explaining product perceptions in both Canada and China.

Strategic Implications of a Decomposed Country of Origin

What are the strategic implications of the above experimental findings? First, managers must be aware of how country–of-origin cues affect consumer perception of product attributes and brand equity. Most CIE studies have investigated the importance of the made-in cue on consumer evaluation of a country's products or services. Only several of these have tried to monetize the impact of CIE on brand equity. The first of these studies (Johansson and Nebenzahl, 1986) attempted to "monetize" the CI effect. In so doing, they determined that manufacturing a Buick or Chevy car in Korea or Mexico, in place of the United States, reduced the value of the cars by approximately 17 percent or in dollar value from $9,000 to $7,500. Nebenzahl and Jaffe (1993) estimated demand elasticities for Korean-made VCRs just starting to be imported into Israel. They calculated that the Korean-made VCRs would have to be discounted by approximately 40 percent in order to be competitive with similar Japanese-made VCRs. This was owing to the poor country image that Korea had at the time. As it turned out, Korean-made VCRs were introduced into the market at a 32 percent discount with limited success. In a more recent study (Seaton and Laskey, 1999) among American consumers, it was found that a change in the assembly location of a $17,000 automobile from the USA to Mexico would result in a change in perceived value of $1,952 (a reduction of 11.5 percent). Shifting assembly to Korea would result in a reduction of perceived value of $1,795, or 10.6 percent.

What the above studies show that utilizing the monetizing models detailed in chapter 3, it is possible to estimate the effect on brand equity as either production or assembly is shifted to countries that have negative CIE images. These measures enable management to calculate whether the cost savings of production/ assembly in these countries are greater than the loss in brand equity. Assuming that, for example, a particular model of an automobile is assembled only in one country, Korea and not in the United States, then pricing strategy is not difficult. However, when assembly of a particular model takes place in more than one country, for example, Volkswagen in Brazil, Mexico and Germany, care must be taken to ensure that only one location is used to source a given target market. Consumers may perceive different brand values for the same model assembled in Brazil versus Mexico. If so, one could expect that there would be different price elasticities of demand for the two models. In practice, a differentiated price strategy would be difficult to implement. A somewhat different example than that contained in the above scenario, was the case of Toyota cars assembled in Australia. Toyota concluded a joint venture with Holden in Australia for the assembly of automobiles; half of the output was given the name Toyota and the other half, Holden, even though the products were identical. However, consumers purchased the Holden cars only if given a price discount.[14] Another example is that Levi Strauss and Wrangler jeans with a "Made in USA" label sold for three times the retail price of the identical product manufactured by the same companies in Europe (*Export Today*, 1994).

In contrast to the above studies that link pricing strategy to country image, Agarwal and Kamakura (1999) argue that country image might not necessarily lead to a competitive advantage in the form of a price premium or discount. They contend that price discounts may be explained by differences in product quality rather than by the perception of country image produced by the made-in cue. Based on a meta-analysis of twelve country of origin studies, Agarwal and Kamakura found that in about 80 percent of the cases, Japanese products were perceived as better than American and German products, and in 75 percent of the cases, American products were perceived to be better than German products. Then, using objective quality and price data from *Consumer Reports*, they estimated price

---

[14] The authors thank Jack Yan for this source.

premiums or discounts above or below the *expected* price from the products' measured quality, which can be attributed to the products' country image. Because Japanese-made products were perceived to be better than either American or German products, it would have been expected that they would command a premium price beyond what could be charged for the difference in objective quality. Although no premium price was found for Japanese products, beyond quality differences, the authors admit that the reason for this might be owing to the Japanese strategy of gaining high market shares, rather than exploiting the competitive advantage of their relatively better country image.

Alternative Marketing Entry Strategies

A company's marketing entry strategies are dependent on a number of factors including the strength of its brand image and made-in country image. Four possible entry strategies are suggested in the 2X2 matrix shown as Table 5.2.

Made-in Country Image	Brand Image	
	Strong	**Weak**
Strong	Made-in Country Global Brand	Made in Country
Weak	Brand Alone Associated Country Decomposition Country of Design Country of Components	Neutralize Country and Brand Price Discount Store Private Label Contract Manufacture Quality Control Niche Markets

Table 5.2 Alternative Market Entry Strategies: Considering Country and Brand Images

The first scenario considers those firms that have both a strong country and brand image. A second scenario looks at firms with a weak country image, but that have strong brand images. A third possibility includes firms with weak brand images, but with strong country images. The fourth possibility is firms with both weak country and brand images. Marketing entry strategies are suggested for all four conditions below.

Strong Country Image – Strong Brand Image

The ideal strategic position of a company is when either the MC or AC has a strong country image and the product has a strong brand image. In this case, the made-in country should be emphasized as well as the brand, especially if it is a global one. Many country-product combinations come to mind; Sony made-in Japan, Buick made-in the United States, Land Rover made in the UK, Zeiss made in Germany, and Volvo made in Sweden, to name a few.

Weak Country Image – Strong Brand Image

The quadrant strong brand image, weak country image generally refers to those products whose production/assembly has been sourced to developing or emerging economies or to a country that has a weaker image than that of the country associated with the brand. In this situation, emphasis should be placed on the brand name, while de-emphasizing as much as possible the country of manufacture/ assembly. For example, a four-roll package of 35mm Fuji film purchased by one of the authors in the United States emphasized the brand name, while de-emphasizing the fact that the film was not produced in Japan. On the barcode strip was the designation "Manufactured for the U.S.A.". On the bottom panel of the package was the information that one of the rolls (a trial roll of 800 ASA film) was made in Japan, while the other three rolls were made in the Netherlands. A three-pack of Kodak 35mm film purchased at Ben-Gurion airport in Israel had a "Made-in France" designation on the box containing the film, but "Kodak (Near East) Inc." followed by Greek lettering on the package. A designated importer, "Kodak Polska" of Warsaw was written below the Greek lettering. Confusing? Apparently, the film was diverted through the gray market to Israel.

Another strategy for products falling in the strong brand image/weak made-in country quadrant would be to emphasize the associated country or decompose country image or both. For example, the Pontiac assembled in South Korea could be advertised as a car designed in Germany and assembled with American technology. In the case of a Chevrolet assembled in the Mexico, an advertisement should emphasize the brand and that the car was designed in the USA and contains components made by American manufacturers.

A made-in Britain study by Wolff Olins found that many people held stereotype images of Great Britain as strike-prone, old-fashioned and out of touch. Such a national image is detrimental to companies operating in a global market. It was this stereotype that led British Telecom to take the "British" out of its brand name (Leonard, 1997):

> *British Telecom did research into the appropriateness of [their brand name]...in overseas markets...we had problems with the name in certain parts of the world - Japan...- where the name British was understood to stand for 'of the past', 'colonial', not about innovation, not about high technology, or the future or moving forward. Given the fact that we are in a fast-moving, highly innovative, creative area in telecommunications, the name British was a problem, and that was why we changed from British Telecom to BT.*

There are also examples where a brand name is created to correspond to an associated country with a strong image for a particular product category. Below (Figure 5.4) is an advertisement for the allmilmö corporation, located in the USA and Canada, an importer of modular kitchen cabinets manufactured in Zeil am Main, Germany. In this case, a corporate brand name was associated with Scandinavia, piggybacking on the design reputation of that region. Shalimar perfume, manufactured by Guerlain of France, was given an oriental brand name to associate the product with that region. Another example of using a foreign sounding brand name to position a product with an associated country is Häagen Dazs, now owned by Pillsbury. The product was founded as a small ice cream business by Reuben Mattus of Brooklyn, New York and subsequently produced in New Jersey. In the late 1950s, Mattus' company was finding it hard to compete with larger competitors. He decided to upgrade the quality of his products, producing what he termed a "superpremium" ice cream. At the time, European ice cream was associated with quality, like the Danish brand Premium Is. So, he made up the name of Häagen Dazs, and printed a map of Denmark, marking Copenhagen on the top of the containers (Cf. Ullmann, 1993). The adoption of a Scandinavian sounding name was intended to associate the product with a region that is known for its high quality dairy products.[15]

Figure 5.4 An Example for Utilization of a Foreign Brand Name and European Source Rather Than Country of Origin (Germany).

---

[15] An amusing anecdote is that no Danish-speaking person would recognize Häagen Dazs as a Danish sounding name (or Scandinavian for that matter).

Strong Country Image – Weak Brand Image

In another category are those products whose country image is strong, but whose brand image is weak. These might be lesser-known Japanese products or those that are perceived to be of lower quality than competitors from the home country. In essence, these brands try to piggyback on a strong country image by emphasizing the made-in cue. Some examples include Korean brands such as Kia automobiles and Worldstar, a manufacturer of computer accessories; Japanese brands like Miranda cameras and Suzuki and Daihatsu automobiles; Telefunken of Germany and Renault Alliance and Encore models of France sold in the United States during the 1980s.[16]

An alternative strategy that seems to work is to utilize word-of-mouth communications by salespersons to emphasize the source country. Nebenzahl (1997) found that salespersons in the consumer durables department of an Israeli department store initiated talking about the country of origin in 19 percent of their conversations. In November 2000, an acquaintance of the authors purchased a VCR in a store in Northern New Jersey. Here is how he described his experience: "I looked at VCRs by Sony and JVC. The salesman told me that now-a-days you don't know where Sony is made while JVC is still made in Japan. I purchased the JVC."

Weak Country Image – Weak Brand Image

Finally, there are those products that have a weak brand image as well as a weak country image. This was the situation that most Japanese products faced in the 1960s, and South Korean products faced in the 1980s. Most of the suggested entry strategies shown in the matrix result in a sacrifice of profits, for market penetration in the short run. Another alternative is to piggyback on a strong brand in the target market. Taking one of the South Korean products for example, Samsung, gained entry into the United States for its microwave ovens by having them distributed by General Electric under the GE label. South Korean household consumer products penetrated the Israeli market in the late 1980s, either by price discounting as mentioned above, or by selling though a large retail chain under the chain's label. Selling products at well known, reputed retailers can overcome country-of-origin problems (Chong, 1992). Other examples include Mitsubishi's entry into the United States through the Chrysler distribution network and Video Technology of Hong Kong's entry into

---

[16] The authors thank Jack Yan for some of these examples.

the Australian marker under the local and well-known brand name of Dick Smith. Since many countries require a made-in country label to be affixed on the product, consumers are cued to this fact. Assuming that the product functions well, and contains the same attributes of more established and better perceived competitors, a strong advertising campaign should begin to improve the country image, which should also reflect upon the brand image (Lampert and Jaffe, 1996).

In the long run, the product can break out of the less profitable strategies of private label and price discounting. This is what happened to both Japanese and Korean products in the United States, Western Europe and Australia.

Market entry strategies of weak country image manufacturers have also been successful in smaller markets like Israel. Today, not only are most South Korean home electronic products sold under their own brand name in Israel, but their success lead to the importation of South Korean made cars that now have a market share of 11 percent, taken mainly at the expense of Japanese models.[17] After penetrating markets by one of the strategies suggested above, South Korean products were heavily advertised focusing on product quality and performance combined with company brand name awareness and image. While prices were slowly increased, at the time of this writing they are still below those of competing Japanese products. Over time, the improved brand image, along with consumer awareness of the intrinsic characteristics of the country's products, may favorably effect consumers' evaluation of them.

Another possibility is to neutralize not only the made-in country cue, but also the brand name. Japanese manufacturers initially used "country-neutral" brand names such as Canon, National (Matsushita), Sharp, Citizen[18] and Brother in order to associate them with the United States in their efforts to penetrate North American Markets. A similar strategy was followed by South Korean manufacturers, for example, Goldstar (consumer appliances), Worldstar (computer accessories) and Lespo (bicycles).

---

[17] This share resulted before the bankruptcy of the Daewoo automobile division.

[18] However, by 1998, respondents in Canada and Hong Kong could recognize the associated country of both Citizen (85% of respondents in Hong Kong and 81% in Canada) and Sharp (81% in Hong Kong and 84% in Canada). This was compared to a 100% recognition of Sony in Canada and a 75% recognition in Hong Kong (Cf. Hulland, 1999).

Product-Country Matches and Mismatches

We have emphasized above that country image is product specific. Cars carrying a Japanese made-in label may be regarded highly, but Japanese clothing may not. This is because the Japanese are not associated with clothing design and manufacture. So, even though Japan's country image is relatively positive, it may not be relevant for all product categories. Therefore, there must be a "fit" between country image and product category. Roth and Romeo (1992) suggest a framework that matches the importance of product category dimensions with the perceived image of the country-of-origin.

Country Image Dimensions

		Positive	Negative
Dimensions as Product Features	**Important**	I Favorable Match *Denmark* **Furniture Porcelain Windmills**	II Unfavorable Match *Mexico* **Computers Cars**
	Not Important	III Favorable Mismatch *Denmark* **Beer Cheese**	IV Unfavorable Mismatch *Mexico* **Beer**

Source: Adapted from Roth, Martin and Jean Romeo 1992. Matching Product Category and Country Image Perceptions: A Framework for Managing Country-of-Origin Effects, Figure 1, *Journal of International Business Studies*, 23, 3, pp. 477-497, Reprinted with permission.

Figure 5.5 Product-Country Matches and Mismatches

The match-mismatch framework is shown as Figure 5.5. A product-country match should occur when important dimensions for a product category are associated with a country's image. For example, a favorable product-country match occurs in quadrant I. In this quadrant the perceived strengths of a country (positive country image) consist of important product features or benefits for the particular product category. A favorable mismatch, quadrant III occurs when the image dimensions for a country are positive, but not important for the product category. An unfavorable product-country match, quadrant II, occurs when the important product dimensions are not the perceived strengths of the country. Finally, an unfavorable match, quadrant IV, occurs when country image is negative and product dimensions are unimportant product features. When a favorable match occurs, consumer willingness to buy a country's products increases.

An example of Danish firms' use of country image to advertise their products illustrates how the match and mismatch matrix may be used. Niss (1996, 14) claims that "Denmark's [country] image is too weak and one-sided to be used as a prominent promotion tool in the marketing of Danish products abroad". Nevertheless, the author does report that producers of certain products do allude to "Scandinavian" as the country of origin in their communication strategy (See Figure 5.5). Suppose that Denmark's manufactures are known for design, prestige and workmanship. For example, manufactures of design goods, furniture and computers do use country of origin, while producers of industrial products do not. Using the above matrix, Danish furniture and other products for which design is an important dimension (e.g. Bang & Olufsen home electronics, Royal Copenhagen china) fit in quadrant I. Therefore, country of origin should be emphasized. Unfortunately, not enough has been done to promote this positive image:

"Made in Denmark" connotes high quality and innovation in product development and design...among those of our foreign customers who know what Denmark is. Unfortunately, a lot of them don't – or they believe that Denmark is the capital of Sweden

Niss, 1996, 14

A favorable mismatch (quadrant III) for Danish products would include beer. In this case, Denmark's positive country image should be used to improve brand awareness of its beer, e.g. Carlsberg. Danish-made industrial products would fit in quadrant II. Product dimensions are important, but Denmark's country image dimensions for this category of products are negative. Strategies that may be used include emphasizing product benefits rather than country of origin and, in the long run, a joint industry-firm campaign to enhance the country's image for this product category.

Taking Mexico as another example, suppose that an image survey shows that the country is weak on the dimensions of design, prestige and workmanship. If so, computers and cars made in Mexico would fit in quadrant II. Since country image is not favorable, the country of design (DC) and the source of components (PC) should be emphasized instead. Mexican beer would fit in quadrant IV. In this case, country origin should be ignored.

Product-Country Matches – Empirical Evidence

There is some empirical evidence of (mostly) favorable product-country matches. Table 5.3 shows ten product categories and those countries that were ranked, first, second and third as being associated most with that product category.[19] These rankings serve as a proxy for associated country images (OC). Table 5.4 provides similar data for leading brands.

Product Category	First	%	Second	%	Third	%
Sports shoes	USA	53	Germany	19	France	4
Cameras	Japan	81	Germany	9	USA	3
Vodka	Russia/CIS	67	Sweden	7	Poland	5
Consumer electronics	Japan	68	Holland	12	Germany	6
Luxury cars	Germany	49	UK	33	Italy	9
Beer	Germany	31	Holland	14	Denmark	13
Computers	USA	80	Japan	5	UK	3
Quality watches	Switzerland	84	Japan	6	France	2
Fashion/ Accessories	France	48	Italy	30	UK	3
Mobile phones	Sweden	19	Finland	16	USA	13

Source: *Country Images II 1997*; Time, Inc. Base: All respondents; Sample: 2,089

Table 5.3 Top Countries Associated with Product Categories

Comparing the data of tables 5.3 and 5.4, we find that there is a good match between countries associated as leaders (ranked first) in product categories with leading brands in each category. The only exceptions are two mismatches in beer (Germany is ranked first in the product

---

[19] According to a survey undertaken by Time Inc. in 1997 among its Reader Panel consisting of Top Management (18%), Middle Management (14%), Professional (28%) and Government (6%) respondents residing in 11 European countries.

category, whereas Heineken of Denmark is ranked first as the leading brand) and mobile phones (Sweden is ranked first in the product category, but Nokia of Finland is ranked first as the leading brand). For the second and third place rankings there is more of a discrepancy.

Product Category	First	%	Second	%	Third	%
Sports shoes	Nike	49	Adidas	27	Reebok	10
Cameras	Canon	27	Nikon	25	Sony	8
Vodka	Smirnoff	36	Absolut	11	Gorbachov	7
Consumer electronics	Sony	51	Philips	15	Panasonic	5
Luxury cars	Mercedes-Benz	33	Rolls Royce	24	BMW	11
Beer	Heineken	17	Carlsberg	13	Becks/ Guinness	5
Computers	IBM	51	Apple	12	Compaq	11
Quality watches	Rolex	36	Omega	13	Seiko	6
Fashion/ Accessories	Christian Dior	16	Armani	10	Gucci	9
Mobile phones	Nokia	29	Ericsson	19	Motorola	11

Source: *Country Images II 1977*; Time, Inc. Base: All respondents; Sample: 2,089.

Table 5.4 Top Brands Associated with Product Categories

In the second place categories there are five correct matches and only one correct match in the third place categories. Can we explain the mismatches found between leading brands and countries? A clue may be found in the theory of learning outlined in Chapter 1. According to this theory, when a person is exposed to information, s/he classifies it in previously known categories. Denmark, Finland and Sweden are identified not only by their respective names but also as being Scandinavian. This leads to some confusion between Finland and Sweden. Furthermore, since Nokia uses an EU made-in label (see Made in Europe below), the consumer has difficulty in associating it with a country. Not having a proper country category for Nokia, it may be misindexed and associated with the category "Sweden" which is known for its mobile phones (Ericsson).

Note that in every case (except for mobile phones); the associated country rankings were higher than for the leading brands. Thus, 80 percent of respondents associated the USA with computers, whereas

51 percent perceived IBM to be the leading brand. Including Apple raises the USA brands to 63 percent, still below the associated country percentage. Similarly, 81 percent associated Japan as the leading country in the camera category, while leading brands included Canon (27 percent), Nikon (25 percent) and Sony (8 percent) accounting for only 60 percent. This was also the only product category where all three brands were associated with the leading country. An explanation for these discrepancies is found in the relative number of brands versus countries with known expertise. The number of leading countries in each product line is much smaller than the number of brands. The world market share of brands is much smaller. Thus, the recalled leading country rankings are higher than those of brands.

What can be inferred from these findings? The strong association between perceived country image and brand image buttresses the contention made in this book about the reciprocity between the two. Second, we also find that country image is product category specific. For example, 81 percent of respondents rated Japan as the top country for camera production, but only 68 percent gave a similar rating for Japanese-made consumer electronic products. Japan is not included at all among the top three countries in sports shoes, vodka, luxury cars, beer, fashion/accessories and mobile phones. The case of mobile phones is most illuminating. While mobile phones are included in the broader consumer electronics category, European consumers identify the weakness of Japan in this particular product line. Likewise, 80 percent of respondents rated the USA as the top country for computers, but only 53 percent for sports shoes and this country is excluded from the list of leading countries in vodka, consumer electronics, luxury cars, beer, quality watches and fashion/accessories. The effect of the home residence of the consumer (HC) on perceived country image is exemplified by luxury cars. European consumers are familiar with Mercedes-Benz, BMW, Rolls Royce, Lamborgini or Maserati and less with Cadillac or Lincoln Continental that are hardly seen on European roads. Also, as we suggested above, individual brands within a product category collectively influence (and are influenced by) country image. However, some brands contribute more than others do, as can be seen by the results shown in Table 5.4. Finally, a relatively strong country image favorably reflects on brand images. This is demonstrated, for example, by the high rating given to Japanese-made cameras and the fact that the three top brands are all Japanese.

Place Branding – Made in Europe

A firm that sources production in a number of European countries, where country of origin equity varies by country, may consider using a made-in Europe or an EU label, rather than specific country labels. When should this strategy be used? The most obvious answer is that a Made-in Europe label should be preferred to a national label whenever consumers perceive the former more positively. A case in point is Nokia of Finland, which has adopted a "Made in Europe" label.[20] However, if consumers perceive large quality differences within a product category originating from different countries, a regional made-in label may have low informational value (Schweiger, et al, 1995). In this case, the made-in Europe option should not be used.

The National Image International Life Cycle

Niss (1996) suggests that use of national image to promote products or services abroad is more frequent in the introduction stage of the International Product Life Cycle (IPLC) than in the growth and maturity stages. Using national image as a promotional device in the beginning of the IPLC helps the exporter penetrate the market faster than by investing in brand awareness. A similar finding was reported by Djursaa et al, 1991. Nearly all the Danish firms in their survey reported a declining use of national image as market penetration evolves. The decline was for all industry sectors included in the study, with the exception of furniture and food. This progression follows the Lampert and Jaffe (1998) image life cycle as postulated above in Chapter 2. Following is an illustration of Danish firms' use of national image over time.

---

[20] Jack Yan reports to the authors that a client software firm located in Slovenia insists on placing a "European" name on postal designations, in the belief that "Europe" is more sophisticated than "Slovenia".

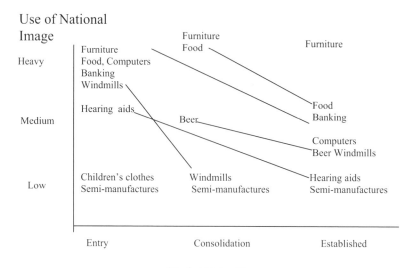

Market Entry Stages

Source: Djursaa et al, 1991. Reproduced by permission of MCB University Press.

Figure 5.6 National Image and Market Entry

For example, Danish manufacturers of windmills emphasize national image during the market entry stage, this use is moderated in the consolidation stage and finally, brand promotion takes over in the established market penetration stage. Some industries only use national image moderately or not at all, such as beer (well-established global brand) and semi-manufacturers for which national image is less important to buyers.[21] Those manufacturers that have been able to build regional or global brands over the market development stages rely less on national image.

Verlegh and Steenkamp (1999) and Laroche, et al (2005) show that country image is a multidimensional construct consisting of cognitive (e.g. product quality, the country's industrial development), affective (e.g. emotional value, consumers' response to the country's people) and normative-conative (e.g. social considerations) components. Amine, et al (2005) studied Taiwan's use of national image over time. Initially, communication campaigns appealed to the cognitive dimension (Taiwan as a "Symbol of Excellence") and later to the

---

[21] Another example of a well-known consumer product is Lego of Denmark, which chooses not to emphasize the national identity of its products.

134

affective dimension (Taiwan welcomes you with a smile"). If the Taiwanese strategy may be generalized, it shows that initial market entry should emphasize cognitive values related to the country's industrial and technological abilities, attributes suited for attracting innovators. Once this objective has been achieved, the emphasis should be directed to more emotional appeals that are better suited for attracting the mass market.

Hsui-Li Chen (2004) examined the effect of country of origin on consumer adoption of a new product (in this case, mobile phones). The study results show that early adopters tend to use made-in country as the source of information, while the majority and laggards tend to use brand-of-origin when they purchase a new product. The author recommends that new products in the introductory stage of the product life cycle should be produced first in developed countries. In the maturity stage, production can be sourced to low-cost countries, emphasizing brand rather than made-in country. In a theoretical analysis that utilizes mathematical modeling, Fruchter et al (2006) reach similar conclusions.

Closely related to market entry is the question of first mover advantage. Chen and Pereira (1999) investigated the relationship between first mover advantages and favorable/unfavorable country of origin effect. They found that as increasing numbers of competitors enter a market, a product's favorable country image begins to lose its strategic importance. This phenomenon may explain why the use of country image tends to decline in advanced stages of market entry (Figure 5.6 above). Conversely, and not surprisingly, it was found that for companies or marketers from a country with less favorable country images, it is more difficult to lead, than to follow. Therefore, the appropriate strategy for a first mover from a weak country image country should try to conceal the origin country.

Conclusion

In this chapter alternative country of origin strategies were suggested that are relevant at the firm level. Images of countries are given as perceived by consumers and the challenge faced by the firm is how to define a strategy congruent with these images. Rarely can a single firm affect country image. Rather, the individual firm must consider country image as a challenge to be handled in the manner outlined above. Nevertheless, country image may be influenced at the national level through a concerted effort by individual firms, trade associations, labor unions, government and other concerned stakeholders. Working together, stakeholders may be able to shape an image that can give associated country firms a competitive advantage. This is the subject of the next chapter.

CHAPTER 6

Managing Country of Origin Effects by Industry and Government

Countries contribute to product brand values and in many respects have brand values in their own right. Yet how many countries actively market themselves as brands, or indeed market themselves at all?

Derek Bowden, Saatchi & Saatchi

Introduction

Industry groups such as chambers of commerce, councils, tourist boards and government agencies are partners in the effort to maintain or improve a country's image. This ongoing endeavor is necessary to mold consumer preference for products sold abroad. On the other hand, industry-government cooperation has also been used as a trade barrier in order to foster demand for domestic goods instead of imports. "Buy local" campaigns are at the heart of this effort. As we have noted in Chapter 4, they are most effective among the segment of ethnocentric, patriotic consumers. "Made in" labels prominently placed on domestic merchandise buttressed by promotional campaigns is generally the way in which the strategy is implemented.

Place Branding

Hardly a month goes by without a media report about how a given country suffers from a negative image, or how a city is launching a new campaign to attract investment and tourism, or how a region is communicating its own separate identity from its parent country. Place marketing has also been used to support domestic producers through "buy national" campaigns. Place branding has been defined (Papadopoulos, 2004) as "...the broad set of efforts by country, regional and city governments, and by industry groups, aimed at marketing the places and sectors they represent".

Place branding has become more important recently (Papadopoulos, 2004) as the major industrialized nations now compete for inward investment with emerging economies, some of which have become members of the European Union. Another area, tourism, has been significantly affected by threat of terrorism, especially since September 11. Efforts to encourage investment and tourism have led to aggressive marketing campaigns on the part of nations. An integral part of these campaigns includes the attempt at developing either national, regional or municipal brands, or all three. As Van Ham (2001) has pointed out, an unbranded nation will find it difficult to gain economic and political exposure in the media, so that image and reputation are becoming integral parts of a nation's strategic equity. The following sections discuss how nation branding strategy can be used as a marketing tool, including case examples of both successful and unsuccessful branding attempts.

Developing a *National Brand*

What is nation branding? It is using marketing strategies to promote a country's image, products and attractiveness for tourism and foreign direct investment (de Vincente, 2004). It consists of developing an image based on a country's positive core values and communicating it both internally and externally (Domeisen, 2003, 14).

Should a country be "branded" by strategically developing its image? The answer has both theoretical and practical aspects. The categorization theory of learning reviewed in Chapter 1 provides the motivation for such branding. When a country image category is formed in the consumer's mind, s/he will associate products of that country with its image. This categorization process is a key determinant of the image of new brands of products. Familiar brands have categories of their own. For these brands, country image is just an attribute. On the other hand, when a consumer is faced with a new brand for which s/he has no existing category, the brand is likely to be associated with the made-in country and acquire its attributes. Thus, if the country image is negative, new brands face an entry barrier that hinders their acceptance and future familiarity. In contrast, when a brand is associated with a country that has a positive image, it will gain acceptance. It can be concluded that theory suggests that like a company brand, country image should be strategically determined and controlled.

According to Anholt (2003), "nations behave in many ways, just like brands…they are perceived in certain ways by large groups of people both at home and abroad; they are associated with certain qualities and characteristics". Therefore, a nation has a personality (Han, 2001) much like products and brands; some countries are perceived as friendly (i.e. Western-oriented), credible (i.e. an ally), or aggressive (i.e. expansionist) and unreliable (i.e. a "rogue" state).

It should be emphasized that all nations have respective images. By branding, attempts are made to mold, modify, or at least influence the shaping of these images. Nations need branding because image and reputation are becoming essential parts of their strategic equity (Han, 2001). As such, nation branding is no longer a choice but a necessity (de Vincente, 2004). And, there are those who believe that a nation's reputation capital (as embodied in its brand) can influence consumer choice (O'Shaughnessy and O'Shaughnessy, 2000).

In practice, can a nation be branded like a company? If so, such a national "brand" would be the image by which the country's products and services are identified in the minds of consumers. What are the essentials necessary to build a national brand? According to the consultant Wally Olins at least three conditions must be met (Olins, 1999):

1. The brand would have to be used consistently over many products or services.

2. Companies using the brand must have corporate values consonant with those determined by the organizers of the brand campaign, such as a chamber of commerce or government agency.

3. Participating companies will have to agree to the brand agenda.

To these we may add a fourth requirement:

4. The leading companies of the country should participate in the program.

Some researchers believe that the task is fraught with difficulties, and, therefore, branding should be undertaken with a great deal of caution. For example, Ritson (2004) takes a cautious approach when stating that "Cities and countries aren't like corporations. While their logos are alterable, their fundamental spirit, corporations and constitution are not". On the other hand, there are those who believe that a nation cannot be branded like a product. For example, Olins is quoted as saying that "The idea of a nation as a brand – as Kellogg's Corn Flakes is a brand – is a very big mistake" (Frost, 2004),

A major difference between product branding and place branding is that the branding of the latter involves many stakeholders and interests (Therkelsen and Halkier, 2004) including national, regional and local authorities as well as business organizations and even individuals. These stakeholders include manufacturer organizations, tourist agencies both on national and municipal levels, economic sectors as diverse as high-tech and agriculture, and the public at large. Even citizens of a country have a stake in their national brand because it identifies a country's values to the outside world. Integrating these different interests into a joint branding process and campaigning a unified image is the ultimate goal. How this goal may be achieved is discussed in the following sections.

Critical to the success of country branding is the development of a core message about a country that can be used by different industrial sectors. Another requirement is that all agents; government, industry and companies actively participate in the development and subsequent use of the country brand.

These objectives are not easily achieved. While all three agents generally agree that such a campaign is necessary, not all agree on how to do it or how to finance it. A major obstacle to the development and implementation of a national brand is the diversity of industries in any given country. How can countries that have strong primary industries (and country images that reflect them) such as Denmark (beer, bacon and butter) and New Zealand (sheep, rugby and trees) create a national brand that will be capable of promoting pharmaceutical and high-tech industries?

For example, a survey among business firms in the UK by the Chartered Institute of Marketing found that 53 percent agreed that a branding campaign would benefit industry, while 28 percent said it would make no difference. When asked whether the idea of a British identity would help position industry as competitive and strong, 45 percent agreed, while 24 percent said it would make no difference.

However, 52 percent of the respondents said that they would not be prepared to pay for such a campaign (Bainbridge, 1999).[22]

Umbrella Branding

In umbrella branding the same brand name is used for several products and/or services. It is applied so that a unified image is attributed to all involved. The Korean conglomerates, such as Samsung, who utilize the same brand name for diverse products and services, from automobiles to banking, are a good example of umbrella branding.

An application of umbrella branding for a nation in its simplest form would be using the same brand for the nation and all its component parts such as tourist agencies, investment authorities and municipalities. The advantages of umbrella-nation branding include economies of scale - applying the same marketing strategy to several areas – and the possibility of synergy when a unified national image is consistently projected to the external world (Therkelsen and Halkier, 2004).

Without an umbrella brand, each country agency such as industry, tourism and investment would have a separate brand and logo. This is illustrated in Figure 6.1. Potential consumers of a country's products and services may be the same people; they are exposed to some of the country's exports and may also be targeted as tourists. However, in the first case they are communicated to with different brands. This is an example of uncoordinated or fragmented branding. An umbrella brand for different functional sectors such as tourism and investment would require the design of a logo and slogan that would be common to both. Such a "national brand" is illustrated in Figure 6.2.

---

[22] Only 2 percent of respondents were willing to pay more than £1,000 as a business levy. Four percent were willing to pay between £500 and £1,000.

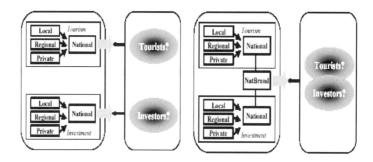

Figure 1
Fragmented international place branding

Figure 2
International umbrella place branding

Source: Therkelsen and Halkier, 2004

Figures 6.1 and 6.2: Fragmented and Umbrella Place Branding

What are the requirements for coordinated, umbrella branding? The most important requirement is a realization that place branding involves a multitude of stakeholders and interests: National, regional and local authorities, diverse private sectors like tourism, IT and agriculture and the local population. Involving most, if not all stakeholders in the branding process is essential to its success. Once an organization has been set up comprising all or most stakeholders, the next, albeit difficult task, involves devising a common set of values that can form the basis for the brand. The danger here is that over emphasis on one set of interests to the detriment of another set of interests may alienate an important stakeholder. But, even if a consensus among stakeholders may be agreed upon, a common brand aimed at different target markets that have varying demands may not be effective. For example, potential tourists are interested in leisure time activities, cultural pursuits and perhaps the exotic, while potential investors are interested in the economy, the infrastructure and political climate. Certainly, each target market has widely different needs.

To illustrate the difficulty of implementing a common umbrella brand, we show in 6.3 below the website for Denmark's investment authority (an arm of the Foreign Ministry and Trade Council), and in Figure 6.4 that of Denmark's national tourist agency. Note first of all that both brands are different. The "Invest in Denmark" logo contains the national emblem with the state seal including lions and crown that gives an impression of authority. If you download the website on your computer, you will find that the page contains information about the sponsor, information about firms that have successfully invested in Denmark and some attempt to point out the competitive advantage of doing business in the country. On the other hand, the "official travel guide" to Denmark website contains information about Denmark's natural environment, people, and cuisine among others. Note that the brand embodies the national flag in a heart-shaped logo, which is much different from the investment logo. While there are some common features on both websites, e.g. Danish people are featured on both, albeit in different situations, and Danish design capabilities are publicized, there is more that is distinct than is common. This illustrates the difficulty in designing an umbrella brand for two sectors, let alone additional sectors that need promotion such as municipalities.

Figure 6.3 Investment in Denmark

Figure 6.4 Visit Denmark

To sum up, the requirements of umbrella branding seem to be the following:

1. Defining the common functional requirements of diversified stakeholders, such as tourism and investment authorities.

2. Finding a common core of values from the functional requirements.

3. Building a brand that will communicate the core values to all target audiences.

Case Examples of Country Branding

Following are examples of country-industry attempts at national branding for the United Kingdom, Scotland, Germany, New Zealand, the USA and Latvia. [23]

---

[23] Several USA states have also initiated brand strategies. For example, the Oregon Economic Development Department encourages manufacturers to incorporate Oregonian" attributes such as "natural beauty" and "environmental awareness" in their promotional campaigns whenever possible. While the so-called "Brand

144

United Kingdom

To most people in China or Brazil, and even to many in the United States or Russia, Britain has neither a positive nor a negative image. It simply has no clear image at all.
Mark Leonard, author of Britain™: Renewing Our Identity

In the 1990's British industrialists, advertising agencies and some government offices were trying to determine what the perception of the UK's image abroad was. Concern was raised that Britain was seen as stuffy and traditional. Research conducted by the BMP DDB advertising agency in 1994 and 1997 in 30 countries asked respondents to pick from a list of 40 adjectives, five that best, and five that least, described Britain. In both surveys the British were described as proud, civilized and cold. The only difference between responses in 1994 and 1997 was that "arrogant" was replaced by "witty." What the British weren't seen as was emotional, temperamental, aggressive and adventurous (Bainbridge, 1999).

According to an executive of the Wickens Tutt Southgate consulting firm, "This [the traditional image of the UK], and the way that Britain is marketed abroad as a glorified historical theme park, makes it impossible for modern businesses to derive marketing capital from their Britishness" (Curtis, 1997). This led some, like the marketing director of British Airways, to suggest promoting the airline as a global, rather than as a British brand. The chairman of Jaguar said "We should not just be selling ourselves on changing the guard and Buckingham Palace" [sic!] (*Brand Strategy*, 1999). The criticism led to a branding campaign supported by British industry in 1997 entitled "Cool Britannia". The idea behind the campaign was that it was possible to give Britain an image that was hip and trendy.

A comment by Warren Hoge, the London bureau chief gives an objective résumé of the attempt (Friedman, 1999, 190-191): "…out are scenes of village cricket, tea and scones, baronial castles, Beefeaters, grouse hunts on heathery moors, ceremonial celebrators in wigs and tights, tepid amber ale and Union Jacks fluttering triumphantly. In are images of pulsating telecommunications, global business transactions, information technologies, buccaneering entrepreneurs, bold

---

Oregon" campaign does not have a state brand or logo, manufacturers are encouraged to use "Oregon" along with their brand name. (The authors thank Heather Francis of the University of Tasmania for calling this to their attention). For additional examples, see the section on "Branding Municipalities".

architecture, cheeks advertising, and daring fashion. Britpop music, nightclubbing – anything, in short, that is youthful, creative and, in the word most uttered by the leaders of this updated land, 'modern'…The style offensive is being undertaken by the new Labor Government at the suggestion of Demos, a social policy research center close to Mr. Blair, which recommended … that it was time to 'rebrand' Britain as 'one of the world's pioneers rather than one of its museums.' 'I'm proud of my country's past but I don't want to live in it,' said Tony Blair. The British Government tourist agency got it just right when it decided in 1997 to change the country's logo from 'Rule, Britannia!' to 'Cool Britannia…'"

The "Cool Britannia" campaign failed to brand Britain successfully. The campaign lacked substance and was under- financed. The "Cool" image may have represented music, fashion and arts industries, but was hardly representative of manufacturing and technology. The *Economist* reported that two year's of government attempts to project a more modern, dynamic and creative image of Britain had not succeeded (*Economist*, November 27, 1999, 36).

Because of this failure, another attempt was made to design a national brand. The British Tourist Authority (BTA) launched a new campaign, "Branding Britain". An integral part of the campaign was the establishment of core values that could be communicated to overseas markets. Actually, there was more than one brand. London, England, Scotland and Wales were viewed as distinct, regional brands. Each region's core values and characteristics were branded individually, but with the same message: "Britain is a land of contrasts". The slogan was meant to convey that on the one hand, Britain has a traditional culture and heritage, and on the other hand, it is "quirky, unconventional, innovative and creative". Yet, this campaign was not successful either. Research showed that the country was associated with the past. The tourist industry in Britain was losing market share to competitors. Britain's share of the world tourist market declined from 5.2 percent in 1990 to 4.4 percent in 1999. The number of tourists to Britain had been static or declining since 1996. Apparently, the lack of success of this campaign was owing to a failure to create an umbrella brand for all four destinations and the fact that each destination had its own tourism board, which operated independently, not always in coordination with the campaign objectives. The difficulty in creating an umbrella brand stemmed from the fact that each location had different core values: Britain was perceived as a contrast between traditional heritage and the unconventional, Scotland as a land of fire and stone and Wales as a land of nature and legend.

Following this campaign, a further attempt was made to re-brand Britain. In May, 2002, a private agency was hired to work with the BTA to establish a new brand. The organizing group consisted of members from the BTA, the Wales Tourist Board, Visit Scotland and the London Tourist Board and a representative from one of the English regional tourist boards. Their task was to produce a strategy for projecting a positive, modern image of Britain, to enhance business and tourism and, if possible, to de-emphasize heritage. Research was conducted in major target markets, including the Netherlands, France, Poland, Sweden, the USA, Japan and China. Britain was found to be "aloof" and "emotionally inaccessible" and Britain's sense of place needed to be balanced with more of the "people". Scotland was found to have a positive image of "Romance" (Hall, 2004). Additional research revealed a number of key values that would make up the brand: Spirit of the Place and Sprit of the People". A series of advertisements depicting these "Spirits" were devised, including the one in Figure 6.5 that contains the core values determined in the research, albeit, with a picture that passes an incongruent image.

Source: www.VisitBritain.org

Figure 6.5 A Branding of Britain Advertisement

Scotland

"Scotland the Brand" is an example of a government campaign to raise awareness abroad of Scotland and its quality products.[24] It is actually an attempt to mold the country's image: "whether we are selling whisky or education or promoting tourism or the arts we must get across the message of a dynamic competitive country...." (The Scottish Office, 1997).

Scotland the Brand was established in 1994 as a joint venture of industry and government for the promotion of Scottish trade, tourism and culture. The organization has been partially funded by Scottish enterprise, which recognized the economic benefits of the promotion of a distinctive Scottish image internationally.

The aim of using a national logo on exported products is to "encourage cohesion in image and marketing to deliver greater commercial value and contribute to raising Scotland's profile and status in the global marketplace." The chosen logo is shown as Figure 6.6 and it started to be used on November 1997 by Rt. Hon Donald Dewar, who was Scotland's First Minister. Within a year of its creation, Scotland the Brand had 100 companies on board that had a combined annual turnover of £5 billion, employing over 100,000 people. In order to become a member of Scotland the Brand, a company's products and brands must have quality regimes in place and be committed to ongoing quality within the organization. Member companies are from a wide range of industry sectors including arts and culture, food and drink, finance, manufacturing, sport, transport and utilities. A major piece of international research was conducted by CLK and sponsored by Marks and Spencer, United Distillers, Stagecoach and British Airways, with the objective of determining how Scots perceive themselves and how others perceive them. The research was conducted in focus groups in England, France, Spain, Japan, the United States and Scotland. In total over 600 people were interviewed.

---

[24] For a sociological study of the development of Scotland the Brand, see: McCrone, et al 1995.

Source: Scotland the Brand
Figure 6.6 The Scotland Logo

Scots on Scotland

The Scots believe that they have a clear identity with civilized, educated, astute and responsible people with a dislike of being "dependent". However, the Scots do believe that they are searching for an identity in a modern world and although there is a strong feeling of pride it conflicts with their dislike of boasting.

World on Scotland

The world considers Scotland to be a small, remote country possessing a rich heritage and a beautiful landscape, inhabited by hard working, honest, warm and likeable people, who retain the sorts of traditional values many others have lost. Howsoever, the Scots are associated with having little or no technology or business infrastructure, even though Scotland provides 36 percent of Europe's branded PCs, 80 percent of its workstations and 13 percent of the ATM machines. This view might be summarized as follows: For many throughout the world Scotland represents a likeable, somewhat idealized country which is, in theory, capable of joining the 21st century, but has yet to demonstrate its capacity to do so. Table 6.1 summarizes the conclusions derived from these studies.

A further survey of Scottish businessmen conducted externally for Scotland the Brand in 1999, showed that 77 percent of the respondents felt that having a Scottish identity was important to them, 67 percent felt that their Scottishness gave them a distinct advantage in the marketplace and 77 percent supported the creation of a national brand.

KEEP	LOSE	GAIN
Integrity	Isolation	Inventiveness
Tenacity	Obstinate	Communication
Spirit	Warring	Participation
"Island"	Pettiness	Accessibility
Timeless	Grumbling	True Timelessness
Craftsmanship	Nostalgia	Positive Attitude
Courage	Stuck in the Past	Vision
Lyricism		Subtlety

Source: By permission of Scotland the Brand.
Table 6.1 Branding Study Attributes of Scotland

The long-term objective of the campaign was: "In ten years time all developed and emerging counties will not only choose to buy Scottish products and services (where there is a choice)...but also rate the distinctive Scottish way of life and values about most others."

Visit Scotland conducted brand research in late 2001 and early 2002 to determine why people visited Scotland and what the country represented as a brand. The research found that three key words represented the brand:

1. Enduring – in the buildings and architecture, history, culture and tradition.

2. Dramatic – scenery, light and the drama of the changing weather.

3. Human – the Scots are seen as down to earth, innovative, solid and dependable and full of integrity and pride.

These key words were quite different from the desired themes such as "spirit"; "lyricism" and "integrity" (see Table 6.1 above). The reality was that Scotland evoked strong associations with the environment and education, but not well with innovation and inventiveness. Nevertheless, among tourists, the survey showed that they felt their expectations were fulfilled when visiting Scotland and that there was nothing synthetic about the country (Scotland's Brand Promise, 2003).[25]

---

[25] A website in Scotland posed the question: "What is Scotland's Brand?" Most of the replies were by Scots and not very positive. For example, "Until the industry

In all, the Scotland the Brand campaign failed to live up to its promises, even though £10 million had been spent on its promotion. In May 2004, it was decided to end operations and have the trademark managed by Scottish Enterprise. A contributing factor to the demise of Scotland the Brand was competition from the Scottish government itself, which had formed a "Promoting Scotland Unit" in 2003. This unit was managed by the Scottish Executive, an agency of the devolved government, which wanted to move away from the "tartanised" image represented by the Scotland the Brand logo. The executive wished to implement a strategy that had a wider appeal, i.e. for political objectives as well as attracting investors and tourists and skilled workers. According to the Executive, the goal was "...for all our public agencies, Scots abroad, our top companies, the UK government and Scotland's devolved government to speak to the world with one voice, all with their particular message to their particular audience...."[26] Whether or not this ambitious objective of appealing to wide and divergent audiences can succeed was questioned by a leading Scottish public relations manager:

We are not convinced of the rationale for the generalized promotion of Scotland [advanced by the Executive, EJ]...We would question whether pipe bands, a ministerial visit and associated events are effective in promoting Scotland's international relationships...[27]

Germany

In 1999, ZDF, the German television network approached identity consultants Wolff Olins to create a national brand for Germany. The campaign's main objective was to change consumer perceptions of Germany from what was found to be a nation of "mechanical perfection", that lacks "creativity and dynamism" to a country that is also "exciting and surprising". This perception of Germany was partly a creation of German manufacturers. Witness the advertising campaign of the Audi 80 in the late 1980s. The ad ran:

---

moves into the 21st century why bother with a brand. Any tourist that comes to Scotland still has trouble doing anything after 5 p.m. and if they don't speak the language they've no chance" (www.footstompin.com).

[26] www.scottish.parliament.uk/business/committees/europe/reports-05/eur05-01-0, retrieved 28-09-2005

[27] op.cit.

> *The three magic words of Audi are **Vorsprung durch Technik.***
> *There is more to them than a mere slogan… [it] is the leitmotiv of*
> *our company philosophy. To fully understand **Vorsprung durch***
> ***Technik** you need a fine grasp of German and the mind of a*
> *German engineer. However, you can experience it simply by*
> *driving the new Audi 80 (Head, 1988).*[28]

According to the consultants, Germany should create an image that shows it to be a source of energy and productivity without weakening its image of commercial and technical prowess. It is suggested that this idea can be translated into visual terms by first showing that Germany is an integral part of the European Union. European integration is demonstrated by replacing black in the national colors with European blue. Also, DE, the internet and e-mail suffix for Germany should be used as a symbol on products (See Figure 6.7). DE stands also for Deutschland Europa, symbolizing the country's Europeaness. Olins suggested six steps in order to implement the German image campaign (Wolff Olins, press information, no date):

1. Set up a national brand steering committee under the leadership of the Chancellor or President of the Republic,

2. Create a research and development team responsible for reporting to the steering committee,

3. Begin a process of national consultation involving representatives of all the Länder as well as national figures in industry, commerce, media, culture and the arts,

4. Commission extensive research into perceptions of Germany overseas, benchmarking these studies against data on perception of other nations,

5. Carry out a thorough review of how and where the national brand could appropriately be utilized,

---

[28] For those of our readers who are not fluent in German, Head (1988) reports the following: "… one of the UK's best-known TV weatherman, Ian McCaskill, remarked, 'I don't like this cold European weather, but at least I've discovered what Vorsprung durch Technik means. It means 'My car won't start.'"

6. Draw up and submit for the Bundestag approval a program of implementation for the brand options adopted by the national steering committee.

Source: Wolff Olins, Branding the Nation – A Debate about a New Image for Germany, 1999

Figure 6.7 Deutschland Europa: Branding Germany

Still, a German brand has not evolved. An opinion poll released by the Goethe Institute in July 2003, revealed that British youth have negative feelings about Germany based on its Second World War past. Apparently, these sorts of images about Germany are held by peoples elsewhere. As a result, the BBC News (August 8, 2003) reported that the Goethe Institute held a brainstorming session in London with corporate and cultural representatives with the aim of re-branding Germany. However, the conference chair was quoted as saying that "we discovered that it would be too hard to change Germany's brand, as many of the images associated with the country are too deep set".

New Zealand

Research undertaken by the New Zealand Trade Development Board showed that while the country was generally regarded as distant and friendly, having a strong "clean and green" association, this was usually a vague understanding and could not be used to gain a competitive advantage for goods and services. In some developing markets, consumers had little or no perception of New Zealand at all. The concept was explained thus: "New Zealand is a land little affected by industrial pollution, over-population, traffic congestion, noise, urban decay. It is a country associated with national parks, scenic beauty, wilderness areas, beautiful deserted beaches, green pastures and a friendly population – an image which is carefully cultivated in tourism brochures and in our trade promotions"(Buhrs and Barlett, 1993).

The "New Zealand Way" national brand represented by a Fern symbol (see Figure 6.8) was launched in 1993. The country's top ten foreign currency earning firms who pooled a percentage of their marketing budgets towards the campaign financed it. At this writing, more than 170 "Brand Partners" have been accredited to use the Brand, accounting for more than $4 billion in exports, or 20 percent of New Zealand's foreign exchange earnings. The logo has been registered in 29 countries. However, early indications are that the branding campaign has so far failed to meet its objectives. Internally, a survey of New Zealanders in 2000 found that 42 percent of the respondents believed that the concept was a myth, despite its high recognition among the general population.

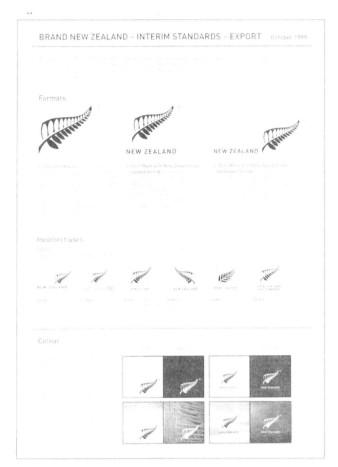

Source: Trade New Zealand
Figure 6.8 The new Zealand Logo Formats

The use of the fern brand was allied with a new slogan, "100% Pure New Zealand" (See Figure 6.9), introduced between July 1999 and February 2000. The campaign was aimed at incoming tourists primarily from Australia, Germany, Japan, Singapore, the UK and USA. The goals of the campaign were to create a global brand, recapture market share from New Zealand's main competitor, Australia, and double tourism receipts (Morgan, et al 2002). While the first objective was attained, it is more difficult to assess the second. Between 1999 and 2003, New Zealand's (incoming) tourism receipts increased by 51 percent, while those of Australia increased by 14.4 percent (Statistics New Zealand, June 2004; Australian Bureau of

Statistics, 2004). Certainly, the increase in New Zealand's tourist receipts was more impressive, but whether this increase was at the expense of Australia is not evident from these data. In any case, the increase of 51 percent in New Zealand's tourism receipts is a significant accomplishment; how much of this was due to the branding campaign is hard to tell. However, it is safe to assume that the campaign was a contributing factor to the successful effort. The campaign has been criticized by those who feel that New Zealand's environmental record does not measure up to it. Much of the added interest in New Zealand can, at least anecdotally, be attributed to the films of Peter Jackson and the *America*'s cup win at the turn of the century; the campaign can be said to have "piggy-backed" off it.

The 100% pure campaign was an attempt to buttress the traditional perception of the country as "clean and green". However, it was directed mainly at the tourist industry. New Zealand's Prime Minister, Helen Clark was interested in communicating a more contemporary positioning, such as a "framework for growing an innovative New Zealand". She was quoted as saying: "Government will work with the private sector to develop a consistent brand image of New Zealand across our industry sectors. As well as being seen as clean and green, we need to be more widely perceived as smart and innovative" (www.alternative.co.nz). As one observer put it: "…while clean and green is a good story, it is not enough where we are moving into high tech infrastructure…."[29] Whether the new brand strategy can communicate an image of New Zealand as an industrialized country (New Zealand was ranked 21 in economic performance of OECD countries in 2002), attractive to foreign investors, remains to be seen.

Figure 6.9 The Tourism Brand New Zealand

---

[29] Rod Mackenzie, former senior trade commissioner for New Zealand, in *Locum Destination Review*, Winter, 2002, 55.

Brand USA

Unlike the other countries surveyed here, the United States never had a national brand or brand slogan, but rather regional or city brands (see some examples below). The first real attempt to communicate an American image abroad by a central authority occurred when Charlotte Beers, a former chairperson of the J. Walter Thompson advertising agency, was appointed Under Secretary of State for Public Diplomacy and Public Affairs on October, 2001. While her job title put her in charge of public diplomacy, her task was not to improve relations with other nation states, but rather to improve America's image abroad, especially in Muslim countries. According to Secretary of State Colin Powell, her objectives were to "brand and market the department and promote American values to the world" (Teinowitz, 2001). Such a promotional effort was deemed necessary because of the deterioration in America's image abroad following its operations in Iraq after 9/11/2001.[30] As a consequence of the image deterioration, some recent advertising studies have shown that branding products as American may no longer be an asset (Fullerton, 2005; Avraham and First, 2003; Elliot, 2003).

Using the slogan "Shared Values", a communication campaign with a budget of $15 million, was aimed primarily at countries with predominately Moslem populations in order to emphasize "those things we have in common" (Tan, 2003). However, Charlotte Beers resigned her position in March 2003, less than three years after her appointment. She was replaced by Margaret Tutwiler, a State Department veteran, who herself resigned after serving in the position less than one year. What went wrong?

Some believe that a $15 million budget was insufficient to mount the campaign, although the appropriation was raised to nearly $300 million in 2003 to cover all public diplomacy efforts around the world (*U.S. Public Diplomacy*, 2003). The appropriation was increased to $685 million in 2004. Others aver that marketing tools do not work very well for propaganda campaigns (Grimm, 2003), some admit that while the marketing of Brand America is probably the most complex positioning problem of all time", it is still doable (Solver and Hill, 2002). The major reasons for the failure are that on the one hand, target audiences are so diverse, and on the other, the "product" itself is "complex, diverse and intangible" (Jurgensen, 2003). A more objective

---

[30] For up to date surveys of America's image in selected countries, see, e.g. *The Pew Research Center* surveys http://Pewresearch.org.

reason for the failed campaign was that many countries refused to air it and in others that did, it proved largely ineffective (Fullerton, 2005).

The "Brand USA" episode is a unique case. Unlike other nations' attempts to develop a brand that could be used to promote exports and investment, the American campaign was one of public diplomacy aimed specifically at Middle Eastern countries. In marketing terms (Henrikson, 2004), the brand experience was not consistent with a message delivered to an already skeptical audience. The message conveyed was that the USA stands for tolerance, freedom and democracy, a message that was not perceived as being consistent with the country's support of authoritarian regimes.

As we pointed out above, designing a national brand is a task best performed by a number of stakeholders working together; government, business, and as much as feasible, the public. It doesn't come as a surprise to learn that the chairman of the DDB Worldwide advertising agency has attempted to organize a group of US brand executives to save Brand USA (Reinhard, 2003).[31]

Emerging Countries: Latvia and Slovenia

Nation branding may be more important for emerging countries like those in the Baltic and Eastern Europe. The economic, political and physical changes that are occurring in these countries have to be communicated to the rest of the world if they are to attract tourism and investment. Many of these countries, like Lithuania, Latvia, Slovenia and Croatia have had negative images because of their membership in the Soviet bloc. Many people hold stereotyped images of these countries stemming from a lack of knowledge about the transformations that these countries are experiencing. Therefore, re-branding has become a necessity.

While the necessity of establishing a national branding strategy for Latvia has been expressed, especially by tourism authorities, not much progress has been made. Two slogans have been used by the Latvian Tourism Development Agency; "The Land that Sings" (2002), standing for nature, culture, business and people. The slogan has been found to have questionable effectiveness (Frasher, et al 2003). The connection between a "singing" nation and nature or business is rather dubious. A year later, during 2003, another slogan was devised, "Growing Green in Latvia", intended to emphasize the unspoiled

---

[31] Karen Hughes was appointed the new Undersecretary for Public Diplomacy in 2005.

natural environment with which Latvia is amply endowed. However, neither logos were developed as the result of market research, nor was their effectiveness tested in target markets (Endziņa and Luņeva, 2004).

The only comprehensive research intended to suggest a national brand for Latvia was executed by MBA students at the Said Business School of Oxford University, commissioned by the Latvian Institute (Frasher, et al 2003). They found that Latvia's image problem was that either people know nothing about the country or have negative perceptions about it. Moreover, the problem was not only one of recognition, but also one of differentiation from its Baltic neighbors of Estonia and Lithuania.

The Said Business School team first identified key target markets. For tourism, they are upmarket German and Swedes and for investment, economic analysts in Germany, Denmark, Sweden, Russia and the UK. The core idea or a brand emanated from the assumption that Latvia represents the spiritual essence of the Baltic region. It is located at its center and can thus serve as a keystone, connecting all surrounding areas, north, south, east and west (Frasher, 2003, 43). The aim of the strategy is to position Latvia's capital, Riga, as the hub of the Baltics, both for tourism and investment. The suggested slogan for this objective is Latvia, the Keystone of the Baltics.

Assuming that the suggested branding strategy is acceptable to all stakeholders, resources are needed to implement it. What is needed is a coordinating institution that would have the responsibility for finalizing and communicating the branding campaign. Such an institution has not been forthcoming. In addition to the problem of a coordinating body, financial resources, political will and professionalism have been lacking as well (Endziņa and Luņeva, 2004). A good opportunity to promote an agreed upon national brand will be during the World Ice Hockey Championship games to be held in Latvia during 2006. Perhaps by then consensus will be reached among stakeholders for a national brand strategy.

What the above country branding schemes demonstrate is that there is growing recognition that a country's image may be managed on the national level if there is cooperation among stakeholders. Both the British and New Zealand campaigns demonstrate the importance of this cooperation across industries. The failure to obtain it was probably the main reason for their lack of success. Another lesson to be learned is that while a national branding campaign may support a favorable image for one industry sector, it may have little effect on other sectors.

This indicates the difficulty in forming an overall country image. Necessarily, such an image should focus on overall country strengths (such as innovativeness, workmanship, design, etc.) that apply to as many industry sectors as possible. This should also help in recruiting firms from diverse product areas, as was the case in Scotland. Another possibility is for clusters of industries to join forces to influence the image of their product category. An example would be food (cheese and chocolate), and the watches and heavy equipment clusters in Switzerland.

Another possible explanation for the lack of success of the above national branding attempts is insufficient budgets. It takes hundreds of Million of Dollars to introduce a new brand to the global market. Compare, for example, the "Scotland the Brand" campaign cited earlier that spent £10 million globally in 2003-2004 on its promotion, with advertising budgets of the automobile industry. According to Nielsen (2005), the automobile industry spent in the first half of 2005 $6.73 billion for advertising in the USA alone. This is equivalent to $13.46 Billion per annum. Of this sum, $1.70 billion per annum were spent for introducing new automobile brands. The average budget for promoting the top five new brands was $143 million per annum per brand. With this level of competitive spending on new brands, the £10 million "Scotland the Brand" campaign can hardly make a dent. Furthermore, changing existing perceptions, as was attempted, requires even greater marketing efforts than the introduction of new ones. It is unreasonable to expect nations to reposition their national brands at a fraction of what companies are allotting for similar efforts.

Finally, lack of unique concept can also share in the demise of past national branding campaigns. The German, Danish, British and Scottish campaigns reviewed above have all targeted at presenting their respective nations as being modern, innovative and technologically advanced. Intentionally or not, practically all emerging economies are equally positioned. To be successful in present day highly competitive global village, it takes more to succeed than just tooting a slogan about being innovative.

Regional Branding

Tourists and investors are not only attracted to particular nations, but also to specific areas within nations. Tourist destinations are regionally defined such as Alsace and Provence in France, Tuscany in Italy, and so on. In the United States, the first exit on major highways crossing state borders is the "Tourist Welcome Center" or "Tourist Information

Center" of the State just being entered where the State and its key touring regions are being promoted. As is obvious from the booklets provided at these centers, some states, such as Texas, are making a concerted effort at a unified branding of the state. High-tech start-up firms locate in silicon valleys, whether they are in California (Highway 101), Massachusetts (Route 128), Herzliya Silicon Valley in Israel or Silicon Glen in Scotland. Like nations, regions compete with one another for tourism, investment and residents. Faced with losses of jobs and population, many older industrial regions have tried to copy the success of California's Silicon Valley and Massachusetts's Route 128 corridor in developing high-tech industries. For example, other states in the U.S., such as Ohio and New Jersey, have sought to encourage such development by establishing science and technology programs, promoting ties between local industries and universities, and investing in university-based research which shows promise of commercialization. Branding of agricultural products by regional location has also been used as a marketing tool, e.g. wine appellations in France such as Chabli, Burgundy and Bordeaux, and McLaren Vale, Hunter Valley and Coonawarra in Australia. In addition, there are regional brands of organic milk in Scotland (*Farmer's Guardian*, July 30, 2004).

There are many examples of regions competing with one another for tourists, product purchases, and investors. Regions compete with others for tourism (Benelux countries, Alsace in France), and regional economic policies are designed to attract inward investment to by means of regional investment incentives of the major trading blocs, as are attempts to develop regional "brands" for food products (Wirthgen, et al 1997).

Regional economic integration has also spurred place marketing. Consumer attitudes toward regional economic blocs such as the EU, NAFTA or MERCOSUR may influence purchase intention of a member country's products. In a study of consumer attitudes towards products made in Mexico (Agarwal, et al 2002), it was found that perceptions of NAFTA influences confidence, attitude and purchase intention of Mexican-made products. Thus, the country of origin effect is moderated by what Agarwal, et al (2002) call the "bloc of origin" effect. The relatively poor country image of Mexico prior to entering NAFTA was improved by its association with the regional economic bloc of countries.

The Difference between Place and Product Branding

While we can use many of the same branding techniques for products and for entities such as nations and regions, there are some conceptual differences between place and product branding. The major difference between the two lies in target markets. There are far more stakeholders that have to be considered in place marketing, and they are diverse. Wolff Olins described the difference between corporate, product and regional branding, thus:

> *Product brands only have to please one audience, consumers…Corporate brands have more audiences to please, such as owners, managers, workers and customers. Branding a geographical entity is still more complex, especially when it involves national characteristics and loyalties. Brands that involve whole populations need popular permission.*

> www.wolff-olins.com/oresund.htm

The Case of the Øresund Region

Regional identity is the image and visibility that a designated area has both internally and externally. In order to gain recognition externally, a region must first be identified as such by its inhabitants. It is a question of whether national identity at the country level and regional identity can co-exist (Gregg Bucken-Knapp, 2001). The political intention behind the branding strategy for the *Øresund* region was to motivate residents to identify with the region rather than with either of their "home" countries of Denmark or Sweden (Pedersen, 2004).

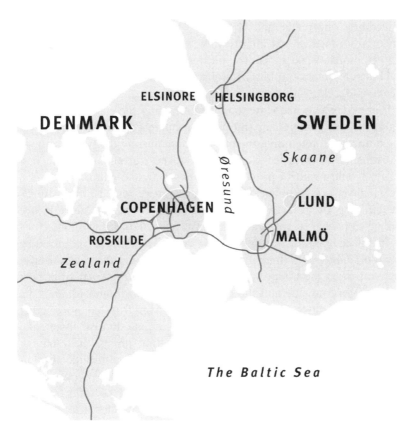

Figure 6.10 The Øresund Region

The *Øresund* region is comprised of Copenhagen, Denmark, Malmö, Sweden, and the surrounding areas (Zealand, Denmark and Skane, Sweden, see Figure 6.10). The region has a population of some 3.6 million and is spread over an area of approximately 21,000 square kilometers. It is the most densely populated area in Scandinavia, representing about 25 percent of the population of both countries. Two-thirds of the region's inhabitants live in the Danish sector. Of note, *Øresund* has a well advanced infrastructure, including ports in both countries, the international airport in Copenhagen and the largest educational complex in Scandinavia, which includes universities and research centers in Copenhagen and Lund. In addition, the area also contains a Medicon Valley, a major international center for biotechnological and pharmaceutical activities, one of the strongest in Europe in featuring cross-border partnerships between industry, universities, hospitals and investors. The investment in Medicon Valley's bio-medical research is the third highest in Europe, exceeded only by London and Paris. The cluster formation of both the medico and biotech sectors employs about half of Denmark and Sweden's total area employees.

There were two major reasons for promoting the region (Pedersen, 2004): a joint commercial and political interest in increasing growth and attracting foreign investment, and an interest in justifying the huge investments made in infrastructure. A successful pursuit of the first reason would result in providing an economic and cultural return on the taxpayer's investment. Both countries were joined physically by the building of a seven kilometer tunnel and six kilometer bridge linking Copenhagen and Malmö that was opened on June 1, 2000.

The place branding strategy of the *Øresund* region was organized by the Wolf Olins consulting firm. The idea to brand the region began early on when the bridge was in the planning stage. Apart from both national governments and the cities of Copenhagen and Malmö, the planning committee consisted of representatives from counties, other cities located in the region, state administrations, tourist bodies and business groups. Working with the consulting group, the planning committee developed core values designed to reflect the ideology of the region. Terms such as "tolerance", "competence", "openness", "responsibility" and "well-being" were mentioned as reflecting the welfare state image of both countries. Proposals for names were solicited from the general public via local radio stations. Some examples received included *Coma*, *Scanport* and *Sewedana*, a combination of Malmö, Copenhagen and Scania (Pedersen, 2004). However, the final decision for branding was left mainly to the consultants who developed a core concept called "human capital", which represented the "quality of life" inherent in the region. Finally, a brand name, *Øresund*, was selected for the region after being tested in focus groups in Frankfurt, London, Singapore and New York. The resulting logo is shown in Figure 6.11.

Figure 6.11 Øresund Region Logo

Has the *Øresund* region been successful in achieving its objectives? Success can be judged by two indicators: Economic/social and cultural/political. Economic indicators include increased activity such as higher GDP growth (by a half a percent) than the rest of Denmark and Sweden and higher employment growth. Higher educational opportunities have also increased. The percentage of Swedes receiving study grants in Denmark has increased from 3 to 6 percent of all Swedish students studying abroad, while the number of Danish students in Sweden has increased from 5 to 8 percent of the total number of Danish students studying abroad. Moreover, about the same number of Swedish medical students study in Copenhagen as in Lund.

Yet, these measures of success could be attributed to the improved accessibility between Denmark and Sweden provided by the tunnel and the bridge. According to many observers (Bucken-Knapp, 2001; Hospers, 2004; Pedersen, 2004; Langer, n.d.), the region has yet to become solidified on cultural/political dimensions. First, the territory encompassing *Øresund* has not been well defined (Hospers, 2004). While the region includes most of Sjælland and Skåne, most in the region (and outside it) conceive the area as consisting of the greater Copenhagen and Malmö areas.[32] Second, regional consciousness is nearly non-existent; most Danes and Swedes have low levels of identification with the region (Bucken-Knapp, 2001; Hospers, 2004). Pedersen (2004) believes that one of the reasons for low public association with the region may be owing to the fact that they were not involved very much in the branding process. The planning group dominating the decision making progress to the exclusion of the local population on both sides of the bridge, thereby resulting in low levels of interest and commitment to the region. Before Wolff Olins' poll, the industry decided that the region needed a more practical name than Øresund "it was ... so difficult to pronounce and to spell. Many were of the opinion that Copenhagen should be included in the name. Copenhagen - Scania was one of many suggestions (Scania is Latin for Skåne). Others wanted a name that evoked positive vibrations, such as Eco Region" (Karlsson, 2005).

The lesson to be learned from this is that regional branding first requires a bottom-up process of internal marketing either before or during strategy development (Hospers, 2004) in order to gain grassroots support for the branding effort.

---

[32] An article in the *Berlingkse Tidende* (June 24, 2001) was quoted as writing: "It wasn't a region that was built. It was just a bridge. A very nice bridge, but still, just a bridge." Cf. Bucken-Knapp (2001), 53.

Branding Municipalities

Many cities around the world have undertaken branding campaigns to either change consumer perceptions, such as Glasgow, Scotland (from a "smokestack" image to one of a "city of culture") or to create an image as a high-tech, quality of life and place to work, e.g. Denver, Colorado. According to Greenberg (2000, 230), city agencies and business groups have designed and implemented branding strategies in order to "forge emotional linkages between a commodified city...and its consumers (i.e. new potential residents, investors, corporate partners, tourists and so on) in such a way that the name of the city alone will conjure up a whole series of images and emotions and with them an impression of value". For example, Glasgow's "Scotland with Style" (See Figure 6.12) campaign was aimed at portraying the city as a modern metropolis, offering the tourist art, fashion, music and landscapes. Apparently, the branding campaign has been successful as evident in the increased number of tourist arrivals since the re-branding was launched in March, 2004. In one year, tourist arrivals increased by nearly 200,000 and one million passengers a month arrived at Glasgow airport, a Scottish record.

Figure 6.12 Glasgow's City Brand Logo

On the other hand, Denver's branding campaign (See Figure 6.13) was undertaken as a response to increased urban competition to attract investors and skilled workers. However, other cities such as Austin, Dallas, Texas; Salt Lake City, and Portland, Oregon, have made the same claims and it remains to be seen whether Denver has a perceived competitive advantage.

Figure 6.13 Denver's Logo

Case Study – Branding Aalborg, Denmark[33]

Located in the Northern part of mainland Denmark, the city of Aalborg is a typical case of the transformation in which the old field of industrial production has been pressured by the global economic competition at the same time as local and regional stakeholders have shifted their attention towards culture, creativity and innovation. Major shipyards and other heavy production facilities have been 'phased out' since the late 1980's.

Branding Aalborg – the History and the Process So Far

According to the Municipal Branding Secretariat the idea for the 'Branding Aalborg' campaign dates back to 1998. Prior to that year, the City Mayor and the County Council Mayor (both Social Democrats) had discussed the future development of both the city and the wider region. In November 1998, Henning G. Jensen, the Lord Mayor of Aalborg, got in contact with the worlds' leading 'branding guru' Wally Olins in England and organised a meeting with him the following spring. In May 1999, a delegation from Aalborg went London to meet Olins.

Hereafter, the process continued with a conference in Aalborg on the 'vision for the future' in August 1999 and was followed up by several meetings in 2000. In the beginning of 2001 a working group started planning the target, organisation and process for the Branding Aalborg campaign. After this, the rest of 2001 was used for setting up a steering committee for Branding Aalborg which was comprised by a number of local stakeholders within politics, business and culture as well as civil servants. In 2002 an exploratory investigation was made by the research institute (*Jysk Analyseinstitut*), and further work was carried out in the working group. In the spring of 2003, the steering committee's vision and value proposals were drafted up and a qualitative analysis of the 'product' was made. The Lord Mayor was presented with the work and after his approval; the City Council approved it in November. After this, it was decided to present the Branding Aalborg project as a public EU project tender. In the beginning of 2004, the Municipality met with the eight selected stakeholder groups to hear their opinion about the competition material. In June 2004, fifteen proposals were examined by an

---

[33] Excerpted from Ole B. Jensen, "Branding the Contemporary City – Urban Branding as Regional Growth Agenda?" Plenary paper for Regional Studies Association Conference, *Regional Growth Agendas*, Aalborg, 28-31 May, 2005. Reproduced with permission of the author.

assessment committee and three proposals were selected for the final. In August the winner was found, and the regionally based marketing company Dafolo Marketing A/S won the first prize.

The winning branding campaign proposal was presented to the Lord Mayor and the City Council and a press conference was held in November 2004. Hereafter there was an official kick-off presentation of the 'Branding Aalborg' campaign in the local concert hall on November 24th, which was followed up by a presentation of the campaign in Copenhagen later the same month. At the end of 2004, the Aalborg Brand Board commiserated on the action plan for 2005. According to this the current phase (spring/summer 2005) was reserved for the search of two pilot projects, where two local firms are to implement the branding values and use the campaign explicitly in their professional work. Furthermore, there are plans for carrying out a future analysis, leading to the development of scenarios. During this process, the selected stakeholder groups are going to discuss the results on a continuous basis. Interestingly, the branding material so far (April 2005) has only been written in Danish! The secretariat is working on a translation of both the branding booklet and the video. So it seems (and quite sensible indeed) that the work has been focusing on the 'internal side' of the brand articulation process first. The Municipality of Aalborg has allocated one million Danish Kroner per year for the next five years to support the branding campaign. Simultaneously, the branding board is working on getting sponsors from the business community in the city to join forces as well.

'Aalborg – Seize the World'
–The Content of the Branding Campaign

The Branding Aalborg campaign has chosen 'Aalborg – seize the world' as the motto for the campaign (Aalborg Municipality 2004). Under this heading four 'values' are identified that supposedly are quintessential to the identity of Aalborg:

- Diversity
- Wide prospects
- Teamwork
- Drive

On the basis of the four values a short vision is presented;

Aalborg wants to be an anti-dote to the traditional metropolis. Larger by heart, smaller by extension – and with wider prospects. We will nurture the contrasts and make room for diversity. Seize the world. And through teamwork and drive create the conditions for a life in development

Aalborg Municipality 2004, my translation, OBJ

Unsurprisingly, the very wording and articulation of the identity pillars has been critiqued heavily in the public debate and media. Some find them just too generic and general to be specific to Aalborg and thus not emblematic of the place-bound identity and character of the city. The main critique raised on this point has therefore mainly been an issue of identification and what sort of city the citizens think they live in. Others find that the four values are too broadly formulated, and thus not able to guide future branding actions accordingly. One of the other issues in the public debate has been whether the money spent (5 million Kroner) would have been better used on other types of public services like care for the elderly or maintenance of the municipal infrastructure – an argument to which the Lord Mayor countered 'it's no use that someone points at holes in the road when we are working to make more jobs' (cited from *Nordjyske*, November 26th 2004).

The motto 'Aalborg – seize the world' is accompanied by a logo that also met a fair amount of critique (see figure 6.14). One of the main critiques was centred on the abstractness of the graphic representation. However, the claim for 'realism' in a graphic logo like this is probably close to impossible as a strategy for urban branding. Rather, and this seems to the general trend, it is a matter of capturing some of the symbolism present in the motto as well as in the 'real city' – the latter clearly being the most challenging.

Figure 6.14 Logo for Aalborg – Seize the World

As a final clue to the understanding of the branding process in Aalborg, one should also pay attention to the fact that a variety of different types of merchandise has been produced, that the Branding Secretariat uses for public relation purposes, but which also can be bought by firms and others that wish to brand themselves by virtue of the new branding artefacts. With a quote from the British rock-band Dire Straits, one could speak of the commercial flow of 'Badges, Stickers, Posters and T-shirts' – key elements in the marketing campaigns of any travelling rock-n'-roll show.

The branding story of Aalborg and how this medium sized city tries to articulate a discourse of global connectivity as well as local identity illustrates an interesting example of how urban interventions are dependent on a specific representational logic. Here the attempt has been to represent the globally aware city with an eye to the 'new economy' in parallel with not escaping the old antagonisms of national under/over-dog narratives.

Buy National Campaigns

Buy national campaigns are intended to increase sales of locally made products at the expense of imports. Thus, they serve as a barrier to trade. Their effectiveness is dependent upon the existence of a significant patriotic segment of consumers who will be sympathetic to an appeal to prefer locally made goods. Almost every country has had an industry group, labor union or nation-wide campaign to promote domestic products. Empirical evidence about their success is sparse. Examples include Australia, Canada, New Zealand and the United States.

Australia

One of the first recorded "Buy Local" campaigns was sponsored by the Australian Natives Association in 1923 via a "Made in Australia" Week (Conley, 1986). Little is known about its success. More recently, Australia's government launched and financed a "Buy Australian Made" campaign in 1986. The campaign was launched by the then Prime Minister, Bob Hawke, who said that its aim was to shift consumers' preferences towards domestic made products by giving them a sense of national pride and purpose when choosing Australian products. Slogans such as "Think Australian – Buy Australian – Be Australian" were used to induce patriotism. Manufacturers could use the "Australian Made" symbol if at least 51 percent of their product was manufactured locally and they paid a participation fee.

Claims were made that the campaign contributed to an A$350 million increase in GDP and 6,500 jobs in a period of ten years.

Considering that the contribution was only A$35 million per annum, the increase was only marginal in relation to the Australian economy. However, interest in the campaign waned and it was dropped in 1998 (Bainbridge, 1999). According to a study of its effectiveness made by Elliot and Cameron (1998), there was a high level of awareness of the campaign's specific appeals and attitudes were favorable to its concept and operation. Moreover, these positive attitudes were associated with a predisposition to purchase locally made goods, suggesting a potential for behavioral change as a result of the campaign. However, a longitudinal study was not done over the period of the campaign, so no conclusion could be made about actual changes in purchase behavior, if any.

Fischer and Byron (1997) also made a study of the campaign. They concluded that the buy national campaign had little effect on consumer choice. Although 93 percent of the respondents believed that buying Australian products benefit the domestic economy, price, quality and value for money were more important factors in the decision making process than country of origin.

USA/Canada

Buy national campaigns began in the United States before independence from Great Britain. Probably the most infamous of these campaigns was the "Boston Tea Party" in 1773, where colonials opposed to British rule dumped 90,000 pounds of British-made tea in the Boston harbor. However, even this act was preceded by a Boston town meeting in October 1768, where it was decided to boycott a long list of British imports (Dana Frank, 1999, p. 6). While these early buy national campaigns were motivated by political considerations, later ones have been motivated by economic determinants. Economic recessions and subsequent unemployment are key factors in these campaigns. The shift of production overseas and competition from imports – textiles and automobiles, for example – have led to buy national promotions.

A made in the USA campaign called "Crafted With Pride in U.S.A." was sponsored mainly by corporations in the U.S. textile and apparel industry. Ettenson, Wagner and Gaeth (1988) made a pre-post study of the campaign's effectiveness over a four-month period. They concluded that the campaign had no effect on the purchase decisions of respondents. Moreover, research carried out by the Crafted With Pride organization found that there was a large gap between respondents' desire to buy American and their actual shopping behavior. The main effect of the buy American campaigns was to make consumers feel guilty about purchasing imports (Dana Frank, 1999, p.241). Likewise, Liefeld (1991) reported that a Buy Canadian campaign funded by the government did not generate a significant increase in the sales of domestically made goods.

On the other hand, a retail sales test conducted in 1992 for a trade organization in Nashville, Tennessee and Cincinnati, Ohio, showed a net 24 percent increase in sales of U.S.-made items during a twelve week period when they were prominently labeled as such, with no other effort made to increase their attractiveness to consumers (no additional promotional effort or price reductions) (FTC, 1996).

In food marketing in the United States, many commodity commissions and state departments of agriculture have tried to appeal to regional patriotism by promoting the use of labeling and certification marks to increase the sale of locally grown and processed food products. Some examples are "Tennessee Certified", "Grown in NY State" and "A Taste of Iowa" (Centner et al, 1989). There is no evidence one way or another as to the effectiveness of such exhortations.

New Zealand

The New Zealand Manufacturers Federation and the New Zealand Council of Trade Unions initiated the Buy New Zealand-Made campaign in 1988, funded by membership dues paid by cooperating businesses. Its purpose was to induce both household consumers and industrial buyers to favor the purchase of domestically produced goods. The impetus for the campaign resulted from prior liberalization of trade regulations, which gave rise to an increase of imported consumer products. According to Wooding (1993), foreign made goods were generally preferred because domestic manufactures were perceived as being of lower quality. Although more recent research by A. C. Nielsen showed that 75 percent of New Zealanders preferred to buy locally-made products (www.buynz.org.nz/about_us.htm). Domestic companies are encouraged to use a made in New Zealand logo (shown in Figure 6.15), which can be obtained for a license holder's fee.

Figure 6.15 New Zealand's Logo

Fenwick and Wright (2000) attempted to determine the effectiveness of the campaign over a five year period by measuring changes in sales and employment of those firms that participated in the campaign versus a matched sample of those that did not. Four industries were surveyed: Apparel, furniture, food and industrial products. The authors concluded that there was "no significant effect of the Buy New Zealand-Made Campaign on member firms in terms of the Campaign's stated objective of retaining employees in manufacturing, nor in terms of increasing domestic sales of members relative to nonmembers." However, the results may have been confounded by an increase of sales and employment among non-participating firms that reaped benefits coincidentally. Moreover, the made-in labels of familiar products that had a poor reputation probably obscured any positive effects of the campaign on unfamiliar local brands. The affixing of a "made-in" label on products of marginal quality may serve to worsen perception about them (Maronick, 1995).[34]

Russia

Concern in Russia over increased imports of food products has led to a "Buy Russia" campaign appealing to both patriotic consumers and nostalgia for home-grown, traditional food products, such as sausages, milk products, chocolates and cookies (Akin, 1997). While there is no empirical evidence about the success of the campaign that is financed by several entrepreneurs, it is interesting to note that a butter product imported from Finland uses a Russian brand name, *Yeliseevsky*, and Sanyo electronic products are labeled as "designed *for* Russia". Apparently, these tactics aid the promotion of the products.

Summarizing the empirical evidence regarding the effectiveness of Buy Local campaigns, we may conclude that there is little evidence to

---

[34] In November 2000, a "Buy New Zealand Made" campaign was revived with the same logo as used in 1998.

support the premise that they can bias purchase preference in favor of domestic made products. At most, they probably serve to reinforce already developed attitudes among ethnocentric and patriotic consumers. As such, their value as a protectionist device must be treated with caution.

Our discussion of national branding and buy local campaigns leads to the conclusion that the contribution of advertising campaign alone is questionable at best. Are there any other alternatives? Can a country's image be managed over time by other means? Following are two case examples that demonstrate some of the forces that contributed to changes in the image of Japan and Israel.

The Evolution of the Japanese Country Image since WWII

At the end of World War II, Japan was a devastated country perceived to be highly traditional with a backward industry. For the first two post-war decades, Japan's image was that of a source for cheap imitations of Western products. Low cost labor was considered its main competitive advantage. Forty years later, the image of Japan was that of a highly developed country that is the world leader in innovative high quality consumer products, especially in the photography, home electronic, computing and automotive industries. How did this change in image come about? The answer is found in the Japanese quality control programs.

Quality control was introduced to Japan in 1950 by Edwards W. Deming in an eight-day seminar at the invitation of the Union of Japanese Scientists and Engineers that continued with one-day seminars for company presidents and top managers. Educational programs of quality control in Japanese companies followed this initiative from companies' top management down to the last worker. In addition to the formal education system, courses in quality control were also offered on radio and through television programs. By the end of the 1960s, the quality of Japanese products in terms of number of defects and overall reliability reached or exceeded Western standards. The 1970s were devoted to total quality control (TQM); extending quality concepts from production processes to determining customers need with an aim to produce products that customers truly want. It took ten more years before the image of Japan caught up and became congruent with the level of products it brought to the international market (Burrill and Ledolter, 1999, 44-48).

Quality became a national strategy that was promoted, supported and controlled by the Japanese government. In 1960, it declared November as National Quality Month (Burrill and Ledolter, 1999, 47). The Japanese Ministry of International Trade and Industry was heavily involved in setting quality standards and monitoring the quality of exports (Dale, 1994, 90). This governmental intervention guaranteed that minimum quality standards were met by all exporting companies while strong companies lead by exceeding them.[35]

Improving CI by Attracting Leading Brands - The Israeli Experience

The 1990s decade had seen the image of Israel being transformed from a source of agricultural produce, polished diamonds and traditional industrial products to a high-tech center that challenges Silicon Valley. While the new image has probably not filtered down to the consumer level outside of Israel, it is perceived by those involved in hi-tech industries, including technology companies and venture capital sources. Consumers may not be aware of the Israeli roots of names like Checkpoint, ICQ, Magic, and DSPC, but those in the field do. This new image has brought about an influx of resources to Israel. How did this change come about? The answer is found in government supported R&D and industrialization support programs.

While the initiation of the Israeli technology industry was forced on it by defense needs, its growth into civilian markets benefited from a number of government programs including participation in the costs of R&D, support of technological incubators and the provision of venture capital. Leading multinational companies, including IBM, Digital, Motorola and Intel were lured by these programs and opened R&D facilities in Israel. Provision of land, participation in investment and tax breaks convinced companies such as Intel to open production facilities in the country. The association with these leading names played a major role in changing the Israeli image within the corresponding industries. The emerging image serves as a magnet to attract hi-tech companies and venture capital (Nebenzahl, 1999). However, like the co-branding of PCs with the slogan, "Intel Inside", it will take a long, concerted campaign among consumers to promote Israel's image as a major developer and producer of technological

---

[35] For an example of Taiwan's image advertising campaign from 1990 to 2004, see: Amine, Lyn and Mike Chao (2005).

products "Israel Inside", and not just technology that is utilized by others.

A number of lessons can be learned from the Japanese and Israeli experiences. First, that a change in country image is a slow long-term process that takes decades rather than years. Second, there should be consistency in those image attributes that are to be changed. Third, it takes concerted effort by all involved to lead a successful image campaign. Cooperation and coordination between industry, trade associations and the government are required for a significant change to take place. And, this cooperation has to be in place over the long run. However, as Wally Olins points out[36], governments (and their representatives) usually operate in a short term environment, making commitment to a national branding campaign very difficult. Fourth, such campaigns are expensive to launch. Government cannot finance the task by itself. As in the Scotland case, industrialists must significantly contribute to a national brand campaign. Last but not least, a prevailing change in country image must be preceded by corresponding actual changes in products and services. Advertising and public relation campaigns can only support *real* improvements in products and services by bringing them to the attention of the target markets. They cannot, by themselves, bring about a significant change in attitudes.

---

[36] In an interview with Jack Yan, reported to the authors.

CHAPTER 7

Legal Aspects of Country Image

Ignorance of the law excuses no man

John Selden (1584-1654)

Made-In Labels – What Do They Mean?

A Federal Trade Commission (FTC) advertising copy test was made to determine consumer perception of the "made-in" label. Does it mean that the entire product was made in the United States? If not, how much of it has to be locally made in order to be considered a domestic product? In addition, is a product assembled in the United States from foreign-made parts perceived to be an American product? In answer to these questions, 70 percent of the respondents believed that a product bearing a made-in label was manufactured with parts made all, or almost all, in the United States. Asked if this requirement includes both parts and labor, 77 percent replied in the affirmative (FTC 1991 Copy Test, 20). When the same test was run in the context of a specific product, the results were somewhat different, but still significant. When shown an advertisement for a Huffy bicycle, 58 percent of the respondents believed that it was made entirely of U.S. parts and labor. In the same sort of test, 43 percent believed that a Smith Corona typewriter was "made-in" the United States (*Ibid*. p.29). Only about 50 percent of the value added of both products was attributed to by American sources.

In a later survey (FTC Attitude Survey, 1995), respondents were asked the open-ended question: "What does a 'Made in USA' label mean?" Nearly two-thirds of the respondents simply repeated the phrase in the question; namely that "Made in the USA" means "Made in the USA"! However, when presented with a scenario in which a product contained 70 percent U. S. content and assembled in the United States, respondents were more specific. In this case, 67 percent agreed[37] that the product could have a "made-in" label. In answer to a question similar to that asked in the American survey, only 7 percent of Australian respondents could accurately describe what "made in" means (Australian Federal Government, 1999).

There are those who believe, however, that consumer perception of the "made in" label is synonymous with "brought into being", which could include local assembly with imported parts or components (FTC, 1996, Appendix). To buttress this assumption, attention is drawn to the FTC 1991 Copy Test survey wherein respondents were asked whether "Made in the USA" implied that the product was assembled in the United States. Almost half (49 percent) replied "yes." This, and the majority of respondents who answered that "Made in the USA" means just that (in the 1995 survey above), does not necessarily imply that they mean all, or virtually all of the manufacturing and processing has been done in the United States.

Country of Origin Labeling Requirements[38]

Given that significant numbers of consumers express a preference for domestically made products, many countries require country of origin labels. For example, the United States Congress passed product marking statutes for the expressed purpose of enabling consumers to make wiser purchasing decisions.[39] This section will deal with the legal requirements of labeling and some of the problems that have arisen because of these requirements. The subject is problematical due to two issues: (1) what are the local content requirements that determine country of origin and (2) on what products and where on the product country of origin labels should be placed.

Most countries require some sort of country of origin labels on imported products. However, the requirements for such labeling differ. A summary of labeling requirements for selected countries is shown in Table 7.1.

---

[37] 26% "strongly agreed", 41% somewhat agreed", 20% "strongly disagree", 11% disagree", 2% "neither agree nor disagree".
[38] The following sections are informative and not recommendations.
[39] United States v. Friedlander & Co., 27 C.C.P.A. 297, 302 (1940).

Country or Organization	"Product of" Label	"Made in" Label
USA	A product must be "wholly domestic" or "all or virtually all" made in the United States.	"Where a product has undergone its principal assembly in the United States that assembly is substantial, and the product was last substantially transformed in the United States."
CANADA	At least 51% made in Canada, the last substantial production operation was performed in Canada, resulting in a new and identifiable product.	No such label.
AUSTRALIA	"Product of" Label 100% (or near) local content, "all or virtually all."	"Made in" Label Product must be substantially transformed in Australia and 50% or more production costs have been incurred.
NEW ZEALAND	At least 50% of the cost of manufacturing incurred in New Zealand, where the last process of manufacture must take place.	No such label.
SWITZERLAND	At least 50% Swiss material and labor and assembled in Switzerland.	Unqualified designations such as "Made in Switzerland" can be used only on Swiss watches.
UK	There is no requirement for goods to bear marks indicating their origin, nor is there anything to prevent voluntary marking. Where marks are used, goods are deemed to have been manufactured or processed in the country in which they last underwent a treatment or process resulting in a "substantial change."	

To be continued on the next page

Country or Organization	"Product of" Label	"Made in" Label
NAFTA	Over 50 percent of the product is of domestic origin using the net cost method. More than 60% of the product is of domestic origin using the transaction value method.	No such label.
EU	In December 2003, the EU Commission recommended three policy options for EU origin marking (see below).	
WORLD TRADE ORGANIZATION	Harmonized rules of origin now under formulation.	
Legal requirements at the beginning of the year 2000. Food labeling legislation is usually regulated under separate guidelines. For example, in the EU, place of origin must be indicated only if failure to do so might mislead a purchaser about its true origin.		

Table 7.1 Country of Origin Labeling Requirements in Selected Countries

A number of preliminary observations may be made from the contents of this table. First, the United States has the most stringent requirement for labeling a product as "made in."[40] This standard requires that products advertised or labeled as "Made in USA" be "all or virtually all" made in the United States. This means that all or nearly all[41] significant parts and processing that go into the product are of U.S. origin. While the FTC regulates claims of U.S. origin under its general authority to act against deceptive acts and practices, primarily the U.S. Customs Service regulates foreign-origin markings on products (e.g., Made in Japan"). Where an imported product incorporates materials and/or processing from more than one country, Customs considers the country of origin to be the last country in which a "substantial trans-formation" took place. A substantial transformation is a manufacturing or other process that results in a new and different article of commerce, having a new name, character and use that is different from that which existed prior to the processing. For most goods, neither the Customs Service nor the FTC requires that goods made partially or wholly in

---

[40] An exception is fresh produce. Retailers are only required in the State of Florida to label fresh imported produce as to its country of origin. Cf. Rosselle, 1999.

[41] In technical terms this means that a *de minimis,* or negligible amount of foreign content can be used to qualify as "Made in USA".

the United States be labeled with "Made in the USA" or any other indication of U.S. origin.[42] However, the fact that a product is not required to be marked with a foreign country does not mean that it is permissible to promote that product as "Made in USA" (Enforcement Policy Statement, 1997).

For example, assume that a television set is assembled in Korea incorporating an American-made picture tube. The set is shipped to the United States for sale. The U.S. Customs Service requires that the set be marked "Made in Korea" because this is where the last substantial transformation occurred. Now assume that the importer advertises the set claiming that "although our televisions are made abroad, they contain U.S.-made picture tubes." This claim is not deceptive. However, making the statement without disclosing the foreign origin of manufacture may imply a broader claim, e.g., that the television set is largely made in the United States. The conclusion is that if an advertisement implies that any foreign content or processing is negligible, the advertiser must substantiate the claim. In this case, the advertiser would not be able to substantiate such a claim of the implied "Made in the USA" because the product was substantially transformed in Korea.

Other countries do not share a standard as stringent as the all or virtually all criterion, most requiring at least 50 or 51 percent local content, requiring in addition that the last transformation takes place domestically.[43]

In today's global economy, exemplified by the sourcing of production in many parts of the world, consumers have been exposed to many products that are assembled locally (or elsewhere) from imported parts. Thus, many American manufacturers and members of Congress assert that most consumers no longer assume that a product labeled "Made in the USA" is "all or virtually all" made in the United

---

[42] For a limited number of goods, such as textile, wool, and fur products, there are statutory requirements that the U.S. processing or manufacturing that occurred be disclosed.

[43] Not only do standards differ around the world, but also apparently within different United States agencies. The Buy American Act gives preference in the government procurement of goods that are "substantially made" in the United States (41 U.S.C. § 10a). To qualify for this preference, U.S. made components must exceed only 50% of the cost of the product's total components. Also, the Commerce Department will provide export assistance to U. S. produced goods that have "substantial inputs [at least 50 percent of the good's total value] of materials and labor originating in the United States" (62 Fed. Reg. 29,710 [1997]).

States.[44] Consequently, the FTC began to re-think the viability of its "wholly domestic" standard for the "Made in USA" requirement. In 1996 the FTC held a public workshop in which interested parties – manufacturers, importers, distributors, and consumers – could voice their opinions about this subject. The views expressed at this, as well as at other related workshops, form three groups:

- Supporters of the "all or virtually all standard".
- Supporters of a percentage content (domestic parts and labor) standard (most favoring a 50% criterion).
- Supporters of a "substantial transformation" standard.

Tests for Substantial Transformation

United States Federal Courts have interpreted whether substantial transformations of imported products have taken place. Four tests for transformation have been identified from the adjudications of these courts. They are:

- name, character and use test
- essence test
- value-added test
- article of commerce test.

These four tests are diagrammed in Figure 7.1.

---

[44] American labor unions and some trade associations (e.g., Association of Home Appliance Manufacturers) however, are strong proponents of the "all or virtually all" standard. American Congressmen have added emotional pleas for the standard, e.g. "Our responsibility is to fight for jobs, fight for American workers and fight for American consumers, and that's what we intend to do" (Representative Ted Strickland, D-OH); "If we change the meaning of the 'Made in USA' label...we are lowering our standard of living, our concern for health and safety, and our concern for the environment to the lowest world standard" (U.S. Representative Danny Davis, D-IL); "Weakening this standard to 'substantially all', interpreted... to mean 75 percent American-made, is at best a dishonest proposition that will undermine the faith that we have in the quality and reliability of products that are 'Made in USA'" (U.S. Representative Ted Barrett, D-WI). [Made in USA Policy Comment, 1997).

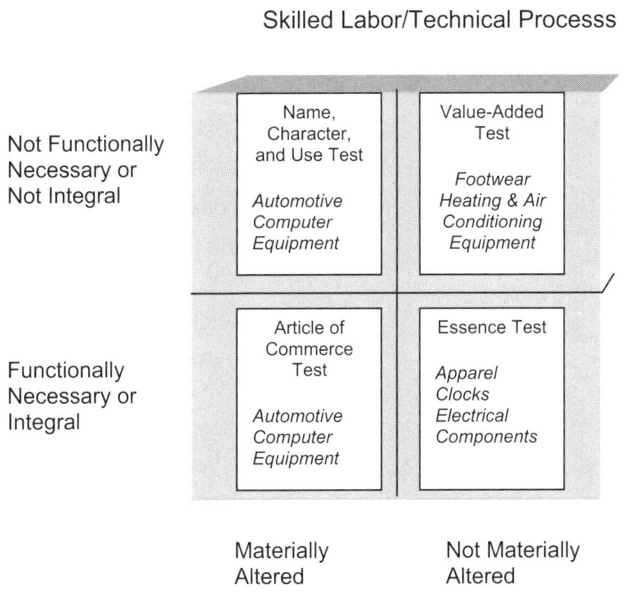

Skilled Labor/Technical Processs

	Materially Altered	Not Materially Altered
Not Functionally Necessary or Not Integral	Name, Character, and Use Test *Automotive Computer Equipment*	Value-Added Test *Footwear Heating & Air Conditioning Equipment*
Functionally Necessary or Integral	Article of Commerce Test *Automotive Computer Equipment*	Essence Test *Apparel Clocks Electrical Components*

Figure 7.1 A Matrix of Test Choice

Table 7.2 provides an introduction to the application of each test.[45]

Tests	Application
Name, character and use test	Fundamental characteristics are materially altered; Technical process; Major manufacturing process; Skilled labor
Essence test	Functionally necessary; No separate commercial value; Technical process; Skilled labor; Destruction with disassembly

To be continued on the next page

[45] This section is reprinted with permission from the Journal of International Marketing, published by the American Marketing Association, Irvine Clarke III, Margaret Owens and John Ford, 1999, Vol. 7, No. 2, pp. 83-91.

Tests	Application
Value-added test	Cost of production, skilled labor/technical process;
	Feature of consumer interest;
	Combination versus material alteration
Article of Commerce test	Producer to consumer good;
	Change in tariff classification under tariff schedules;
	Material alteration;
	Technical process;
	Skilled labor

Table 7.2 Tests of Transformation

Name, Character, and Use Test

The first test states that an imported product is transformed substantially if it is transformed into a new and different article with a distinctive name, character, or use. The criteria of name, character, and use are used to determine whether and when substantial transformation has occurred for the purpose of determining the country-of-origin marks to be placed on a product. It is necessary that the fundamental characteristics of the product be changed so that its characteristics or use be altered substantially.

A simple example is the making of an imported wooden handle into a hairbrush. The manufacturer imports the handle from Japan, and the word "Japan" is marked on the handle, but in a place where, when the bristles are attached by the manufacturer, "Japan" is obliterated. Customs wants the handles individually marked so that the ultimate consumer will know it was made in Japan (See United States v. Gibson-Thomsen Co. [1940], 27 C.C.P.A. 267). In this situation, the character and use of the imported product changes from a wooden handle into a hairbrush with bristles used to brush human hair. The handle loses its identity in the final product and need not carry "Japan" on the handle. It is important for the marketer to evaluate thoroughly the process to be performed on the imported part. The expected increase in profits from using a foreign part may be lost through confiscation if a manufacturer fails to comply with prescribed marking alterations.

Essence Test

The essence test means that the imported part is substantially transformed when it becomes an integral part of the new article with which it is combined. The imported part is considered integral if (1) it is functionally necessary to the new article versus an accessory, (2) it has no commercial value separate from the new article, (3) it becomes part of the new article by a process that requires some degree of skill, or (4) removal of the imported part from the new article will destroy either the imported part or the new article.

An example of the essence test is as follows: In an attempt to reduce its manufacturing costs, a typewriter ribbon manufacturer decided to import the spool on which it winds the ribbon. The spool was manufactured in a foreign country and imported into the United States, where the manufacturer wound the ribbon on the spool. Although the manufacturer wanted to save money on the production of the spool, it did not want to mark the spool itself with the name of the country where it was made. In this situation, the essence test can be used to advantage because it can be shown that the spools are transformed substantially after importation into new articles with a distinctive use, the spool becoming an integral part of the new article. The empty spools are the vehicles for selling ribbon. The ribbon is the major feature of interest to the consumer and the essence of the finished product (see Grafton Spools, Ltd. V. United States [1960], 45 Cust.Ct. 16, 223 C.D. 2190). Here, the manufacturer was able to achieve significant savings on production costs and maintain the product's desired image in the mind of the retail consumer.

Marketers may find that using foreign labor to produce part of a product can provide a competitive advantage by lowering costs and increasing the quality of the product. Before marketers advise a manufacturer to use foreign labor or components, they should address the following questions: (1) is the imported part functionally necessary to the new article, or is it merely decorative or an accessory? In the previously mentioned example, the spool is necessary to create a useable product. What good would the ribbon be without a spool on which to wind it? (2) Does the imported part have any value apart from the new article? The spool would have no value apart finished product because the consumer would not buy the spool by itself. The spool would therefore have no market value. It is the combination of the spool and the ribbon that has market value. (3) Does it require some degree of technical skill or competence to combine the imported part with the new article? The typewriter ribbon manufacturer had the technical skill to combine the spool and the ribbon to produce a new product. And (4) if the imported part was removed from the new article, would the part or new article be destroyed? In the typewriter ribbon example, the spool could not be removed from the new article without destroying the product. How could the typist use the ribbon in the typewriter without a spool on which to wind it?

Value-Added Test

The value-added test implies that neither the imported part nor the domestic part has a value on its own, but when they are combined, value is added to the final product. Manufacturers relying on this test should be concerned about what processes are being performed on the components of the final product. In determining the country of origin of a finished product, the courts have found it to be the country that incurred the greatest cost in producing a component of the finished product, reasoning that the most costly part adds the most value to the finished product.

An example is an U.S. shoe manufacturer, which has the upper part of its shoes manufactured in country X, incurs a substantial cost in manufacturing the uppers. These uppers are imported into the United States, where the manufacturer attaches the soles and marks the shoes "Made in America." In this case, however, the uppers are considered the essence of the shoes. The soles are not the major feature of interest to the consumer and do not add significant value to the ultimate product. Attaching the uppers to the outsoles is significantly less costly than manufacturing the uppers. The desirability of the final product to the consumer comes from the uppers, not the soles. Unlike empty spools, the uppers are mot merely vehicles to sell the soles. The uppers remain the major feature of interest to the consumer (see Uniroyal, Inc. v. United States [1982], 542 F. Supp. 1026).

In using this test, marketers should examine which part of the product attracts the consumer and which part is more costly to produce. In the case previously described, the manufacturer had to remark the shoes with the proper country of origin, that is, X, which significantly decreased the manufacturer's profits. Marketers need to be aware that if the target market prefers articles from a specific country, the final product must be combined so that the country contributes the part that is more costly to produce and is identified with the part that is of interest to the consumer.

Article of Commerce Test

The article of commerce test determines whether a new article of commerce has emerged from operations performed on the imported article. The manufacturing of calculators, computers and other technology has brought this test to the forefront. For example, a U.S. manufacturer imports several components from Taiwan, which were made from materials imported into Taiwan from several foreign countries and the United States. Final assembly of the product is in the United States. The manufacturer wants Taiwan to be the country of origin for the imported materials to reap duty-free benefits due to a developing country, which benefits pass ultimately to the U.S. manufacturer.

Materials received in Taiwan are imported for making integrated circuits (ICs) and photodiodes used in the final product, a calculator. Silicone slices are imported, which must be manufactured further to produce chips. Mold compounds, black for the ICs and transparent for the photodiodes, are used to encapsulate the IC chips. The manufacturer then imports all the component parts into the United States for final assembly. Under this scenario, the imported parts undergo operations in Taiwan to become a new article of commerce. The operations require employees who are technically trained in various skills. The courts have ruled that to obtain the desired country-of-origin marking of the final product, it must be transformed from a producers' good to a retail consumers' good in the specified country (see *Texas Instruments v. United States* [1982], 681 F.2d 778). With continuing advances in technology, this test is important to marketers now and in the future.

The test actually stands for the proposition that the product is being transformed from a producer good to a retail consumer good. In other words, the producer is using the products to make its final product. A producer good is an item that is not used by or is not capable of use by retail consumers. A consumer good is one that has value and use to the consumer. Integrated circuits and photodiodes have no use to the consumer separate and apart from the calculator. The key issue in the calculator example is that, for the U.S. manufacture to have the final product marked with the desired country of origin (Taiwan, in this case), it must show that the location where the materials were actually transformed into a consumer good was Taiwan and not the United States. This would require that the components imported into Taiwan underwent significant transformations and became a new article of commerce in Taiwan. This must not change when final assembly occurs in the United States. If the expertise to make the article a consumer good was employed in the Taiwanese transformations, Taiwan could be used as the country of origin.

Country Marking Criteria

The country marking of an article that is considered a new and different article of commerce is determined by two main criteria: (1) Where was the article transformed from a producer good to a consumer good? And (2) have the operations underlying the asserted transformation effected a change in the classification of merchandise under the tariff schedules? A marketing manager needs to ask these questions when attempting to determine the country marking of an imported article and the effect that country of origin will have on positioning decisions for the item.

Figure 7.1 shows how alteration criteria may be used as guidelines in relation to the four main tests when attempting to determine where substantial transformation has occurred. A component is *functionally necessary* when it is required to operate or run the finished product or is the vehicle that makes the finished product usable. *Integral* means that the component becomes part of the finished product, such that its removal would destroy both the component and the finished product. The degree of labor or technology used in the transformation also is a determining factor.

To assist marketing managers in their assessment of the transformation tests and demonstrate an application of the tests, Table 7.3 lists various products and the test appropriate for country-of-origin marketing requirements.[46]

---

[46] Current federal case law, customs court rulings, international court rulings, and the Code of Federal Regulations were used in preparation of Table 7.3.

Product	Name, Character, and Use Test	Value-Added Test	Article of Commerce Test	Essence Test
Adhesives	X			
Air conditioning equipment		X		
Apparel			X	X
Automotive			X	X
Building materials	X			
Canned fish/seafood	X		X	
Canned, prepared specialty foods	X	X	X	
Clocks	X			X
Computer equipment	X		X	
Dies, jigs, tools	X			
Electrical appliances	X		X	
Electrical components	X		X	
Fabricated metal products				X
Farm machinery			X	X
Footwear		X		
Frozen foods	X			
Furniture	X			
Hardware	X			
Heating equipment		X		
Household appliances	X		X	
Household video equipment	X		X	
Industrial machinery			X	X
Refrigerator equipment		X		
Sports, recreational instruments				X
Surgical and medical instruments	X		X	
Television equipment	X		X	X
Watches	X			X

Table 7.3 A Product's Country of Origin Test Chart

189

Table 7.3 is divided into common standard industrial classifications to offer marketing managers guidance in the application of trans-formation tests. Merchandise not mentioned in Table 7.3 may be classified according to similitude with one of the articles shown. Table 7.3 and the respective tests provide the importer or marketer with a starting point for determining under which test a particular product will likely fit.[47]

Because global country-of-origin marking tests are being modeled increasingly after those of the United States, the four primary tests of transformation discussed herein probably will become the standard by which country marking decisions are made.

A manufacturer or marketer should look carefully at the processes being used and/or what effect the foreign part will have on the ultimate product. Each situation will call for a different analysis, and it is important that the manufacturer or marketer look at the current law relating to country-of-origin marking requirements.[48] By understanding how country markings are prescribed and the tests that determine them, marketers can devise transformation strategies that blend the advantages of global sourcing with the desired country-of-origin markings to achieve maximum benefit. By using the test(s) that best fit the product class, marketers can take a proactive role in the transformation of their products to achieve a desirable marking. Marketers who understand transformation tests are no longer captive to customs rulings; rather, they can develop approaches acceptable in the greatest number of potential target markets to use as a basis for strategic marking decisions. To make the proper strategic marking decisions, marketers should answer several questions:

1. What is the specific product being marketed?

2. Who are the potential consumers, and what are their beliefs or perceptions about foreign versus domestic products?

---

[47] Table 7.3 illustrates what tests the courts have used. These classifications are for illustration only and should not be relied on by manufacturers or marketers in making their decision about the use of foreign labor or foreign parts in the manufacture of their particular product.

[48] This section was written from the perspective of the U.S. marking statutes. Even with WTO changes, each country may have its own way of dealing with country-of-origin markings, and the international strategic marketer should be cognizant of the regulations in foreign target markets.

3. What is the preferred country of origin for the product?

4. How can the product be manufactured or assembled to obtain the desired country-of-origin marking?

For example, a marketer of household audio or video equipment should look at what foreign components and/or labor are needed to manufacture the product. In addition, it is necessary to study the potential consumer market and determine consumer perceptions about foreign versus domestic producers. When these two decisions are made and depending on the results of the research, the marketer should have the imported article undergo its last substantial transformation in the desired country of origin. This would be the country in which (1) the fundamental characteristics of the product would be materially altered, (2) the product would be transformed from a producer good to a consumer good, or (3) the components would become integral to the final product. When the country has been chosen, if the imported product requires some type of manufacturing process, the marketer may also want to consider employing skilled labor in the chosen country and/or using some recognized technical process in performing the work, because the courts appear to add some weight for this in determining country of origin.

The same analysis can be made for any type of product, and the ultimate sourcing and marketing decisions will be made of the basis of the analysis. Marketers familiar with the tests of transformation used in global markings can consider some of the practical strategic implications that surfaced during this examination of the U.S. marking cases and statutes.

Country of Origin Marking

It is not our objective to review the many standards of different countries, as this would be an insurmountable task. We will however, review the standards of the United States, NAFTA, the EU and the WTO.

Marking in the USA

The Customs Service determines the USA standard for country of origin labeling. According to the Tariff Act of 1930 (19 U.S.C. 1304), "*every* [our emphasis] article of foreign origin imported into the United States shall be marked in a conspicuous place as legibly, indelibly, and permanently as the nature of the article (or container) will permit, in such a manner as to indicate to the ultimate consumer in the United States the English name of the country of origin of the article." The term "conspicuous" has been contentious because of the different shapes, sizes and packaging of products. For example, take the case of a company that packaged CD-ROM drives assembled in the United States of almost all Chinese-made parts in boxes covered with an American flag and eagle, with the statement "Made in China" in small print on the bottom or side panels of the package. This would mislead or deceive most consumers and would be in violation of both FTC and U.S. Customs requirements.

Another example concerns footwear. The Customs Service requires that a country of origin statement on footwear and its packaging must appear in close proximity to any non-origin reference. This is not the case for clothing. For example, a decoration on wearing apparel made in a foreign country may be in the form of some American symbol or design (implying USA origin). However, the manufacturer is not required to attach a made-in label proximate to the design, but only on the inner label affixed to the garment (Department of the Treasury, §134.46). This ruling holds as long as the decoration or design does not mislead or deceive the consumer. And, what about an innocuous product such as manhole covers? Here, the customs has ruled that they have to be marked on the top surface with the English name of the country of origin by means of die stamping or other permanent method of marking.

Separate legislation regulates labeling requirements for automobile, textile and apparel products. Automobile labeling is governed by the Automobile Labeling Act of 1992. This legislation requires that cars and light trucks bear labels that stipulate the percentage of U.S. and Canadian components and the two top countries that contribute 15 percent or more of the vehicles component value. In addition, the label must show where the vehicle was assembled and the engine and transmission's country of origin. However, parts of the legislation defeat their purpose. The origin of components requirement, for example, is not for a particular vehicle, say, a Buick Century made in Mexico, but for all Centuries wherever they are made. Thus, it is possible to find the same domestic parts content for a Buick Century made in Mexico as for one made in the United States. Another problem is that the same car could be labeled as having 50 percent U.S/Canadian components if the suppliers were United States' wholly owned, or less than 50 percent domestic U.S. content if the suppliers were not United States' wholly owned. Of course, in order to comply with the law, automobile manufacturers must be able to specify the ownership of all parts suppliers, a rather burdensome task.

Misleading or Deceiving Labeling

Some examples of non-origin markings of products made in foreign countries that the U.S. Customs has ruled to be misleading or deceiving to the consumer are as follows:

1. "A product of ABC Corp., Chicago, Illinois"

2. "Manufactured by ABC Corp., California, U.S.A."

3. "Manufactured and Distributed by ABC, Inc., Denver, Colorado"

4. "Packed for ABC Corp., Greenville, South Carolina"

5. "Distributed by ABC Inc., Colorado, U.S.A."

6. "Made for XYZ Corp., California, U.S.A."

7. "Designed in U.S.A."

8. "Well Made in the USA"

9. "A [name of product] Born in the U.S.A."

In all of these cases the distributor would be required to affix the name of the country of origin in close proximity and in comparable size lettering to such markings.

In addition to misleading labeling, advertising claims of "Made in USA" for products that contain significant foreign components misrepresent the extent to which they are made in the United States. Two case examples serve to illustrate this point (Federal Trade Commission, January 19, 1999):

American Honda Motor Co., Inc. is an U.S. subsidiary of Honda Motor Co., LTD of Japan incorporated in California. It is the domestic distributor for all Honda automobiles, motorcycles, and power products, including lawn mowers. The FTC's alleged that advertisements provided by Honda and placed by local dealers for three American Honda lawn mower models carried the logo "Made in

America by Honda." Neither model could meet the "all or virtually all" criterion because a significant proportion of the components was of foreign origin.

Johnson Worldwide Associates, Inc. markets outdoor recreation products, such as fishing gear, watercraft and motors. It advertised its Super Mono fishing line as "Made in the USA of American and Japanese components", i.e. assembled in the United States from both American and Japanese parts. However, it was found that the fishing line was made *totally* in Japan, while only the packaging and some incidental materials contained U.S. made components or processing.

The Marking Rules of NAFTA

The North American Free Trade Agreement initiated new requirements for country of origin markings that differed from those used by the Customs Service since 1940. Basically, under NAFTA, a tariff-shift requirement is used to determine whether country of origin markings is required.[49] Therefore, imports to the United States under NAFTA would be regulated differently from non-NAFTA imports, which would be treated under the traditional substantial transformation principles described above. However, the U.S. Court of International Trade ruled in *CPC International*[50] that Customs must treat NAFTA goods under both the tariff-shift requirements and substantial transformation criteria.

The World Trade Organization (WTO Standards)

The WTO is in the process of codifying country of origin labeling standards based on the "harmonized system description and coding system" agreed upon in the Uruguay Round "Agreement on Rules of Origin."[51] These standards will apparently favor the tariff-shift approach for defining where substantial transformation occurs. Basically, origin would be based on a three step approach (Bade, 1977). The first part would be based upon the tariff-shift provisions like those contained in the NAFTA agreement. A product assembled in Mexico from imported components could be labeled as a "Made in Mexico" product and also be exported to Canada and the United States duty free if it also meets a second test that would determine if the assembly was sufficient to confer (Mexican) origin. Finally, a third test

---

[49] For a discussion of this provision, see (Bade, 1997).

[50] CPC Int'l, Inc. v. United States, 933 F. Supp. 1093, 1094.

[51] Uruguay Round, Pub. L. No. 103-465, § 101(d)(4), (10), 108. Stat. 4809 (1994).

would be based on value-added criteria. How much value was added to the components in Mexico? In order to determine this, some threshold (and how it should be calculated) is necessary, whether it is 25, 35 or 50 percent. Once finalized and agreed upon, these requirements will apply equally to all member nations. Although the harmonization work has not yet been completed, significant progress has been made.

European Union

In December 2003, the European Commission Directorate-General for Trade published a document entitled "Made in the EU Origin Marking – Working Document of the Commission Services". Current EU legislation requires a *declaration* of origin to accompany imported goods, but does not require any origin *marking*, except for some agricultural products. At the national level, compulsory origin marking for imported goods is prohibited. However, there is no prohibition against *voluntary* origin marking of either EU (e.g. "Made in France" or foreign-made goods (e.g. made in Malaysia"). In summary, there is currently [as of 2006, EDJ] no legal requirement for an EU origin label.

A major objective of the new European Commission initiative to foster origin labeling was to provide:

> *"...comprehensive and accurate information to consumers on the country of origin of products, and in a way that would promote in parallel the image and attractiveness of EU products... [in order to] enhance European companies' competitiveness in the global arena against foreign competitors producing at lower costs and investing less in consumer protection"*
> European Commission, Directorate-General for Trade, 2003, p. 3.

Another objective of the proposal was to consolidate the concept of "made in the EU" as a symbol of the EU's single customs union and single market.

The idea to have a "made in the EU" marking, if accompanied with an EU brand, would constitute a regional brand as we have discussed in the nation branding section of Chapter six. However, there was no plan to include an EU brand in the proposal. Nevertheless, the proposal met with considerable objection from member states. Government representatives of Germany, for example, claimed that the marking scheme would be disadvantageous for German-made goods, since they were believed to be of higher quality than competing products made in other EU nations. In addition, governments of the UK and Denmark were also vociferous opponents. A Danish government representative was quoted as saying that "it has not been proven that consumers prefer goods produced in their own country to foreign-produced goods (*sic!*)" (*The Copenhagen Post*, January 16, 2006).

Importers' and consumers' groups in many of the 25 member states were also opposed to any compulsory marking. They claimed that the measure was protectionist. Typical of this way of thinking, was the head of the International Trade Division of Danish Trade and Services, who was quoted as saying (*The Copenhagen Post, op.cit.*):

It stinks of protectionism. It's a barrier to a specific type of product and to specific types of countries...it gives the wrong message and it puts up an unequal barrier to trade, as those who import goods from countries outside the EU would need to use money on labeling, while importers of goods from countries like Italy wouldn't.

Another group opposing the measure was multinational companies who had production facilities in developing countries. They would not be able to use the EU marking on products made, e.g. in Asian countries. This, they believed, would be a disadvantage. Anyway, they claimed, brand name was more important to consumers than country of origin.

Given the wide opposition to the proposal, the EU Commission dropped it on July, 2004. Thus, origin marking in the EU remains purely voluntary. However, it can still be used by manufacturers in EU countries who believe that their country image is less favorable than that of the EU. So, a "made in the EU" label would in this case be preferable to a "made in Country X" marking.

In conclusion, the review of legal requirements for country of origin marking, the difficulties of enactment processes and the heated debates all point to the importance of the subject in the mind of political leaders and businesspersons alike. As noted in our presentation of legislation in the USA, consumer perceptions are at the heart of the debate. The tools and techniques presented in the earlier chapters of this book provide the means for assessing consumer perceptions. Their application can contribute to future legislation by having it based on valid data.

EPILOGUE

*Barriers to trade – language, education, buying power –are fast
disappearing. No longer is it so important that a product was
'Made in China', or Canada, or France. Labels of country of
origin have been largely a matter of semantics for years. Now,
with new trade agreements among nations, the only label that
might make sense is "Made on Earth.*

> Cesare R. Mainardi, Martin Salva and Muir Sanderson

Given an era of rapid globalization epitomized by open borders to the
movement of goods, capital and people, and the consequent sourcing
of production, the distinction between domestic and foreign-made
products is becoming blurred. For example, brands often identified or
associated with certain countries, are in fact wholly or partly foreign
owned. Some illustrations were given above, namely, Rolls Royce,
Daewoo, Mazda and Land Rover. Others include Burger King,
Pillsbury, Stouffer's frozen foods and Carnation evaporated milk (all
identified with the United States (OC), but foreign owned). Does this
phenomenon mean that made-in labels and the stimuli that they
represent are becoming less meaningful to consumers in their
evaluation of imported products?

Both experimental research and consumer intention surveys have
shown that the country-of-origin cue is still an important factor in the
evaluation of imported products. Consumers continue to associate and
evaluate given product lines (e.g. cosmetics, furniture, cars, and
fashion articles) with specific countries. As shown above, even in the
case of hybrid products, the country of assembly is an important factor
in the consumer's evaluation of imported products.

In addition, more countries are turning to professional image-makers
in an attempt to strengthen, change (re-branding) or build a national
identity (as illustrated in chapter 6). As we pointed out above, images
change over time, either from a concerted effort on the part of firms,

industry and government, or in some cases, from a lack of effort. This last point was emphasized recently by the breakdown in quality control on the part of several Japanese manufacturers. The revelation that Mitsubishi Motors had concealed consumer complaints for twenty years about problems with airbags, brakes and fuel leaks lead to the resignation of Katsuhiko Kawasoe, the president of the firm. This was followed by another mishap for the Japanese *keiretsu*, in the recall of 45,000 television sets by Mitsubishi Electric because they were prone to ignite. Adding to this bad publicity was the recall of tires by Bridgestone because of defects. All of these events have put to question the efficacy of Japanese quality control, which was one of the factors responsible for its strong country image, known for quality, workmanship and durability. The question is of course, what effect will these "mishaps" have on both the manufacturers' brands and the "Made in Japan" label? Both are bound to deteriorate if awareness of the above events becomes widespread and if countervailing action is not taken. An image that took decades to improve and consolidate may deteriorate over a relatively shorter period of time.

Building a national identity is not a one-time media event. All stakeholders must support it over the long run. This support must come in the form of prominent and consistent use of the country brand on all qualified export products. Not all of the country's exported products should qualify to use the national brand, but only those that adhere to strict standards. This is necessary in order to maintain a uniformly high product standard across industries. Of course, the maintenance of a positive country image, or any improvement of an image, will benefit not only those who have invested in it, but all stakeholders, including perhaps those products that are below the desired standard. A strong country image may induce manufacturers of lower quality products to improve them. If not, consumers will have the final word in the marketplace.

This book has summarized much of what is known about country image and place branding. What remain to be explored are several areas that need attention. The first is e-commerce.

E-Commerce

Many products advertised for sale on the Internet do not stipulate country-of-origin. The authors determined this fact by an extensive search of e-commerce suppliers' web pages. Three types of use (or lack) of country-of-origin information were found. First, full information was provided. For example, we found a J.C. Penney advertisement for a Sony digital camcorder that mentioned Japan as the country of manufacture. The same retailer also advertised Reebok athletic shoes made in China. Another example was a Paragon travel utility kit made in China that was offered by CompuServe Netmarket.

Second, are cases where country of manufacturer is not designated, but only the country from which the product was imported. This designation is weaker, since the consumer cannot be certain where the product was made. Examples of this practice include a microwave oven imported from Thailand and a snowboard imported from Canada, both advertised by J.C. Penney.

Third, are advertisements where country of origin or country of importation is not specified. Here we found Kitchenaid hand mixers and Pierre Cardin luggage advertised by CompuServe Netmarket. Additional cases where no reference was made to country appeared in an eToys advertisement for a Pokemon backpack and cameras and telephone equipment offered by Circuitcity.

How do consumers react to these three types of e-commerce advertising? Will consumers refrain from buying those products for which country of origin information is missing? Given the fact that many consumers do indeed search for the made-in label before purchasing, the lack of such information in e-commerce advertising may constrain their decision to buy from the net. Another possibility is that consumers may place greater reliance on brand names or on the reputation of the virtual store. This is a fruitful area for future research.

In the previous chapter we documented the fact that many countries require country of origin labeling on imported products. However, the Internet does not recognize territorial boundaries. This fact was exemplified from the search described above. A paradox is created where the same product sold in a traditional store in a given country must by law have a country of origin label, but where the same product may be sold in a virtual store by the same company without this information. It has been suggested that legislation be passed requiring companies to use top-level domains that stipulate their home country. For example, the domain XYZ.nl, will identify XYZ as a company domiciled in the Netherlands. However, when the company is an e-commerce store, this solution does not provide any country of origin information about products advertised on the Internet. Apparently, legislators have not dealt with this problem because country of origin labeling requirements is territorial in application, while the Internet is extra-territorial. A solution to this problem requires international cooperation.[52]

Another issue yet to be addressed by e-commerce practitioners and researchers is how to obtain a better understanding of consumer perception of brand and country image over the net. The traditional marketing concept distinguishes between a consumer orientation versus the earlier production approach. While the production approach stresses product and channel attributes, the consumer approach gives greater weight to consumer perceptions and needs. In an attempt to extend Aaker's (1996) ten measures of brand equity to online commerce, Christodoulides and de Chernatony (2004) conducted a comprehensive review of the online branding and consumer behavior literature as well as sixteen interviews with online branding experts. Their efforts resulted in ten Internet-specific brand equity measures. These measures are: Online brand experience, interactivity, customization, relevance, site design, customer service, order fulfillment, quality of brand relationships, communities, and website logs and revisits view time. We note that practically all these measures follow the production rather than the consumer approach. This is in contrast with the original measures of Aaker (1996) that included loyalty, perceived quality, perceived value, organizational associations and brand awareness, measures that focus on consumer perceptions. Therefore, research is needed to assess the relative weights that consumers assign to brand and country of origin when purchasing on the internet.

An Additional Research Agenda

Another area that still needs research involves determining which product categories are more prone to CI influence on purchasing decisions. While it is widely agreed that CI is product specific, little is known about how purchasing behavior is modified by trade-off strategies for given product categories, e.g. price versus a strong brand made in a weak country-image country, CI effects on perceived risk and the role of emotion and CI. The subject of emotion and buying behavior has received increased attention recently in the marketing literature (Chaudhuri, 1998; Mick and Fournier, 1998; Luce, et al, 1999; Travis, 2000). It has been averred that successful brands (and

---

[52] An example of such cooperation could be on the regional level, e.g., among EU countries. But even within the EU cooperation is a problem, exemplified by the recent debate over the "Rome II Green Paper" regarding the regulation of e-commerce.

perhaps a country's image?) form an emotional connection with consumers (Travis, 2000). If so, the question is how emotion-laden is country image in explaining a consumer's product choice? Is emotion a strong influence on some product categories, but not on others? The answers to these questions should provide some new direction for determining communication strategy.

Research is also needed to determine the influence on country image of country compositioning or national co-branding. Can the addition of another country name (as a co-brand) to the made-in country from a strong image country compensate for a weak brand, a weak image country, or both? Additional questions that need an answer include: (1) what is the joint effect of brand and country on consumer evaluations of brand/country alliances? (2) are there spillover effects on both the brand and country images as a result of the brand/country alliance? (3) does brand and/or country familiarity moderate attitudes toward the brand/country alliance?

Finally, an area that has received scant attention is services. Does CI affect services and service providers in the same way as products? Given the differences between the two categories (tangibility, distance between consumer and provider, etc.) there is reason to believe that CIE should be different. In summary, while we know quite a bit about CIE, there are still areas that deserve the attention of researchers. We hope that this book will serve as an inspiration to them.

Appendix

Appendix 1

Household electronic products made in COUNTRY X are ...

	STRONGLY AGREE				STRONGLY DISAGREE		
expensive products	1	2	3	4	5	6	7
products I'll be proud to show my friends	1	2	3	4	5	6	7
products I like	1	2	3	4	5	6	7
inexpensive products	1	2	3	4	5	6	7
high quality products	1	2	3	4	5	6	7
products my friends would buy	1	2	3	4	5	6	7
expensive products	1	2	3	4	5	6	7
products I'll be proud to show my friends	1	2	3	4	5	6	7
products I like	1	2	3	4	5	6	7

A person who buys household electronic products made in COUNTRY X…

	STRONGLY AGREE						STRONGLY DISAGREE
is making the best choice	1	2	3	4	5	6	7
is a gambler	1	2	3	4	5	6	7
looks for established brand names	1	2	3	4	5	6	7
is stingy	1	2	3	4	5	6	7
is paying top price for top quality	1	2	3	4	5	6	7
is a poor person	1	2	3	4	5	6	7
is getting a good deal	1	2	3	4	5	6	7
is ignorant, foolish	1	2	3	4	5	6	7
prefers domestic products	1	2	3	4	5	6	7
is a lower class person	1	2	3	4	5	6	7
will be satisfied	1	2	3	4	5	6	7
is unthinking, rash, naïve	1	2	3	4	5	6	7
is correct in choosing the product	1	2	3	4	5	6	7
doesn't care about quality	1	2	3	4	5	6	7
is knowledgeable about the product	1	2	3	4	5	6	7
is a local chauvinist	1	2	3	4	5	6	7
is buying a good but expensive product	1	2	3	4	5	6	7
is getting ripped off	1	2	3	4	5	6	7
cares about quality	1	2	3	4	5	6	7
is mistaken in choosing the product	1	2	3	4	5	6	7
demands high quality	1	2	3	4	5	6	7
will be dissatisfied	1	2	3	4	5	6	7
is not knowledgeable about the product	1	2	3	4	5	6	7
wants to help the domestic economy	1	2	3	4	5	6	7

Appendix 2

CETSCALE

1. Americans should only buy American-made products.
2. Only those products that are unavailable in the U.S. should be imported.
3. Buy American products. Keep Americans working.
4. American< products first, last, and foremost.
5. Purchasing foreign-made products is un-American.
6. It is not right to buy foreign-made products.
7. A real American always buys American-made products.
8. We should purchase products manufactured in America instead of letting other countries get rich off of us.
9. It is always best to purchase American products.
10. There should be very little trading or purchasing of goods from other countries, unless out of necessity.
11. Americans should not buy foreign products because this hurts American business and causes unemployment.
12. Curbs should be put on all imports.
13. It may cost me more, but I prefer to buy American products.
14. Foreigners should not be allowed to put their products on our markets.
15. Foreign products should be taxed heavily to reduce their entry in the U.S.
16. We should buy from foreign countries only those products that we cannot obtain within our own country.
17. American consumers who purchase products made in other countries are responsible for putting their fellow Americans out of work.

Source: Shimp and Sharma (1987)

Bibliography

Aaker, David A. (1991) *Managing Brand Equity,* The Free Press, New York, N.Y.

Aaker, David A. (1996), "Measuring Brand Equity AcrossProducts and Markets,"*California Management Review,* 38, 3, 102-120.

Agrawal, Jagdish and Wagner Kamakura (1999), "Country of Origin: A Competitive Advantage?," *International Journal of Research in Marketing*, 16, 255-267.

Ahmed, Sadrudin, Alain d'Astous and C. d'Almeida (1994), "A Study of Country-of-Origin Effects in Africa," in E.J. Wilson and W.C. Black (eds.) *Proceedings of the Academy of Marketing Science*, Nashville, Tennessee, 299-304.

Ahmed, Sadrudin, Alain d'Astous and Simon Lemire (1997), "Country-of-Origin Effects in the U.S. and Canada: Implications for the Marketing of Products Made in Mexico," *Journal of International Consumer Marketing*, 10, 1/2, 73-92.

Ahmed, Sadrudin and Alain d'Astous (1999), "Product – Country Images in Canada and in the People's Republic of China," *Journal of International Consumer Marketing*, 11, 1, 5-22.

Akin, Melissa (1997), "Move Over Cola, Russia Wants Kvass," *Christian Science Monitor*, (October 15), 9.

Alba, Joseph W. and Wesley J. Hutchinson (1987), "Dimensions of Consumer Expertise," *Journal of Consumer Research*, 13, 411-454.

Albaum, G. and R. A. Peterson (1984), "Empirical Research in International Marketing 1976-1982," *Journal of International Business Studies*, (Spring-Summer), 161-173.

Amine, L. S. (1994), "Consumer Nationality as a Determinant of Origin Preferences and Willingness to Buy," In S. K. Sokoya, editor, *Proceedings of the 1994 Conference of the Association for Global Business*, Las Vegas, 135-145.

Amine, L. S. and S. Shin (2002), "A Comparison of Consumer Nationality as a Determinant of COO Preferences," *Multinational Business Review*, 10, 1, 45-53.

Amine, L. S. and M. C. H. Chao (2005), "Managing Country Image to Long-Term Advantage: The Case of Taiwan and Acer," *Place Branding*, 1, 2, 187-204.

Andrew, I. And E. Valenzi (1971), "Combining Price, Brand Name and Store Cues to Form an Impression of Product Quality," *Proceedings of the 79th Annual Convention of the American Psychological Association.*

Anholt, Simon (2003), *Brand New Justice:The Upside of Global Branding.* Oxford: Buttersworth Heinmann.

Ashill, N. and A. Sinha (2004), "An Exploratory Study into the Impact of Components of Brand Equity and Country of Origin Effects on Purchase Intention," *Journal of Asia-Pacific Business*, 5, 3, 27-43.

Anonymous (1994), "Canada Takes a New Look," *The Economist*, November 19, 46-47.

Australian Federal Government (1999), "Consumer Fact Sheet," Department of Industry, Science and Resources, www.isr.gov.au/labeling/industry/factsheet.html.

Avraham, E. and A. First (2003), "I Buy American: The American Image as Reflected in Israeli Advertising," *Journal of Communication*, 53, 2, 282-298.

Bade, Donna (1997), "Beyond Marking: Country of Origin Rules and the Decision in *CPC International*," *The John Marshall Law Review*, 31, 179-205.

Baily, William and Sheila Gutierrez de Pineres (1997), "Country of Origin Attitudes in Mexico: The Malinchismo Effect," *Journal of International Consumer Marketing*, 9, 3, 25-41.

Bainbridge, Jane (1999), "The Case for Branding Britain," *Marketing*, (March), 37.

Baldauf, Artur, Karen S. Cravens and Gudrum Binder (2003), "Performance Consequences of Brand Equity Management: Evidence from Organizations in the Value Chain," *The Journal of Product and Brand Management,* 12, 4/5, 220-234.

Batra, Rajeev, Venkatram Ramaswamy. Dana Alden, Jan-Benedict-Steenkamp and S. Ramacahnder (2000), "Effects of Brand Local and Nonlocal Origin on Consumer Attitudes in Developing Countries," *Journal of Consumer Psychology*, 9, 2, 83-95.

Baumgartner, Gary and Alain Jolibert (1977), "The Perception of Foreign Products in France," in H. K. Hunt (ed.), *Advances in Consumer Research*, 5, Ann Arbor, MI: Association for Consumer Research, 603-605.

Boosi-Yehoshua, Irit (2003), "Developing Scales for the Measurement of Brand Image," Unpublished Ph.D. dissertation, Bar-Ilan University, Ramat-Gan, Israel (Hebrew).

Bilkey, W. and E. Nes (1982), "Country of Origin Effects on Product Evaluations," *Journal of International Business Studies*, (Spring/Summer), 89-99.

Brand Strategy, (November 22, 1999), 1.

Brodowski, Glen (1998), "The Effects of Country of Design and Country of Assembly on Evaluative Beliefs About Automobiles and Attitudes Toward Buying Them: A Comparison Between Low and High Ethnocentric Consumers," *Journal of International Consumer Marketing*, 10, 3, 85-113.

Brodowski, G., J. Tan and O. Meilich (2004), "Managing Country-of-Origin Choices: Competitive Advantages and Choices," *International Business Review*, 13, 729-748.

Bruner, Jerome S., J. Jacqueline Goodnow, and George A. Austin (1956), *A Study of Thinking.* New York: John Wiley and Sons, Inc.

Bruskin Report (1985), *A Market Research Newsletter*, Report No. 132, New Brunswick: NJ.

Bucken-Knapp, G. (2001), "Just a Train-ride Away but Still Worlds Apart: Prospects for the Øresund Region as a Binational City," *GeoJournal*, 54, 1, 51-60.

Buhrs, T. and R. Bartlett (1993), *Environmental Polocy in New Zealand-The Politics of Lean and Green.* Oxford University Press.

Burrill, Claude W. and Johannes Ledolter, (1999), *Achieving Quality Through Continual Improvement.* New York: John Wiley & Sons, Inc.

Caldwell, N. and J. Freire (2004), "The Differences between Branding a Country, a Region and a City: Applying the Brand Box Model," *Journal of Brand Management*, 12, 1, 50-61.

Cameron, Ross and Gregory Elliott (1998), "The 'Country-of-Origin Effect' and Consumer Attitudes to 'Buy Local' Campaigns: Australian Evidence," *Australasian Marketing Journal*, 6, 2, 39-50.

Capon, N., J.P. Berthan, J. Hulbert and L. Pitt (2001), "Brand Custodianship: a new Primer for Senior Mangers," *European Management Journal*, 19, 3, 215-227.

Cattin, P., A. Jolibert and C. Lohnes (1982), "A Cross-cultural Study of "Made in" Concepts," *Journal of International Business Studies*, 13, 3, 131-141.

Centner, T., S. Turner and J. Bryan (1989), "Product Differentiation Protection: Developing a Strategy for Multiple Producers of Regional Supply Crops," *Journal of Food Distribution Research*, 20, 2, 13.

Chao, Paul (1998), "Impact of Country-of-Origin Dimensions on Product Quality and Design Quality Perceptions," *Journal of Business Research*, 42, 1-6.

Chao, Paul (1989), "The Impact of Country Affiliation on the Creditability of Product Attribute Claims," *Journal of Advertising Research*, (April/May), 35-41

Chasin, J. B. and E. D. Jaffe (1979), "Industrial Buyer Attitudes Towards Goods Made in Eastern Europe," *Columbia Journal of World Business*, (Summer), 74-81.

Chasin, J. B., H. Holzmueller and E. D. Jaffe (1989), "Stereotyping, buyer familiarity and ethnocentrism: A cross-cultural analysis," *Journal of International Consumer Marketing*, 1, 9-25.

Chasin, J. B. and E.D. Jaffe (1987), "Industrial Buyer Attitudes Towards Goods Made In Eastern Europe: An Update," *European Management Journal*, 5, 3, 180-189.

Chaudhuri, Arjun (1998), "Product Class Effects on Perceived Risk: The role of Emotion," *International Journal of Research in Marketing*, 15, 2, 157-168.

Chen, Hwei-Chung and Arun Pereira (1999), "Product Entry in International Markets: The Effect of Country-of-Origin on First Mover Advantage," *Journal of Product & Brand Management*, 8, 3, 218-229.

Chinen, Kenichiro, Minjoon Jun and Gerald Hampton (2000), "Product Quality, Market Presence, and Buying Behavior: Aggregate Images of Foreign Products in the U.S.," *Multinational Business Review*, Spring, 29-38.

Chong, Ju Choi (1992), "A Note on Rivalry in East Asia – The Case of Sourcing," *Journal of World Trade*, 26, 5, 99-103.

Clarke III, Irvine, Margaret Owens and John Ford (1999), "The Harmonization of Product Country Marking Statutes – Strategic Implications for International Marketers," *Journal of International Marketing*, 7, 2, 81-92.

Cohen, Joel B. and Kunal Basu (1987), "Alternative Models of Categorization: Toward a Contingent Processing Framework," *Journal of Consumer Research*, 13, 455-472.

Conley, J. (1986), "When the Going Gets Tough the Patriots Cry 'Be True Blue and Buy Australian'," *The Age*, (September), 6.

Crawford, J. and B. Garland (1988), "German and American Perceptions of Product Quality," *Journal of International Consumer Marketing*, 1, 1, 63-78.

Croft, Martin (1995), "National Origin and their Relevance to Branding Products and Services," *Brand Strategy*, (December 25), 22.

Curtis, James (1997), "Should Brands Fly the Flag?" *Marketing*, March 20, 19-22.

d'Astous, Alain and Sadrudin Ahmed (1992), "Multi-Cue Evaluation of Made-in Concept: A Conjoint Analysis Study in Belgium," *Journal of Euromarketing*, 2, 1, 9-29.

Dale, Barrie G., (1994) "Japanese Total Quality Control" in Dale Barrie G., ed., *Managing Quality* 2nd ed. Hertfordshire, UK: Prentice Hall Europe.

Darling, John R. and Frederick B. Kraft (1977), "A Competitive Profile of Products and Associated Marketing Practices of Selected European and non-European Countries," *European Journal of Marketing*, 11, 7, 519-531.

Darling, John R. and D. Arnold, (1988), "Foreign Consumers' Perspective of the Products and Marketing Practices of the United States versus Selected European Countries," *Journal of Business Research*, 17, 237-248.

Department of the Treasury, United States Customs Service (1997), Country of Origin Marking, 19 CFR Part 134, Washington, D.C.

Djursaa, Malene (1988) *Med Britiske Briller*, Copenhagen: Teknisk Forlag.

Djursaa, Malene (1989), "Dragging Denmark out of Obscurity," *Magazine for Anglo-Danish Relations*, 1, 2.

Djursaa, Malene (1990), "British Image of Themselves vs. Others," *Marketing Intelligence and Planning*, 8, 7, 29-32.

Djursaa, Malene, Simon Kragh and Jan Möller (1991), "Danish Sells – Whatever They Say," *Magazine for Anglo-Danish Relations*, 4, 10-11.

Dodds, W., K. Monroe and D. Grewel (1991), "Effects of Price, Brand, and Store Information on Buyers' Product Evaluations," *Journal of Marketing Research*, 28 (August), 307-319.

Dornoff, R. J., C. B. Tankersley and G. P. White (1974), "Consumer's Perception of Imports," *Akron Business and Economic Review*, (Summer), 26-29.

Dubin, R. (1978), *Theory Development*, New York: The Free Press.

Dubois, Bernard and Claire Paternault (1997), "Does Luxury have a Home Country? An Investigation of Country Images in Europe," *Marketing and Research Today* (May), 79-85.

Durvaula, Srinivas, J. Craig Andrews and Richard Netemeyer (1997), "A Cross-Cultural Comparison of Consumer Ethnocentrism in the United States and Russia," *Journal of International Consumer Marketing*, 9, 4, 73-93.

Dzever, Sam and Pascale Quester (1999), "Country-of-Origin Effects on Purchasing Agents' Product Perceptions: An Australian Perspective," *Industrial Marketing Management*, 28, 2, 165-175.

Elliot, G. and R. Cameron (1994), "Consumer Perception of Product Quality and the Country-of-Origin Effect," *Journal of International Marketing*, 2, 49-62.

Elliot, S. (2003), "American Companies are Adjusting Almost Everything that Represents them Overseas," *The New York Times* (April 4), C5.

Endziņa, I. and L. Luņeva (2004), "Development of a National Branding Strategy: The Case of Latvia," *Place Branding*, 1, 1, 94-105.

Enforcement Policy Statement (1997), Federal Trade Commission, Washington, D.C.

Engel, James F, David T. Kollat and Roger D. Blackwell (1973), *Consumer Behavior*, New York: Holt, Rinhart and Winston, Inc.

Erickson, G. M., J. K. Johannson and P. Chao (1984), "Image Variables in Multiattribute Product Evaluations: Country-of-origin Effects," *Journal of Consumer Research*, 11 (September), 694-699.

Eroglu, S. A. and K. A. Machleit (1989), "Effects of Individual and Product Specific Variables on Utilizing Country of Origin as a Product Cue," *International Marketing Review*, 6, 6, 27-41.

Ettenson, R., J. Wagner and G. Gaeth (1988), "Evaluating the Effect of Country of Origin and the 'Made in USA' Campaign: A Conjoint Approach," *Journal of Retailing*, 64, (Spring), 85-100.

Ettenson, R. (1993), "Brand Name and Country of Origin Effects in the Emerging Market Economies of Russia, Poland, and Hungary," *International Marketing Review*, 10, 5, 14-36.

Etzel, M. J. and B. J. Walker (1974), "Advertising Strategy for Foreign Products," *Journal of Advertising Research*, (June), 41-44.

Export Today, January, 1994.

Farmer's Guardian, July 30, 2004, 19.

Federal Trade Commission (1991) Copy Test, www.ftc.gov/jointvent/madeusa/ftp/usa/043.txt.

Federal Trade Commission (1995), "Comments Regarding 'Made in USA' Advertising Claims," December 15, 1.

Federal Trade Commission (1995), File number P894219.

Federal Trade Commission (1996), document P894219, January 16, 2.

Fenwick, Graham and Cameron Wright (2000), "Effect of a Buy-National Campaign on Member Firm Performance," *Journal of Business Research*, 47, 135-145.

Fischer, Wolfgang and Peter Byron (1997), "Buy Australian Made," *Journal of Consumer Policy*, 20, 89-97.

Frank, Dana (1999), *Buy American: The Untold Story of Economic Nationalism*. Boston, Beacon Press.

Frasher, S., M. Hall, J. Hildreth and M. Sorgi (2003), *A Brand for the Nation of Latvia*. Said Business School, Oxford University.

Friedman, Thomas (1999), *The Lexus and the Olive Tree*, London, HarperCollins.

Fullerton, J. (2005), "Why Do They Hate Us? International Attitudes Towards America, American Brands and Advertising," *Place Branding*, 1, 2, 129-140.

Gaedeke, R. (1973), "Consumer Attitudes Towards Products 'Made In' Developing Countries," *Journal of Retailing*, 49, 14-24.

Gallup (1985), *Key results of Consumer Preference Research Studies*. New York: NY.

Gardner, D. (1974), "Is the Price/Quality Relationship Important? Working Paper # 186, Faculty Working Papers, College of Commerce and Business Administration, University of Illinois.

Gilley, Bruce (1996), "Lure of the West," *Far Eastern Economic Review*, 159, 70.

Gorfinkle, Joseph I. (1966), *The Eight Chapters of Maimonides on Ethics.* Columbia University Oriental Studies; Vol. VII. New York, AMS Press Inc.

General Motors Corporation (1999), *Annual Report*, http://www.gm.com/company/investor_information/docs/fin_d ata/ar1999/download/gm_ar_part2.pdf.

Greenberg, M. (2000), Branding Cities A Social History of the Urban Lifestyle Magazine," *Urban Affairs Review*, 36, 2, 228-263.

Gregory, James R. (2001), *Branding Across Border.* New York: McGraw Hill.

Grimm, M. (2003), "Now the Loser: Brand USA," *Brandweek* (October 20), 44, 38, 19.

Gupta, Sunil and Lehmann, Donald R. (2003), "Customers as Assets," *Journal of Interactive Marketing,* 17,1, 9-24.

Gupta, Sunil, Lehmann, Donald R. and Stuart, Jennifer A. (2004), "Valuing Customers," *Journal of Marketing Research*, 4, 1, 7-18.

Gupta, Sunil and Lehmann, Donald R. (2005), *Managing Customers as Investments,* Upper Saddle River, NJ: Pearson Education, Inc.

Halfhill, D. (1980), "Multinational Marketing Strategy: Implications of Attitudes Toward Country of Origin," *Management International Review*, 20, 4, 26-30.

Hall, Jonathan (2004), "Branding Britain," *Journal of Vacation Marketing*, 10, 2, 171-185.

Hallberg, Annika (1996), "Country-of-Origin Effects of Tourism," in Wolfgang Framke, Anne-Mette Hjalger, Karen Pederson and Peter Strunge (eds.), *Proceedings of the Nordic Tourism in a Global Environment Symposium,"* Copenhagen, October 17-20, 1995, 149-165.

Hallberg, Annika (1999), "The Impact of International Tourism on Consumers' Attitudes and Behaviours Towards Products – A Cross-National Study of Product-Country Images," *Proceedings of the 7th Nordic Symposium in Hospitality and Tourism Research 1998*, 253-264.

Han, C. Min (1988), "The Role of Consumer Patriotism in the Choice of Domestic versus Foreign Products," *Journal of Advertising Research*, 28, 3, 25-32.

Han, C. Min and V. Terpstra (1988), "Country-of-Origin Effects for Uni-National and Bi-National Products," *Journal of International Business Studies*, (Summer), 235-255.

Han, C. Min (1989), "Country Image: Halo or Summary Construct?", *Journal of Marketing Research*, 26, 222-229.

Han, C. Min (1990), "Testing the Role of Country Image in Consumer Choice Behaviour," *European Journal of Marketing*, 24: 6.

Head, David (1988), "Advertising Slogans and the 'Made-in' Concept," *International Journal of Advertising*, 7, 237-252.

Heimbach, A. E., J. K. Johansson and D. L. MacLachlan (1989), "Product Familiarity, Information Processing and Country-of-Origin Cues, *Advances in Consumer Research*, 16, 460-467.

Henrikson, A. K. (2004), "U.S. Public Diplomacy in the Middle East Lessons Learned from the /charlotte Beers Experience," Anna Tiedeman Seminar on Geography, Foreign Policy, and World Order, Fletcher School of Diplomacy, Tufts University, May 4.

Heslop, L. A., J. Liefeld and M. Wall (1987), "An Experimental Study of the Impact of Country-of-Origin Information, In R. Turner, ed., *Marketing,* Administrative Science Association of Canada, 179-185.

Heslop, L. A. and N. Papadopoulos (1993), "But Who Knows Where or When: Reflections on the Images of Countries and Their Products," in N. Papadopoulos and L. A. Heslop (eds.), *Product-Country Images: Impact and Role in International Marketing*, New York: International Business Press, 39-76.

Hoeffler, Steve and Kevin L. Keller (2003), "The Marketing Advantage of Strong Brands," *Journal of Brand Management,* 10, 6, 421-445.

Hong, S. and J. F. Toner (1989), "Are There Gender Differences in the Use of Country-of-Origin Information in the Evaluation of Products?" *Advances in Consumer Research*, 16, 468-472.

Hong, S. and R. S. Wyer, Jr. (1989), "Effects of Country-of-Origin and Product Attribute Information Processing Perspective," *Journal of Consumer Research*, 16, 2, 175-187.

Hooley, G. J., D. Shipley and N. Krieger (1988), "A Method for Modeling Consumer Perceptions of Country of Origin," *International Marketing Review*, (Autumn), 67-76.

Hospers, G. (2004), "Place Marketing in Europe: The Branding of the Oresund Region," *Intereconomics*, 39, 5, 271-279.

Howard, D. (1989), "Understanding How American Consumers Formulate their Attitudes about Foreign Products," *Journal of International Consumer Marketing*, 2, 2, 7-22.

Hsieh, Ming-Huei (2003), "Measuring Global Brand Equity Using Cross-National Survey Data," *Journal of International Marketing,* 12, 2, 28-57.

Hulland, John (1999), "The Effects of Country-of-Brand Name on Product Evaluation and Consideration: A Cross-Country Consideration," *Journal of International Consumer Marketing*, 11, 1, 23-40.

"Imagination," Microsoft® Encarta® Online Encyclopedia 2000 http://encarta.msn.com © 1997-2000 Microsoft Corporation.

Insch, Gary and J. Brad McBride (1998), "Decomposing the Country-of-Origin Construct: An Empirical Test of Country of Design, Country of Parts and Country of Assembly," *Journal of International Consumer Marketing*, 10, 4, 69-91.

Interbrand (2004) www.Interbrand.com/best_brands_2004_fac.asp

International Mass Retail Association (1994), *Consumer Attitudes Toward Product Sourcing*, Arlington, VA.

International Trade Center (ITC) (2000), "Country-Specific Trade Profiles".

Jacoby, J., J. C. Olson and R. A. Haddock (1971), "Price, Brand Name and Product Composition Characteristics as Determinants of Perceived Quality," *Journal of Applied Psychology*, 55, 570-579.

Jaffe, E. D. and I. D. Nebenzahl (1984), "Alternative Questionnaire Formats for Country Image Studies," *Journal of Marketing Research*, 81, (November), 463-471.

Jaffe, E. D. and I. D. Nebenzahl (1988), "On the Measurement of Halo Effect in Country of Origin Studies," In H. C. Meissner, editor, *East-West Economic and Business Relations: Systematic Analysis and Perspectives of Development*, Proceedings of the 14th annual meeting of the European International Business Association, Berlin, December 11-13.

Jaffe, E. D. and I. D. Nebenzahl (1989), "Global Promotion of Country Image - the Case of the 1988 Korean Olympic Games*,"* *Proceedings of the 15th annual European International Business Association*, Helsinki, December 15-17.

Jaffe, E. D., I. D. Nebenzahl and S. I. Lampert (1994), "Towards a Theory of Country-of-Origin Effect: An Integrative Paradigm," In K. Obloj, editor, *High Speed Competition in a New Europe*, Proceedings of the European International Business Association, Warsaw.

Jaffe, E. D. and Carlos Martinez (1995), "Mexican Consumer Attitudes Towards Domestic and Foreign Made Products," *Journal of International Consumer Marketing*, 7, 3, 7-27.

Jensen, Ole (2005), "Branding the Contemporary City – Urban Branding as Regional Growth Agenda?," Plenary paper presented at the Regional Studies Association Conference, Aalborg University, May 28.

Johansson, J. K., S. P. Douglas and I. Nonaka (1985), "Assessing the Impact of Country-of-Origin on Product Evaluations," *Journal of Marketing Research*, 22, (November), 388-396.

Johansson, J. K. and I. D. Nebenzahl (1986), "Multinational Production: Effect on Brand Value," *Journal of International Business Studies*, 17, 3, 101-126.

Johansson, J. K. (1989), "Determinants and Effects of the Use of 'Made In' Labels," *International Marketing Review*, 6, 1, 47-58.

Jurgensen, J. (2003), "Marketing and Image Conflicts with Perception as Aggressor," www.nancysnow.com/puttingahappyface.htm. Retrieved 20.09.2005.

Karlsson, P., "A Region is Born," www.oresundregion.nu/lookasse/birthregion/artikler/oresundregion-businessborn.htm. Retrieved May 31, 2005.

Kaynak, Erdener and Tevfik Dalgic (1988), "Irish Consumer Attitudes Towards Foreign Products: Retail Policy Implications," In E. Kaynak (ed.), *Transnational Retailing*, Berlins de Gruyter, 103-112.

Keller, Kevin L. (1993), "Conceptualizing, Measuring, and Managinjg Customer-Based Brand Equity," *Journal of Marketing,* 57, 1, 1-22.

Khanna Sri Ram (1986), "Asian Companies and the Country Stereotype Paradox: An Empirical Study," *Columbia Journal of World Business*, 21, 2, 29-38.

Kiecker, P. and D. Duhan (1992), "The Influence of Origin Evaluation and Origin Identification on Retail Sales," Paper presented at the American Marketing Association's summer educator's Conference, Chicago.

Klein, Jill Gabrielle, Richard Ettenson and Marlene Morris (1998), "The Animosity Model of Foreign Product Purchase: An Empirical Test in the People's Republic of China," *Journal of Marketing*, 52 (January), 89-100.

Klein, Jill Gabrielle, Richard Ettenson and Balaji Krishnan (2000), "Extending the Construct of Consumer Ethnocentrism: When Foreign Products Are Preferred," unpublished manuscript.

Knight, Gary A. and Roger J. Calanton (2000), "A Flexible Model of Consumer Country-of-Origin Perceptions. A Cross-Cultural Inverstigation," *International Marketing Review*, 17, 2, 127-145.

Kotler, Philip (1997), *Marketing Management: Anlysis, Planning, Implementation and Control*, 9th ed., Upper Saddle River, NJ: Prentice Hall International, Inc.

Lampert, S. I. and E. D. Jaffe (1998), "A Dynamic Approach to Country-of-Origin Effect," *European Journal of Marketing*, 32, 1-2, 61-78.

Lampert, S. I. and E. D. Jaffe, (1996), "Country of Origin Effects on International Market Entry," *Journal of Global Marketing*, 10, 2, 27-52.

Lande, Stephen and Jeffrey Crigler (1995), *A Buyer's Guide to American Products: From Automobiles to Video Games*, Carol Publishing Group.

Langer, Roy (n.d.), "Placed Images and Place Marketing," Unpublished manuscript, Department of Intercultural Communication and Management, Copenhagen Business School.

Lee, Dongdae and Gopala Ganesh (1999), "Effects of Partitioned Country Image in the Context of Brand Image and Familiarity: A Categorization Theory Perspective," *International Marketing Review*, 16, 18-39.

Leonard, Mark (1997), *Britain^{TM} Renewing our Identity*, London: Demos.

Li, Zhan G., L. William Murray and Don Scott (2000), "Global Sourcing, Multiple Country-of-Origin Facets, and Consumer Reactions," *Journal of Business Research*, 47, 121-133.

Liefeld, J. (1991), "Canadian Food Consumption Patterns," *Proceedings of the New Zealand Institute of Food Science and Technology Conference*, 9-33.

Liefeld, J. (1993), "Country-of-Origin Effects: Review and Meta-Analysis of Effect Size," In N. Papadopoulos and L. A. Heslop, editors, *Product and Country Images: Research and Strategy*, New York: Haworth Press, 117-156.

Liefeld, J. (2004), "Consumer Knowldege and Use of Country-of-Origin Information at the Point of Purchase," *Journal of Consumer Behavior*, 4, 2, 85-96.

Lillis, C. M. and C. L. Naranya (1974), "Analysis of 'Made In' Product Images - An Exploratory Study," *Journal of International Business Studies*, (Spring), 119-127.

Lin, L. and B. Sternquist (1992), "Taiwanese Consumers' Perceptions of Product Information Cues: Country of Origin and Store Prestige," Paper presented at the 1992 Annual Meeting of the Academy of International Business, Brussels.

Liu, S and K. Johnson (2005), "The Automatic Country-of-Origin Effects on Brand Judgments," *Journal of Advertising*, 34, 1, 87-97.

Luce, Mary, John Payne and James Bettman (1999), "Emotional Trade-Off difficulty and Choice," *Journal of Marketing Research*, 36, 2, 143-159.

Lumpkin, J. and J. Crawford (1985), "Consumer Perceptions of Developing Countries," In N. K. Maholtra, editor, *Developments in Marketing Science*, 8, 95-97. Coral Gables, Fl: Academy of Marketing Science.

"Made (badly) in Japan," *Economist*, September 18-22, 2000.

Made in USA Policy Comment (August 8, 1997), FTC File No. P894219.

"Major U.S. Manufacturers Agree to Settle Charges of Making Misleading 'Made in USA' Claims," Federal Trade Commission, January 19, 1999. FTC File Nos. American Honda: 982 3600; Johnson Worldwide Associates: 992 3019.

Manrai, Lalita, Ajay Manrai, Dana-Nicoleta Lascu and John Ryans, Jr. (1997), "How Green-Claim Strength and Country Disposition Affect Product Evaluation and Company Image," *Psychology & Marketing*, 14, 5, 511-537.

Marcoux, Jean-Sebastien, Pierre Filiatrault and Emmanuel Chiron (1997), "The Attitudes Underlying Preferences of Young Urban Educated Polish Consumers Toward Products Made in Western Countries," *Journal of International Consumer Marketing*, 9, 4, 5-29.

Maronick, Thomas (1995), "An Empirical Investigation of Consumer Perceptions of 'Made in USA' Claims," *International Marketing Review*, 12, 3, 15-30.

Martin, I. and S. Eroglu (1993), "Measuring a Multi-Dimensional Construct: Country Image," *Journal of Business Research*, 28, 191-210.

Mascarenhas, Oswald and Duane Kujawa (1998), "American Consumer Attitude Toward Foreign Direct Investments and their Products," *Multinational Business Review*, (Fall), 1-9.

McCrone, David, Angela Morris and Richard Kiely (1995), *Scotland the Brand: The Making of Scottish Heritage*. Edinburgh University Press.

Merriam-Webster Collegiate Dictionary (2000), at: http://www.m-w.com/cgi-bin/dictionary.

Mick, David and Susan Fournier (1998), "Paradoxes of Technology: Consumer Cognizance, Emotions and Coping Strategies," *Journal of consumer Research*, 25, 2, 123-143.

Mescshi, Robert L. (1995), "Value Added," *Financial World*, 164, 17, 52-53.

MOFTEC (2000), China Ministry of Foreign Trade and Economic Development, Beijing.

Morgan, N., A. Pritchard and R. Piggott (2002), "New Zealand, 100% Pure. The Creation of a Powerful Niche Destination Brand," *The Journal of Brand Management*, 9, 4, 335-354.

Monroe, K. (1979), *Pricing: Making Profitable Decisions*, New York: McGraw-Hill Book Company.

Monroe, K. and R. Krishnan (1985), "The Effect of Price on Subjective Product Evaluations," in J. Jacoby and J. Olson (eds.), *Perceived Quality: How Consumers View Stores and Marchandise*, Boston, MA: Lexington Books, 209-232.

Morgansky, M. and M. Lazarde (1987), "Foreign Made Apparel: Influences on Consumers' Perceptions of Brand and Store Quality," *International Journal of Advertising*, 6, 339-346.

De Mortanges, Charles P. and Allard van Riel (2003), "Brand Equity and Shareholder Value," *European Management Journal,* 21, 4, 520-527.

Nagashima, A. (1970), "A Comparison of U.S. and Japanese Attitudes Toward Foreign Products," *Journal of Marketing*, 34, (January), 68-74.

Nagashima (1977), "A Comparative 'Made In' Product Image Survey Among Japanese Businessmen," *Journal of Marketing*, 41, (July), 95-100.

Nations Brands Index – Q3 Report, 2005. www. announcement@gmi-mr.com, retrieved October 27, 2005.

Nebenzahl, I. D. and E. D. Jaffe (1991a), "The Effectiveness of Sponsored Events in Promoting a Country's Image," *International Journal of Advertising*, 10, 223-237.

Nebenzahl, I. D. and E. D. Jaffe (1991b) "Shifting Production to East European Countries: Effect on Brand Value", *Proceedings of the 17th Annual Conference of the European International Business Association held in Copenhagen*, Dec. 15-17, 279-308.

Nebenzahl, I. D. and E. D. Jaffe (1993), "Estimating Demand Functions from the Country-of-Origin Effect," in Nicholas Papadopoulos and Louise A. Heslop (eds), *Product and Country Images: Research and Strategy* (New York: The Haworth Press).

Nebenzahl, I. D. and E. D. Jaffe (1996), "Measuring the Joint Effect of Brand and Country Image in Consumer Evaluation of Global Products," *International Marketing Review* 13, 4, 5-22.

Nebenzahl, I. D. and E. D. Jaffe and S. I. Lampert (1997), "Towards a Theory of Country Image Effect on Product Evaluation," *Management International Review*, 37 1, 27-49.

Nebenzahl, I. D. and E. D. Jaffe and J-C Usunier (2000), "Developing Cross-Cultural Scales for the Measurement of Country Image," *Working Paper WP 1-2000*, Department of International Economics and Management, Copenhagen Business School.

Nebenzahl, I. D. (1998), "Consumers' Awareness of a Brand's Origin Country and Made-in Country: Development of Research Methodology and Initial Results," in Englis, Basil G. and Olofsson, Anna (eds.) *European Advances in Consumer Research*, III, Provo, Utah, 149-153.

Nebenzahl, I. D. (1999), "Knowledge Creation and Transfer: The Emergence of Israel as a High-Tech Powerhouse" in Burton, Fred, Mo Yamin and Mike Bowe, eds., *International Business and the Global Services Economy. Proceedings of the 25th Annual Conference of EIBA*, Dec. 12-14.

Nes, E. B. (1981), *Consumer Perception of Product Risk and Quality for Goods Manufactured in Developing versus Industrial Nations*, Ph.D. dissertation, University of Wisconsin.

Netemeyer, Richard, Srinivas Durvasula and Donald Lichtenstein (1991), "A Cross National Assessment of the Reliability and Validity of the CETSCALE," *Journal of Marketing Research*, 28 (August), 320-327.

Niss, Hanne (1996), "Country of Origin Marketing over the Product Life Cycle," *European Journal of Marketing*, 30, 3, 6-22.

Obermiller, C. and E. Spangenberg (1989), "Exploring the Effects of Country of Origin Labels: An Information Processing Framework," *Advances in Consumer Research*, 16, 454-459.

Okechuku, Chike (1994), "The Importance of Product Country of Origin: A Conjoint Analysis of the United States, Canada, Germany and The Netherlands," *European Journal of Marketing*, 28, 4, 5-19.

Okechuku, Chike and Vincent Onyemah (1999), "Nigerian Consumer Attitudes Toward Foreign and Domestic Products," *Journal of International Business Studies*, 30, 3, 611-622.

Olins, Wally (1999), *Trading Identities*, UK: The Foreign Policy Centre.

Oliver, R. L. (1997), *Satisfaction: A behavioral Perspective on the Consumer,* McGraw-Hill, New York, NY.

Olsen Janeen, Kent Granzin and Abhijit Biswas (1993), "Influencing Consumers Selection of Domestic versus Imported Products: Implications for Marketing Based on a Model of Helping Behavior," *Journal of the Academy of Marketing Science*, 21, 4, 307-321.

Opinion Survey on Foreign Affairs, Public Relations Office, Prime Minister's Office, Tokyo, November, 1998.

Papadopoulos, Nicolas (2004), "Place Branding: Evolution, Meaning and Implications," *Place Branding*, 1, 1, 36-49.

Papadopoulos, Nicolas, Louise Heslop (1986), "Travel as a Correlate of Product and Country Images," paper presented to the ASAC Conference, Whistler, British Columbia.

Papadopoulos, Nicolas, Louise Heslop and G. Avlonitis (1987), *Does "Country-of-Origin" Matter? Some Findings From a Cross-Cultural Study of Consumer Views About Foreign Products*, Report No. 87-104, Cambridge, MA, Marketing Science Institute.

Papadopoulos, Nicolas, Louise Heslop (1990), "A Comparative Image analysis of Domestic versus Imported Products," *Internattional Journal of Research in Marketing*, 7, 283-294.

Papadopoulos, Nicolas, Louise Heslop (eds.) (1993), *Product and Country Images: Research and Strategy*, New York: The Haworth Press.

Papadopoulos, Nicolas, Louise Heslop (2002), "Country Equity and Country Branding: Problems and Prospects," *Journal of Brand Management,* 9, 4/5, 294-314.

Patterson, Paul and Siu-Kwan Tai (1991), "Consumer Perceptions of Country of Origin in the Australian Apparel Industry," *Marketing Bulletin*, 2, 31-40.

Pedersen, S. (2004), "Place Branding: Giving the Region of Øresund a Competitive Edge," *Journal of Urban Technology*, 11, 1, 71-95.

Rao, A. and K. Monroe (1989), "The Effect of Price, Brand Name and Store Name on Buyers' Perceptions of Product Quality: An Integrative Review," *Journal of Marketing Research*, 26, 351-358.

Ratcliff, Robert and Jonathan Griffin (1999), *Through Other Eyes How the World Sees the United Kingdom*, London: The British Council.

Reinhard, K. (2003), "Restoring Brand America," *Advertising Age* (June 23), 30-31.

Render, B. and T. O. O'Connor (1976), "The Influence of Price, Store Name and Brand Name on Perceptions of Product Quality," *Journal of the Accademy of Marketing Science*, 4, Fall, 722-730.

Rosenblatt, G. (2005), "Marketing a New Image," *The Jewish Week*, (January 1).

Rosselle, Tracy (1999), "Florida's Country-of-Origin Law," *Citrus & Vegetable Magazine*, (October), 36-38.

Roth, M. S. and J. B. Romeo (1992), "Matching Product Category and Country Image Perceptions: A Framework for Managing Country-of-Origin Effects," *Journal of International Business Studies*, 3, 477-497.

Ruttenberg, A., A. Kavisky and H. Oren (1995), "Compositioning-the pardigm-shift beyond positioning," *The Journal of Brand Management,* 3, 3, 169-179.

Ruttenberg, A., H. Oren, and M. Honen (1998), "Brand Coding—an approach to developing an optimal compositioning," *The Journal of Brand Management,* 5, 5, 330-345.

Samiee, S. (1994), "Customer Evaluation of Products in a Global Market," *Journal of International Business Studies*, 25, 3, 579-604.

Sauer, P., M. Young and H. Unnava (1991), "An Experimental Investigation of the Processes Behind the Country-of-Origin Effect," *Journal of Intenational Consumer Marketing*, 3, 2, 29-59.

Schieb, A. (1977), "Le Consommateur Face a la Multinationalite des Marques et des Produits," *Revue Francaise de Gastion*, 11, (September-October), 59-62.

Schooler, R. (1971), "Bias Phenomena Attendant to the Marketing of Foreign Goods in the US," *Journal of International Business Studies*, 2, 71-80.

Schramm, Wilbur (1955), *The Process and Effects of Mass Communication* Urbana, IL: University of Illinois Press.

Schweiger, Günter, Gerald Häubl and Geroen Friederes (1995), "Consumers' Evaluations of Products Labeled 'Made in Europe'," *Marketing and Research Today*, February, 25-32.

Scotland's Brand Promise (2003). www.scotexchange.net.

Seaton, B. and R. H. Vogel (1985), "Brand, Price and Country of Manufacture as Factors in the Perception of Product Quality," Paper presented at the Academy of International Business annual meeting, New York, October 17-20.

Seaton, F. B. and H. A. Laskey (1999), "Effects of Production Location on Perceived Automobile Values," *Journal of Global Marketing*, 13, 1, 71-85.

Shimp, Terrance and Subhash Sharma (1987), "Consumer Ethnocentrism: Construction and Validation of the CETSCALE," *Journal of Marketing Research*, 28 (August), 320-327.

Shimp, Terrance, Samiee and T. Madden (1993), "Countries and Their Products: A Cognitive Structure Perspective," *Journal of the Academy of Marketing Science*, 21, 4, 323-330.

Silver, S. and S. Hill (2002), "Selling Brand America," *Journal of Business Strategy* (July-August), 10-15.

Simon, Carol J. and Mary W. Sullivan (1993), "The Measurement and Determinants of Brand Equity: A Financial Approach," *Marketing Science*, 12, 1, 28-52.

Soldner, H. (1984), "International Business Theory and Marketing Theory: Elements for International Marketing Theory Building," In G. M. Hampton and A. P. Van Gent, (eds), *Marketing Aspects of International Business*, Hingham, MA. Kluwer-Nojhoff, 25-27.

Spezzano, Dick (1999), "Country of Origin Labeling – What's the Big Deal," *Supermarket Business*, 54, 5, 200-201.

Supphellen, M. and T. Rittenburg (2001), "Consumer Ethnocentrism when Foreign Products are Better," *Psychology & Marketing*, 18, 9, 907-927.

Tan, P. (2003), "Brand USA: Tarnished?" www.brandchannel.com/print_page.asp?ar_id=1428section=main. Retrieved April 3, 2005.

Thakor, M. and C. Kohli (1996), "Brand Origin: Conceptualizatoion and Review," *Journal of Consumer Marketing*, 13, 3, 27-42.

Thakor, M. and A. Lavack (2003), "Effect of Perceived Brand Origin Assoctaions on Consumer Perceptions of Quality," *Journal of Product and Brand Management*, 12, 6, 394-407.

The Scottish Office (November 10, 1997), "Donald Dewar Launches Scotland the Brand," *News Release – 1701/97*.

Therkelsen, Anette and Henrik Halkier (2004), "Umbrella Place Branding A Study of Friendly Exoticism and Exotic Friendliness in Coordinated Natio0nal Tourism and Investment Promotion," *Discussion Paper No. 26*, Aalborg University, 2004.

Thorelli, H. B., J. Lim and J. Ye (1989), "Relative Importance of Country of Origin, Warranty and Retail Store Image on Product Evaluations," *International Marketing Review*, 6, 1, 35-46.

Tobin, J. (1969), "A General Equilibrium Approach to Monetary Theory," *Journal of Money, Credit and Banking*, 1, 15-29.

Travis, Daryl (2000), *How Successful Brands Gain the Irrational Edge*, New York, Prima Venture.

Tse, D. and G. Gorn (1992), "An Experiment on the Salience of Country-of-Origin in the Era of Global Brands," *Journal of International Marketing*, 1, 1, 57-76.

Tse, D. and G. Gorn (1993), "An Experiment on Country-of-Origin Effects in the Era of Global Brands," *Journal of International Marketing*, 1, 1, 57-77.

Tse, D. and Wie-na Lee (1992), "Removing Negative Country Images: Effects of Decomposition, Branding, and Product Experience," *Journal of International Marketing*, 1, 4, 25-48.

Tülin, Erden (1998), "An Empirical analysis of Umbrella Branding," *Journal of Marketing Research*, 35 (August), 339-351.

Ulgado, Francis M. and Moonkyo Lee (1993), "Consumer Evaluations of Bi-National Products in the Global Market," *Journal of International Marketing*, 1, 3, 5-22.

Ulmann, Arieh (1993), "The Battle of the Superpremium Ice Creams," in Gregory Dess and Alex Miller (eds.), *Strategic Management* (New York: McGraw-Hill), 444-455.

U.S. Public Diplomacy, GAO-03-061, House Committee on International Relations, Washington, D.C., September 2003.

Verlegh, Peeter and Jan-Benedict Steenkamp (1999), "A Review and Meta-Analysis of Country-of-Origin Research," *Journal of Economic Psychology*, 20, 521-546.

Wall, M. and L. A. Heslop (1986), "Consumer Attitudes Toward Canadian Made versus Imported Products," *Journal of the Academy of Marketing Science*, 14, 27-36.

Wall, M., J. Liefeld and A. Heslop (1991), "Impact of Country-of-Origin Cues on Consumer Judgments in Multi-Cue Situations: A Covariance Analysis," *Journal of the Academy of Marketing Science*, 19, 2, 105-113.

Wang, C. and C. Lamb, Jr. (1983), "The Impact of Selected Environmental Forces upon Consumers' Willingness to Buy Foreign Products," *Journal of the Academy of Marketing Science*, 11, 2, 71-84.

Wang, C. K. (1978), "The Effect of Foreign Economic, Political and Cultural Environment on Consumers' Willingness to Buy Foreign Products," Unpublished Ph.D. dissertation, Texas A & M University.

Whetten, D. A. (1989), "What Constitutes a Theoretical Contribution?" *Academy of Management Review*, 14, 4, 490-495.

Wirthgen, B., H. Kuhnert, M. Altmann, U. Demmin and A. Wirthgen (1997), "The Importance of Region of Origin in Influencing Consumer Behavior of Food Products," *Working Paper*, University of Kassel.

Witt, J. and C. Rao (1992), "An Examination of Country-of-Origin Bias in the Context of Brand Reputation," Paper presented at the annual Meeting of the Academy of International Business, Brussels.

Wolff Olins (1995), *Made in UK: An International Business Survey of Attitudes Towards National Identity and UK Commerce and Industry*, London.

Wolff Olins, press information, n.d.

Wood, V. and J. Darling (1992), "The Marketing Challenges of the Newly Independent Republics," *Journal of International Marketing*, 1, 1, 77-102.

Wooding, P. (1993), "New Zealand in the International Economy," in Brian Roper and Chris Rudd (eds.), *Oxford Readings in New Zealand Politics: No. 2*, Auckland: Oxford University Press, 91-107.

Yan, Jack (1995), "Nicole? Papa!" *CAP*, 3, 2, 6-12, 26.

Young & Rubicam Group (2005), "BrandAsset Valuator," https://www.yrbav.com/.

Yoo, Boonghee and Naveen Donthu (2001), "Developing and Validating a Multidimensional Consumer-Based Brand Equity Scale," *Journal of Business Research,* 52, 1-14.

Zeithaml, V. (1988), "Consumer Perceptions of Price, Quality and Value: A Means-end Model and Synthesis of Criteria," *Journal of Marketing*, 52, 2-22.

Ziamou, Paschalina, Yorgos Zotos, Steven Lysonski and Costos Zafiropoulos (1999), "Selling Exports to Consumers in Bulgaria: Attitudes Towards Foreign Products," *Journal of Euromarketing*, 7, 3, 59-77.

Index